T0348366

HOW TO BE
DATEABLE

HOW TO BE
DATEABLE

THE ESSENTIAL GUIDE TO FINDING
YOUR PERSON AND FALLING IN LOVE

JULIE KRAFCHICK & YUE XU

Simon Element

New York   Amsterdam/Antwerp   London   Toronto   Sydney   New Delhi

**SIMON
ELEMENT**

An Imprint of Simon & Schuster, LLC
1230 Avenue of the Americas
New York, NY 10020

First Simon Element hardcover edition January 2025

SIMON ELEMENT is a trademark of Simon & Schuster, LLC

For information about special discounts for bulk purchases,
please contact Simon & Schuster Special Sales at 1-866-506-1949
or business@simonandschuster.com.

The Simon & Schuster Speakers Bureau can bring authors to your
live event. For more information or to book an event, contact the
Simon & Schuster Speakers Bureau at 1-866-248-3049 or visit
our website at www.simonspeakers.com.

Interior design by Laura Levatino

Interior illustrations by Julie Krafchick

Manufactured in the United States of America

10 9 8 7 6 5 4 3 2 1

Library of Congress Cataloging-in-Publication Data has been applied for.

ISBN 978-1-6680-3042-4
ISBN 978-1-6680-3043-1 (ebook)

This book is for all the lovers, dreamers, and hope*ful* romantics out there. Your great love story is right around the corner.

Contents

HOW TO BE
DATEABLE

Date·able:

noun; The type of dater who stands out because they're *able* to show up authentically and take control of their love life, with a level of growth, curiosity, and vulnerability that makes them a desirable person to date

Introduction:

We're in a Love Crisis

A ndrew was a good-looking and successful guy in his early thir-ties who had no problem attracting matches on dating apps. He went on hundreds (yes, hundreds) of first dates. But none of the dates seemed to progress, to the point that Andrew was convinced he had a third-date curse. He didn't understand why this one part of life couldn't fall into place. Andrew had everything else: a job he loved, a close-knit group of friends from college, and a new condo he bought in Lincoln Park, one of the best neighborhoods of Chicago. He had accomplished so much—from graduating magna cum laude at Northwestern University to climbing the ranks at his consulting firm—yet he couldn't seem to make dating work. When his coupled-up friends asked about his love life, he dodged their questions, as he had been ghosted, breadcrumbed, and outright rejected too many times to count. *Am I just not dateable?* he wondered as he tweaked his pro-file for the zillionth time.

You may have felt like Andrew at one point or another. Perhaps you've gone on endless dates that go nowhere or you've had a string of those "what are we?" situations. Like Andrew, you may have got-ten to the point where you'd rather not even update your friends when last week's hot prospect turned into this week's ghost. With the endless cycles of first dates, messaging black holes, and microwave relationships (you know, the ones that heat up so fast only to evaporate just as quickly), you may be wondering if love is even in the cards anymore.

Trust us; you're not alone. We're in a f*cking love crisis. Nearly half of US adults over the last ten years said dating has gotten harder, according to a study by the Pew Research Center. People are deprioritizing love, putting their careers before romantic partnerships or opting not to have relationships at all. Today's daters have seen the fallout of divorce, and we're not sold on the way relationships have been done before. Roughly four in ten adults ages twenty-five to fifty-four are considered "uncoupled," living without a spouse or significant other. More and more adults are delaying marriage–or forgoing it completely. And despite the increase in hookup apps and openness around sex, Americans are having less sex than ever before. According to *The Atlantic*, we're in a sex recession–primarily caused by the decline in couplehood among young people. At the forefront are Millennials and Gen Z, who are more likely to report having no sexual partners at all.

You would think that the explosion of dating apps would make it easier to have sex and relationships, but modern daters would tell you it's quite the opposite. While technology has opened up new ways to connect, it's also magnified the ugly side of dating, where people love bomb, ghost, and treat each other as disposable. From dating app convos that go nowhere to unsolicited d*ck pics, it can feel near impossible these days to form a real connection with someone who's emotionally available. When you've had one too many cringeworthy first dates that make you question humanity, or a slew of never-quite-official situationships that tear at your heartstrings, it's hard to stay hopeful that your person is out there. All this dating trauma starts to take a toll on our mental health and makes us question whether it's even worth it. And the result? We see daters delete their apps, go on a dating sabbatical, or resign themselves to the idea that they're destined to be alone.

Ultimately, this isn't what anyone wants. We need love. The single most significant predictor of human happiness is the quality of a person's relationships. According to the Centers for Disease Control and Prevention (CDC), when people are socially connected and have stable and supportive relationships, they are more likely to make healthy choices and to have better mental and physical health outcomes. And as discovered by the Harvard Study of Adult Development, strong relationships are the biggest predictor of well-being, and a prominent contributor to longevity. There's a reason for the obsession with dating and romantic relationships: we're meant to do life with other people. Healthy relationships provide a sense of belonging, comfort, and joy that enriches our lives with meaning and purpose. If we don't get this love crisis under control, we risk exacerbating the loneliness epidemic. According to the World Health Organization (WHO), loneliness is associated with an increased risk of dementia, heart disease, and stroke, and it has the equivalent mortality rate to smoking 15 cigarettes per day. Loneliness is literally killing us! Even in the short term, today's world of modern dating is anything but healthy, and the impact of these experiences is harmful to our well-being.

IMAGINE A NEW WORLD

It's more pivotal than ever for us to change course. Imagine a universe where dating feels so rewarding, you no longer focus on the outcome. Imagine having authentic connections, seamless communication, and feel empowered to express your true self. Terms such as "ghosting" and "dating fatigue" are extinct because here, people express their feelings and date in a way that truly serves them. Imagine having invigorating conversations filled with laughter and learning, even if they don't lead to romance. No more uncertainty or unanswered messages; everyone keeps true to their word, and there's no one left hanging, wondering about the other person's intentions. In this utopia, the pursuit of love is an enjoyable and thrilling adventure, unburdened by cultural and societal pressures that currently plague the dating scene. There is peace, harmony, and a sigh of relief. Every dater is certain that their person is just around the corner, confident that each step they take brings them closer to love. This book was written to show that this dating utopia is possible. **While every other dating book will show you how to adapt to dating culture, we'll show you how to rise above it and reshape how you approach modern dating altogether.** We'll help you get out of the field of first dates, situationship slope, or wherever else you're struggling to leave. You'll start navigating in a new way, which will eventually help you find love—with yourself and others.

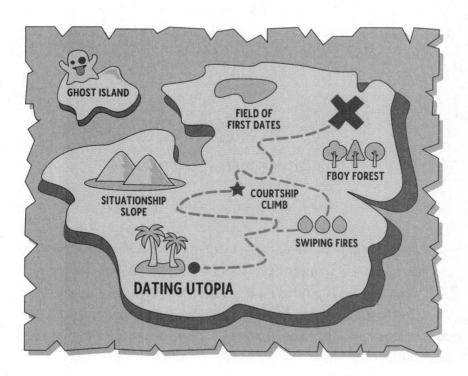

We know you wouldn't be here if you, deep down, didn't want to find love. You wouldn't be here unless you wanted to break through all this dating BS and find a committed relationship where you feel fully seen and heard. This generation of daters has asked for more out of relationships—when and how we choose to have them. This is a good thing! It recognizes that we want equality, substance, and connection in our romantic relationships. It's not just about settling for any old relationship, but rather the right relationship: one that truly aligns with who you are.

And we're here to tell you that it's possible.

SO WHO ARE WE?

First things first, we never set out to be dating experts. But there's a reason why you gravitate toward helping people: usually you've struggled with the same things yourself. We understand how stressful and confusing dating can be while you're in the thick of it. We get how lonely it can feel when all your friends are partnered up and you're the remaining single person in the group. And we certainly know the feeling of just wanting to meet your person already, dammit!

We met in 2015 and became fast friends, bonding over modern dating, as we were both recently back into the dating scene. Julie had just broken up with the person she thought was "the One" and was utterly devastated that she was starting over . . . yet again. Prior to this, she had always felt like a later bloomer, as most of her dating and relationship history consisted of casual situations or unrequited love. As she approached her late twenties and more of her friends started coupling up, she turned to online dating. At first, dating apps were great! She was going on real dates and developing feelings for the people she was seeing. But then the burnout started—it seemed like nothing ever progressed into the serious, committed relationship she longed for. Frustrated by the apps, Julie decided to take matters into her own hands. After working in the Silicon Valley tech scene for over a decade, she created 500 Brunches, a platform that connected people with similar interests to meet in real life–over brunch. Little did she know this would lead her to her first real love (and later, that gut-wrenching heartbreak of parting ways with said person). But more importantly, it would also lead her to Yue.

Yue had recently moved to San Francisco after living in New York City and Beijing. She had just exited a long-distance relationship and wondered why the last time she was in love was almost a decade ago! As a former dating coach, she was confident in her dating skills. She knew how to "win" over dates and understood how men operated (after all, she had heard it all through her vlog *Ask Miss Singlefied*, where she gave advice to guys from a girl's perspective). And with the male-female ratio strongly in her favor in her new tech-driven home, she thought dating would be a breeze. But reality hit hard–the rules and dating tactics she had preached for years were becoming obsolete. Yue had long been a dedicated rules follower–wait three days to text back, never initiate, and under no circumstances pick up the bill– but these tactics were not working for her this time around. Traditional gender roles were thrown out the window. Men were no longer chasing women–and women were often in control, initiating hookups and exploring polyamory. Everyone seemed more concerned about building their professional empires than starting families, so much so that her first date in San Francisco showed up with a business plan for her to review! Dating apps dominated, replacing in-real-life (IRL) conversations. Heteronormative boundaries were changing, and people were experimenting sexually in new and different ways (hello, triads and sex parties!). Something big was happening–a seismic shift in the dating world. This new world of digital dating, changing gender dynamics, and nontraditional arrangements was reshaping our romantic expectations. Was it just San Francisco or were we on the brink of a dating revolution? Spoiler: it was not just San Francisco; the shift was starting everywhere.

One fateful night, over a few too many cocktails, we were out discussing dating (as we usually did). We had a brilliant idea: why don't we start a podcast to document all of the trials and tribulations of modern dating so we could get to the root of why we date the way we do? The next week, we grabbed some recording equipment, headed to Yue's studio apartment in Nob Hill, and recorded our first episodes of *Dateable*. We knew we were onto something when our inbox started overflowing with everything from the OMG-that-happened-to-me-too comments to the I-never-thought-of-it-that-way-before epiphanies. Daters suddenly didn't feel so alone in their quest for love. They could see firsthand how others went through the same challenges they faced. It also proved incredibly therapeutic *for us* as it challenged our own dating patterns and ways of thinking.

Fast-forward to a decade later, and we transformed from active daters to bona fide experts, featured in the *New York Times*, CNN, and places we never imagined seeing our faces. We've interviewed thousands of daters and world-renowned experts to answer our burning question: *why do we date the way we do?* It was simple yet oh so complex. We were determined to uncover the secrets behind the struggle to find love. But more importantly, we were on a mission to provide solutions. We wanted to liberate daters from the mindset that modern dating sucks and share how it's entirely possible to have the love life you've always wanted.

In our years of doing *Dateable*, we closely followed a group of daters and their dating experiences. Over time, we noticed a distinct dichotomy among them. While everyone started out frustrated by modern dating, a subset managed to transcend this frustration. They not only created love lives that worked for them but also genuinely enjoyed dating, with some even finding epic loves. Conversely, the remaining group found themselves trapped in a perpetual cycle of installing and uninstalling dating apps, defeated and worn down.

We, too, underwent a transformation in our approach to dating and started having partnerships that far exceeded our expectations. We started to take note of all the factors that we saw within ourselves and that distinguished the group of successful, happy daters from the rest. What were the strategies that allowed them to rise above and break free from the dating grind? This is what compelled us to write this book for you.

BREAKING UP WITH BAD DATING HABITS

It's easy to blame technology, dating apps, or hookup culture for the chaos of modern dating. We've been taught to keep swiping (because dating is a numbers game, after all!) and that if we can create that perfect dating profile, everything will fall into place. Daters are so caught up in the small levers that they're missing the big picture, losing the skills you need to have a relationship. This may sound crazy coming from dating experts, but we actually think *you shouldn't get good at dating*. And that's because everything in today's dating world is centered around *disconnection* when *connection* is what we all so deeply desire.

We need to challenge the norms of dating culture and break up with bad dating habits once and for all. Because right now, we're all being set up to fail. There's a reason why modern dating feels like a maze you can't get out of: it's designed that way. Some of these dating norms and behaviors have been ingrained in us for years and others have been perpetuated by dating apps and technology. Culturally, we've outgrown the sexist tropes and disempowering advice in the old guard of dating bibles such as *The Rules* or *Why Men Love Bitches*, yet we're still clinging to their advice–often subconsciously at times—as we don't know a different way. We're still operating from a playbook of "how dating works" and what "will or will not" attract a partner.

STOP FALLING FOR THE TRAPS

It's not your fault: you were told this is how you date. Through our years of research, we saw daters falling for **four dating traps** that kept them in this perpetual cycle of dating. In the first part of this book, we'll take you through the traps: **the Expectation of Love on Demand**, **the Settling Paradox**, **the Validation Trap**, and **Relationship Chicken**.

We'll shed light on their destructive nature and why they keep you stuck: how we expect instant connection; why we refuse to "settle" yet we end up settling for dead-end situationships; how dating has become more of a vehicle for validation; and ways we're all playing the game of Relationship Chicken, ultimately leaving us more disconnected and discontent. You may instantly recognize how you fall for a particular trap, while it may take more introspection to discern others.

Throughout this book, we'll share our stories and experiences from when we fell for the traps ourselves to when we started following our own methodology to come out on the other side. Before we go through these traps, you'll learn more about what type of dater you currently are. In the next section, you'll be able to take our quiz to identify your dating archetype—the parts that make you the incredible person you are, but also what's holding you back. Through this lens, you'll be able to view the traps in relation to you. Most of us hold traits of all the archetypes, but you'll see that some may be more or less dominant for you. It's important to point out: there's no good or bad style. All of them are dateable in their own way.

In the following chapters, you'll hear from five characters who are composites of the thousands of daters we've interacted with through our podcast, our courses and programs, the Big Dateable Energy community on Facebook, and our Instagram account (@dateablepodcast). These daters are fictional for the sake of individuals' anonymity, but their experiences and transformations are real. There's a reason we modeled them after certain daters: they're the ones who followed the frameworks outlined in this book and made the necessary changes to be their most dateable selves.

So let's meet our daters!

Andrew: a hetero man in his early thirties from Chicago, who, as we mentioned earlier, is incredibly accomplished in his professional life yet has had quite the challenge to find a partner. Last year, Andrew ended his first serious relationship, but prior to that, he had limited dating and relationship experience. Now he's back in the dating pool, in a very different life stage than his coupled-up friends who are becoming first-time parents. Eventually Andrew wants all these things, too, but his current goal is to make it to the third date with someone. Though it doesn't help that his parents are always asking when they can expect grandkids. . . .

Drea: a hetero woman in her late thirties from Washington, DC, who wants nothing more than to fall in love. As a nurse, she's a giver by nature. This tendency has been problematic in her love life though, as she gravitates toward people who are takers. This was evident in her marriage that ended three years ago and has persisted in her dating life postdivorce. She's found herself in one situationship after another, always building up the "relationship" to be more than it is. But who can blame her? She's a romantic at heart and just wants her second shot at love. . . .

Eli: a gay man in his midforties from Los Angeles who is a notorious serial dater. As the extreme extrovert he is, Eli has no problem meeting men, whether it's on the apps or IRL. He's always on the go—from jet-setting around the world as an influencer to nights on the town in West Hollywood, never spending a night in due to his FOMO (fear of missing out). His friends often tease him because he believes he could meet his soulmate at any given moment—a bar, a Starbucks line, or the gym. He's certainly an active dater but he's ideally looking for something real that can last more than a couple of months. . . .

Maya: a hetero woman in her midtwenties from New York City who is perpetually single. She's a busy marketing professional who takes pride in being self-sufficient. After all, she's been single for the last four years after an unexpected breakup with her college sweetheart. While Maya's on her own, she's never lonely: she has a great group of single girlfriends she goes out with often. She's also on every app but struggles to find men who meet her standards. Her friends tell her she's being too picky, but Maya disagrees. She mostly gets frustrated by the inefficiencies of dating. But as someone who has a vision for her Mr. Right, she's determined to find him. . . .

Tori: a lesbian woman in her early twenties from San Francisco who overthinks her way out of any potential relationship. As a software engineer in a male-dominated industry, she's had to assert herself in her career yet struggles to do the same while dating. Tori often gets caught up in her head, ruminating and analyzing every text message, conversation, or interaction. This leads to a lot of anxiety especially in the early stages of dating when she's unsure of the situation. Tori has never had a serious relationship and struggles to put herself out there fully to take that leap. . . .

As a way to represent the breadth of daters, there's diversity in their genders, ages, sexualities, locations, races, and past dating/relationship experiences. We're both hetero daters of different ethnicities: we understand there's nuance these factors bring. In this book, though, we'll focus more on the overarching commonalities we've seen among all sorts of daters. Because, believe it or not, we've seen the same struggles persist! Please do not get hung up on finding the dater you're the most similar to in terms of demographics; what's more important is that each dater represents one of the dating archetypes we'll get into in the next section. Those are the daters to follow more closely. We know that by seeing how their journeys unfold, you will be able to apply their findings to your love life, too.

We'll also tap into many of the insights we've learned from the multitude of dating experts we've had on our podcast: therapists, dating coaches, authors, podcasters, dating app founders, researchers, and more. Thank you again to all the experts we've referenced and even the ones we didn't (we hope to have you in the next book!).

START FALLING IN LOVE

While it's crucial to reflect on how we may be falling for the traps of modern dating, it's even more pivotal that we help you take action. That's why in the book's second part, we've developed a framework that will make you a more intentional dater, so you can show up authentically and start falling in love. As buzzword-y as it seems, intentionality means dating with deliberate purpose. This way, you're in control—not the apps, not the person unresponsive to your text messages, not the many other ways modern dating is out to get you. You'll start to think about: What type of love life do I want? How do I show up? Am I dating the way I want to be dated? Am I even that into *them*? Dating does not own you. You are in the driver's seat, and you have the power to make it work for you.

Over the past couple of years it took to write this book, we consolidated our personal experiences and the themes we heard on *Dateable* and from the daters we followed. We surveyed our audiences through our Facebook and Instagram communities. We pressed our friends, acquaintances, and family members to share their journeys more in-depth. And when we were together in Austin at South by Southwest while writing this book, it all clicked. It came down to five very distinct phases:

1. **Letting go:** Release the baggage and beliefs that are holding you back.
2. **Gaining clarity:** Uncover what you truly want and need.
3. **Showing up:** Give to dating what you want to get out of dating.
4. **Investing appropriately:** Prioritize your time, energy, and emotions into what matters.
5. **Persevering through it all:** Stay resilient despite the inevitable challenges and setbacks.

While it may be tempting to skip to the end, we highly recommend you take your time with each chapter, as they all play off one another to give you a more holistic perspective. This book is going to be different from other dating self-help books. We're not here to tell you to fundamentally change who you are as a person (because, damn, you're wonderful the way you are). So much dating advice is geared toward presenting in a certain way–be more of this, less of that–to attract more prospects. But we want to do something different. We want to help you get out of your own way and unlearn what you've learned about dating so that you can embrace your most dateable self on your own terms.

We're also not here to give you prescriptive advice, but rather to empower you to take on dating differently. As a society, we're at a tipping point, ready to create our own DIY relationships that break free from the conventional mold. While we want you to find a relationship, it's more important to find the *right* one for you. Because who you pick as a partner is a big decision. The best marriages and long-term relationships make people happier. But mediocre relationships, or those full of turmoil, do the exact opposite. **This book will help you date differently: with your needs at the forefront.**

So if you're expecting hacks, tricks, gimmicks, shortcuts, or ways to game the system, we're sorry to tell you that you're in the wrong place. We're done with the rules and bad dating advice that's hurting your love life and stripping you of your confidence—and we hope you are, too. We're not here to give you bandage solutions that yield short-term gains. No longer will you be stuck overanalyzing profiles or fixated on the person who never texted you back—because you'll quickly start to see that stuff doesn't matter. You'll start to approach dating from a different perspective: one that is real and authentic. You'll be focused on what moves the needle so you can cut through all the dating BS to build a solid relationship that lasts. You'll be armed with the necessary mantras to exude your Big Dateable Energy (BDE). And the best part: you'll start to weed through the people who aren't on the same page and attract others who have subscribed to this new dating culture.

EMBRACE THE PROCESS

Even with all this newfound knowledge, you may not walk outside and magically meet your soulmate tomorrow (but who knows, that would be freaking awesome!). There's a good chance it'll still take time to meet someone right for you. But what if dating being challenging is actually . . . a good thing? It's not a setback, but rather a blessing in disguise. The journey itself, the intricate dance of seeking and discovering love, holds immeasurable value. We're often so focused on the outcome that the process becomes miserable. What if we accept that all of the trials and tribulations are necessary in order to create a healthy, sustainable, long-term relationship with someone?

While it just so happens that both of us are in loving relationships at the time of writing this book, that's not the only measure of success. The most pivotal shift we saw was the transformation within ourselves and the optimism we now bring to modern dating. We'll share how we learned to enjoy the process and how to not fixate on the outcome while still honoring our needs and being intentional about a serious, committed relationship. And most importantly, how we learned to manage the anxiety and emotions from dating disappointments while staying optimistic. Starting to date with purpose (as you will after reading this book) sets you up for that fulfilling partnership that will eventually come your way–that we're sure of!

ENDING THE LOVE CRISIS

We wrote this book to put you in the driver's seat, empowering you to design your own love life. While we do believe you can emerge from this love crisis, part of the work is enjoying the process as you date. Not only will you be a happier dater, but you'll treat the rest of the dating world with more humanity. That ripple effect of warmth and positivity can have immense power on all the daters out there–one date at a time. Think about it: don't you want to leave your date in a better place than before? This book is more than a book; it's a movement: for us all to date with more compassion while staying true to ourselves.

This book is for all the lovers, dreamers, and hopeful romantics out there. It's for the optimists at heart, even if you're feeling down about dating right now. We see you, and we wrote this just for you. Because the last thing we want you to do is give up. In the midst of all the setbacks and disappointments, there's someone out there *right now* who's eagerly searching for someone just like you. We want you to hold on to that belief because finding the right relationship is an absolute game changer in life. Despite the chaos and challenges in the dating world, we wholeheartedly believe epic love is achievable.

So, are you ready to take charge of your love life? Let's go!

What Type of Dater Are You?

Have you ever wondered what's serving you—and what's not—in the way you date? From our years of interacting with thousands of daters through our podcast, courses, programs, and communities, we've been able to identify the **five prominent archetypes** among modern daters. Each dating style has parts that make them incredibly dateable—and other parts that hold them back. Most of us exhibit a little bit of every style, but you'll see that some may be more or less dominant for you. By understanding your most prominent dating archetype (fun fact: most of us have one or two leading ones), you'll be able to go through this book with a better understanding of how you can lean into your core strengths and, more importantly, how you can get out of your own way. Only then can you stop falling for the traps of modern dating and start falling in love! Remember, there's no good or bad archetype—all of them are dateable.

Let's find out what kind of dater you are!

THE FIVE DATING ARCHETYPES QUIZ

For the sake of readability, we've included the simplified version of the quiz in our book. If you want to take a more in-depth version of this quiz, you can go to **www.howtobedateable.com**. You can always take the quiz again once you finish the book to see how your styles may have changed from the insight you've gained.

Instructions: In each group, check all the statements that resonate with you. Remember, everything is in a dating context. Then, tally up the number of check marks in each section to get your score for each group.

Group A:

____ I often think about the future and what's next when dating someone.

____ I tend to focus on meeting certain milestones within certain time frames.

____ I have specific long-term goals in mind such as marriage or children.

____ I believe it's important to keep progressing, whether it's planning the next date or considering a bigger commitment.

____ I will end things if we're not moving at the speed I want.

____ I often find myself comparing where I'm at in life to others.

____ Total

Group B:

____ I believe love conquers all and has the power to overcome challenges.

____ I tend to wear my heart on my sleeve and lead with my emotions.

____ I am a deeply committed and loyal person, sometimes to my detriment.

____ Putting others first is a common tendency for me; my focus is on their needs.

____ I often find myself in undefined romantic situations, unsure of the level of commitment from the other person.

____ I tend to give people more chances than they deserve.

____ Total

Group C:

____ I thrive on the energy from meeting new people and having new experiences.

____ I prefer to date multiple people at once to maximize my time.

____ I think of every place or event as an opportunity to meet my soulmate.

____ Dating is a numbers game: I like to line up as many dates as possible.

____ I value the spark and instant chemistry and am hesitant to go on a second date with someone I didn't feel that with.

____ I am the type to be meeting new people every chance I get.

____ Total

Group D:

____ I pride myself on being independent and self-sufficient.

____ People I date often tell me they're drawn to my confidence.

____ I hold both myself and my potential partners to high standards.

____ I have a hard time letting people in.

____ I admit that I can be judgmental of others.

____ I try hard to avoid conflict or disagreements as much as possible.

____ Total

Group E:
___ I tend to examine every possible scenario or outcome in detail.
___ I often think about how I'm being perceived by others.
___ I am thoughtful about my actions; very rarely am I impulsive or spontaneous.
___ I find myself spending extended periods analyzing interactions or texts.
___ Taking a leap of faith is a challenge for me as I need to gather all available information when making decisions.
___ I often catch myself replaying a situation or conversation.
___ Total

Next up, let's find your most prominent styles! Bring your group totals over here.

Group	Group Total
Group A = Achiever	
Group B = Dreamer	
Group C = Energizer	
Group D = Maverick	
Group E = Thinker	

Score of 5–6: highly present
Score of 3–4: somewhat present
Score of 1–2: minimally present

Which one(s) did you score the highest? This is your most prominent style. While many of you may highly resonate with one or two archetypes, it's also common to have a little bit of all of them. Whatever your case, focus on the top one or two that you identify with the most as you go through this book.

So now that you know your prominent archetypes, what do they mean? Let's break down each one.

ACHIEVER

You tend to date with purpose and conviction. You know what you want for the long term and aren't afraid to go after it! As a natural leader, you often come up with great date ideas and are good at moving the relationship forward. You aren't afraid of commitment, and your bold nature can allow you to take chances and be open about your relationship goals. The people you date tend to know where they stand with you, as honesty and integrity are some of your core values. Your resilience and perseverance allow you to withstand the hardships and challenges of modern dating, which motivates you to keep going on this quest for love. Overall, you're optimistic and believe that you can do anything—and have anything—if you set your mind to it.

Your superpower: You're hyperfocused and make your intentions clear.

What could be holding you back: You often have a goal in mind when dating, but you may lose track of the biggest one of all: finding the *right* person for you. You can get caught up in artificial milestones and timelines—often focusing on what's next instead of developing the connection. When you're living in the future, staying present is nearly impossible—and your dates can feel this! You may approach dating transactionally without even realizing it. With so much focus on progression, you need to be careful you don't stay in the wrong relationships due to a fear of starting over—or that you don't give up on a genuine connection if they're not 100 percent on your timeline. Don't let your impatience and need to beeline to the finish line get in the way of letting the right relationship truly blossom.

> Pay attention to **Andrew,** who has a prominent Achiever style. He tends to have a specific vision of how a relationship should progress— and feels like a failure if he can't make it past the third date. Having his self-worth so closely tied to the outcome makes it challenging for him to enjoy the experience of dating and getting to know a new human being.

DREAMER

You want nothing more than to have your great love story. You tend to see the best in people, and your warm energy draws them to you like a magnet. You often give your all to relationships—determined for them to work out. You wear your heart on your sleeve and love deeply, bringing passion to your relationships. You make time for the people in your life, through your gestures or words of how much they mean to you. You tend to lead with your emotions, encouraging your partners to open up and making them feel loved and appreciated. Your empathy and compassion for others are huge assets you bring to relationships. Your undying commitment and loyalty make you the type of partner others can build a life with.

Your superpower: You make people feel connected to you.

What could be holding you back: Your whimsical definition of love may not always be realistic at times, and you tend to idealize a relationship or get ahead of yourself when dating. You might be inclined to prioritize others over yourself or neglect the practical aspects of a relationship. Instead of recognizing when you're getting subpar treatment, you may be prone to living in a fantasy of what the relationship *could* be instead of seeing the reality of what's happening. You likely also take dating personally and let your emotions take over when you aren't receiving enough reassurance. You may wonder why it's so easy for others to find love, but you're missing the opportunity to take control and create the love you've longed for.

Pay attention to **Drea**, who has a prominent Dreamer style. She often settles for situationships and suppresses her own needs in a relationship. By not being true to herself about what she wants from a partner, she expends time on people who won't ever fully commit— and robs herself of the opportunity to find a true partner.

ENERGIZER

You're full of charisma and people are drawn to you like a magnet. You're generally down to meet new people and your social nature makes you approachable and easy to talk to. You often have a positive energy and adventurous spirit, which draws people to you. You may believe you can meet your soulmate anywhere and at any time. You also take pride in trying new experiences, which makes dating you fresh and exciting. And when in a relationship, this keeps your bond strong, not stale. Since you tend to be more extroverted, you may be more open about your feelings, thoughts, and desires. At your core, you're an optimist who believes in love and wants to find that special person.

Your superpower: Your zest for life gives you a contagious energy.

What could be holding you back: While you live an exciting lifestyle, all that go, go, go can get exhausting and may burn you out. It also may be a struggle to get to know someone at a deeper, more emotional level if you're always onto the next. You may get pulled in based on "the spark" or chemistry, and it can be challenging to take the space to reflect—and, at times, genuinely know yourself and what you're looking for. You might even experience connections that burn out quickly, especially if they start hot and heavy. When you repeat the same patterns expecting different results, it feels like you're going through the motions. It often takes slowing down to speed up, creating enough space to build that lasting connection you so desire.

Pay attention to **Eli**, who has a prominent Energizer style. With a tendency to fall swiftly into relationships that fizzle out just as fast, he unwittingly creates a whirlwind of noise in his love life. As someone who always has a new prospect or is going to a new date spot in town, Eli experiences a lot of highs when dating. But he also experiences low lows, as he doesn't know how to be alone.

MAVERICK

You're self-sufficient, independent, and want the best out of life. Someone would only be so lucky to join in on this ride! You tend to come across as confident and authentic–sometimes with a no-BS attitude, telling it like it is. You may have a high bar, but you aren't trying to change someone once you find them. This goes a long way as your partner can feel truly seen and heard for who they are. Your relationships thrive when you live independent lives and respect each other's interests, aspirations, and boundaries. Your partner doesn't feel smothered or controlled and you may even be more open to nontraditional arrangements. Most importantly, you want someone who is additive to your life and can challenge you in all the right ways.

Your superpower: You don't ever lose your sense of self.

What could be holding you back: While you have a great life, it may be hard for you to make room for others. You might write people off quickly or make them prove themselves first. You may be critical (of yourself and others), which can come off as being judgmental or picky if you're not conscious of it. It may be hard for you to be emotionally vulnerable and show your true self. Since you're so self-sufficient, it also may be a struggle to ask for help or communicate your needs. But if you either avoid conflict or let resentment build, it won't help grow your relationships! While you don't *need* a partner, showing someone you *want* to be with them and approaching dating with more of a "we" attitude can open up a world of options.

Pay attention to **Maya**, who has a prominent Maverick style. She often struggles to form intimate bonds and get close to people. By remaining on the surface of relationships and avoiding emotional depth, she finds herself with stagnant connections that lack the growth she deeply desires.

THINKER

You tend to be a vigilant dater who is consistent, reliable, and dependable—all qualities that make a great long-term partner. You're a steady constant for the people you care about, there even when times are tough. Since you're typically good at solving problems and have a strong attention to detail, you're naturally empathetic and make your partner feel loved and supported. You also have the capacity to work through conflict and any challenges as you strive to understand your partner with an open mind. Your interest in personal development and willingness to take feedback are enormous assets for a lasting partnership. It may take you time to make a decision and go all in, but once you do, you're fully committed to it.

Your superpower: You're able to see a situation from perspectives others don't see.

What could be holding you back: While it's important to be thoughtful about your decisions, your overthinking may send you into a state of analysis paralysis. Dating isn't always logical, and love involves taking risks. You may hold back out of fear of making the wrong decision or incorrect move, often plagued with anxiety. You might also not be as expressive or open with your dates, overly cautious of how you're perceived. Watch out that you don't spend precious time spinning your wheels, contemplating stuff that doesn't matter. You don't want to get caught up in the minor details that you miss the big picture of what could make you happy! You'd be surprised what can happen when you act with more conviction and take that leap of faith.

Pay attention to **Tori**, who has a prominent Thinker style. She often gets in her head after every date—especially when she meets someone she likes. Instead of authentically expressing herself, she exercises extreme caution with every action and every word to project herself as the ideal partner, making dating a major source of anxiety for her.

Remember that these dating archetypes don't define you, but they can give you insight into why you date the way you do. Pay attention to your styles as you keep reading, and you'll likely find that you also resonate with stories and examples outside of your archetype(s). Plus, it's always interesting to think about how the person you're dating operates! Because after all, you'll meet many daters who approach dating much differently than you do. As we keep going, we'll be referring back to these archetypes often. This will help you see how you may be falling for some of the traps of modern dating through the lens of your dating style–and how you can rise above them. Speaking of traps . . . let's get into them!

PART 1:

The Traps of Modern Dating

Chapter 1:

The Expectation of Love on Demand

IT'S TIME TO BREAK UP WITH:

1. **Relationshopping:** The act of looking for your romantic partners like you would shop for items online.
2. **Daterviews:** A date that feels more like a job interview where you're peppered with questions instead of letting the connection naturally unfold.
3. **The Spark:** That elusive chemistry we're all chasing that ends up not being the best predictor of a good partner.

Yue was sitting across the table from a prominent tech founder at a friend's wedding. After he heard about her background as a dating expert, the founder's eyes lit up. "You know what we should build," he started thinking out loud. "There should be a [computer] program that takes all the qualities you're looking for in a partner and spits out the perfect person for you. You can skip the dating part and go straight to getting married. Voilà! No time wasted! My friends would kill for something like that."

While Yue was laughing along, the founder's idea made her think. On the one hand, wouldn't it be great to skip to the end? She had been through it all: countless first dates, the pain of unrequited love, and even a two-year relationship that made her feel more alone than when she *was* alone. At the time of this wedding, she had recently started dating someone new. They hadn't defined their relationship, and she was unsure how their future would unfold. A part of her wanted to fast-forward through the ambiguity of a new relationship and avoid the potential heartbreak she so deeply feared. But on the other hand, she knew that even though this founder's idea sounded like the next unicorn start-up, it would never work in practice. Because love takes time. Seeing whether you're the right fit for each other takes time. Revealing ourselves takes time. And connecting on a deep level takes time. Our **expectation for love on demand**, or the instantaneous and effortless connection that we believe we can have whatever we want, whenever we want, is *exactly* what's contributing to the impending love crisis. So how did we get here?

SORRY, YOU CAN'T ORDER
YOUR SOULMATE ON AMAZON

Today, we can get a car, a meal, or even a date at the touch of our fingertips. In two minutes or less, you can take a virtual yoga class, turn on a movie, or order groceries for delivery. It's also made us increasingly impatient (ever had an Uber say they are coming in over ten minutes!?!). We're used to Amazon Prime, where we find any product we could need, hit a button, and it's on our doorstep within forty-eight hours. And just like with everything else in today's world, daters expect instant attraction and connection when dating. When we match with someone on an app, we expect to chat immediately and meet within a few days. We decide on the first date if we can see a future with this person. And if we don't get a text back within a few minutes, we assume they've lost interest.

Dating apps perpetuate this expectation through their instant results. In fact, they are designed this way. In 2009, Grindr was the first app to feed into this expectation, utilizing Apple's geo-location data so you could meet up with someone nearby within minutes. But when Tinder launched in 2012, it forever changed the game, allowing the masses to create a dating profile in seconds (something that once took *forever* with the original dating sites like Match.com). Daters now had a singles bar at their fingertips where they could instantly match and chat. In the past with OG online dating sites, you'd spend hours crafting a long message, only to wait in limbo for weeks on end, as people weren't glued to their devices like they are today. Now, with everything optimized for your phone and an emphasis on quick scrollable photos over long profiles, you could browse through hundreds of people from anywhere.

Dating apps can feel like you're sifting through Amazon (although, wouldn't it be nice if your potential date could come with a five-star rating and reviews?). It messes with our heads because these aren't products we're shopping for; they are people! It's hard for even the most self-aware of us to context-shift and process information that's displayed similarly but is so fundamentally different.

This mental model makes us think of humans as products and commodities. We start "relationshopping" for our perfect mate by looking at a short list of attributes, a couple of photos, and a short bio, just like a consumer shopping for a product. Add in the gamification aspects that made dating apps so popular, and we start seeing people as disposable. Getting the "It's a match" message drops that hit of dopamine, keeping you engaged and endlessly scrolling to see what else is out there. All this is by design. Tinder followed the hooked model introduced by Nir Eyal, a prominent behavioral designer in the tech industry and the author of *Hooked: How to Build Habit-Forming Products*. There's a trigger that brings you to the product (e.g., a notification updating you on a past match or a new incoming message), followed by an action (in this case, swiping, which is similar to the infinite scroll concept in other apps). Most importantly, there's a variable reward, which is an element of gratification delivered intermittently, meant to keep users repeating the same action in the hope of another reward. Just like with gambling or video games that use the same mechanism, you can get addicted and more focused on "winning" matches than actually forming connections.

To be clear, we aren't anti-dating apps here, as we've both met long-term partners this way. Dating apps can be an excellent method to expand the pool of people you meet—and technology will only continue to grow, not go away. We have to acknowledge, though, that our digital landscape influences how we view dating and relationships. It's up to humanity to catch up to technology to ensure we're using apps and other methods to foster connection, not disconnection. Sure, you can send a message solely with emojis and GIFs, but is that the best way to get to know someone if you're looking for a relationship?

The Expectation of Love on Demand created by technology makes us anything but intentional when we date. Just as consumers scroll through Amazon or other sites out of boredom (often buying things they don't need, just to return them a few days later), daters do the same thing. They mindlessly swipe through hundreds of profiles because it's easy and because they can. So many daters today aren't dating mindfully and being intentional, but rather going through the motions. That's why so many people get stuck in a perpetual loop: blaming apps for all their dating troubles, uninstalling them only to reinstall them one week later. We do believe even in today's world, you can be an intentional dater and it's foundational to have the love life you want. But when you throw whatever to the wall to see what sticks, you'll come back empty-handed. In order to get there though, we must understand the influences around us and how we may sub-consciously fall for these traps.

REMEMBER YOUR DATING ARCHETYPE!

Using this lens will help you connect the dots to see how you may fall for the Expectation of Love on Demand.

- **Achievers:** How can you be less milestone-driven so you can enjoy the process?
- **Dreamers:** How can you not get ahead of yourself when meeting someone you like?
- **Energizers:** How can you put less emphasis on instant-connection chemistry?
- **Mavericks:** How can you let people reveal themselves instead of being quick to judge?
- **Thinkers:** How can you start letting situations play out over time?

LOVE ISN'T A ROM-COM

Let's not only blame technology. The Expectation of Love on Demand runs much deeper than that. As a generation who grew up on Disney movies and rom-coms, we saw how love could save us, change us, and conquer all. Don't get us wrong, we loved movies such as *Cinderella* and *The Little Mermaid*, but the message that one day our Prince Charming would magically arrive to give us the life we've always wanted is kind of f*cked when you think about it.

These movies gave us unrealistic expectations of how dating, love, and relationships work. The message for hetero women was just sit around and be pretty, and passively wait for love. And for hetero men, you just need to keep persisting. Once the two main characters finally get together, the credits roll. We don't see the disagreements, the challenges, or the hard conversations. It further skews our perception that love is effortless, which affects how we date and have relationships. We continue to swipe right if we don't see what we are looking for on date number one. And if our relationship falls short, we'll opt to be alone rather than work through the challenges. For many of us who grew up watching rom-coms, it takes conscious work to unlearn some of the messages we received. When we expect a big rom-com story, we often get ahead of ourselves, creating imaginationships (you know, when you fall for the fantasy of the person, creating a love story that's not grounded in reality).

One of the daters we met, Drea, is your typical Dreamer. As a thirtysomething nurse living in Washington, DC, she has a heart of gold and wants nothing more than her big love story. But whenever she'd meet someone she liked, she'd start to fixate about their future when they'd barely been on a couple of dates. Drea would build their relationship up in her head, believing it was more serious than it was. (They'd been dating for three months! Who cares if they only saw each other a grand total of six times!) She was constantly project-ing who she *thought* her dates were because she barely knew them. She assumed that liking someone was enough, and their great love story would begin. She spent more time in her head, thinking about what they *could* have together, instead of assessing the reality of the situation–and talking to her dates about what they even wanted. And not to mention it created so much anxiety at the beginning because she would be mapping out their next five years when they hadn't even defined the relationship.

Drea was out at a friend of a friend's birthday party one night and instantly locked eyes with a guy across the room. Like in the movies, she felt an immediate spark as they made their way to each other. After chatting for a bit, they ended up going back to her place. They continued to date for a few months–nothing super formal, but they'd text every couple of weeks and meet for a drink or bar trivia. They had even been texting about meeting for a game of bocce ball in the park and had a day date in the books! In Drea's head, there was no doubt they were on their way to becoming a couple. She couldn't wait to introduce him to her friends and become official. But, of course, they never once had a conversation about this.

On the day of their bocce date, Drea texted him to see when they would meet. To her surprise, he replied: Sorry, I totally forgot. I went away to Virginia for the weekend. Rain check? All week she had been looking forward to this date, and he had just forgotten? *At least he said "rain check,"* she justified to herself. In her mind, this was just a bump in the road. Drea was still holding out for that big grand ges-ture that would turn this love story around. But he never showed up with his boom box in the pouring rain. She never shared that his lack of communication hurt her, and their budding relationship began its slow fade. The End. Because this is real life, not a rom-com, after all.

Drea had to finally squash the fantasy and take the "relation-ship" at face value when his texts diminished to 2 a.m. booty calls. It took longer than she'd like to admit to detach from what had turned into a friends with benefits (FWB) situation. Because sometimes it actually can be safer to stay in the fantasy than to put yourself out there. But if you're looking for something real, instead of expecting that love (or like) is enough, you need to be realistic that it takes time—and conversations—to understand someone's mentality and intentions. Instead of falling for imaginationships, try to slow down and stay more objective—especially in the early stages when you don't fully know someone. We're not saying to play games or emotionally pull back, but rather to pay attention to how someone's really showing up. There are so many assumptions made in dating, especially ones that fit a romantic narrative we'd like to hold on to. It's hard not to get ahead of ourselves when we like someone. By staying a bit more objective and less attached to a certain outcome, you can look at each interaction as a way to gauge if this person is partner material. And if they aren't, you can find someone who is. In the early stages, it's all about observing and communicating. Understand that it takes time for people to reveal themselves. The more you can see situations for what they are, the less disappointed you'll be. Because when you build up a relationship as something it's not, you're depriving yourself of the ability to assess whether it's truly a good fit for you.

For whatever reason, our dating logic is different from other areas of life. If you went to a restaurant that was subpar at best, you wouldn't keep going to that spot, expecting it to change. Instead, you'd try the many other neighborhood gems out there! But for whatever reason, even when the person shows us they aren't who we thought they were, we try to regain the initial experience of the connection we envisioned. It's time that we drop the rom-com fantasy and take situations at face value. Ultimately, it'll be much more rewarding to fall in love with the person, not the idea of them—even if it takes more time.

So, how do you start being more realistic about how love works? Let's do a quick reality check:

The Rom-Com Way	Reality Check
Two characters meet, lock eyes, and instantly know they are soulmates.	You may have to swipe through hundreds of profiles, have countless first dates, and hang out multiple times before you know whether someone is a good fit for you. *This is normal!* Even if you meet IRL, you'll likely go on multiple dates and learn a lot more about the person to determine if they are right for you.
The two characters fall madly in love and know they have found "the One." When you know, you know.	You create love over time. You may not know immediately if this person is "the One." All that matters is if you're both on the same page regarding your needs, wants, and desires, and are committed to being together.
A big challenge or disagreement happens, almost breaking up the loving couple. But the hetero man declares his love, boom box in hand, in the pouring rain. All's well that ends well, and love conquers all—the end.	You *both* talk about the challenges, not just sweep them under the rug. Grand gestures and declarations of love do not solve your problems. Your bond strengthens as you learn to communicate effectively and navigate conflict. Love doesn't conquer all, but perseverance, mutual understanding, and realistic expectations of a relationship do. This isn't the end, but the start of deepening your relationship.

It's worth taking a minute to identify any strong ideas you have about dating and relationships. Are they creating expectations of how you think love should work? For instance, are you justifying an on-again, off-again relationship or holding on to the initial chemistry despite blatant incompatibilities? Are you cutting out at the first sign of conflict because you believe relationships should be easy? While it's tempting to think everything will just work out and we don't have to put in any work, these patterns are ultimately detrimental to our dating experience (and mental health!).

BDE (Big Dateable Energy):
The best love story is grounded in reality.

F*CK THE RULES

Many of us grew up reading dating bibles such as *The Rules*, *Why Men Love Bitches*, and *The Game*. They taught us hard-and-fast rules to follow: don't text for three days, don't reveal too much, and never show more interest than they're showing you. *The Rules* sold millions of copies because it held a promise: follow these time-tested secrets and you'll capture the heart of Mr. Right (or Ms. Right or Mx. Right, but yeah, the nineties). Despite the advice being questionable at best, it capitalized on the notion of Love on Demand. Just follow this simple formula of dos and don'ts and ta-da! You're in love!

Bad dating advice reinforced that everything should happen in a particular way: linearly, quickly, and without any difficult conversations. Especially for the Achievers out there, this type of instruction-based dating advice provided a method–but also an expectation of how a relationship should progress, clinging to arbitrary milestones and timelines. We've seen daters treat these resources as textbooks they can use to accomplish their love goals. Because if you study hard enough, you'll reach the desired milestones, right? But love doesn't work this way, though we want to think it does! Even today, decades after these books came out, we hear many dating conundrums centered around these dating norms: "Should I initiate a text if I haven't heard from them in three days?" or "Will they lose interest in me if I sleep with them on the third date?" The dynamics of dating and relationships have completely changed, yet we still hold on to the old, outdated rules to navigate the new way.

While these dating blueprints and rules help create a strategy around dating, all they do is set us up for disappointment. They cause us to act in ways that aren't authentic to who we are and actually *push away* human connection. *The Rules* taught daters to withhold their wants, needs, and desires and "play it cool" to attract a mate. All that does is make dating so petty. Would you deny a friend's weekend invite because they didn't ask you by Wednesday? Would you track how many hours it took your friend to reply to your text? Probably not. And that's why in dating, when things don't go 100 percent to plan, the anxiety kicks in or we decide this person isn't right for us. If they set up the next date a week too late or don't text when you think they should, everything starts to feel off-kilter. Even with the best intentions, people are rarely as predictable as these books make them seem. Like it or not, life happens. It's not an excuse for bad dating behavior, but being rigid doesn't set you and your partners up for success. The problem with the Expectation of Love on Demand is exactly that: it's an expectation.

Advice in *The Rules* results in short-term gains, and doesn't give daters the skills they need to build long-standing loving relationships. Instead of teaching necessary communication skills, this type of dating advice shows us how to play games and hide our true selves. It's not our fault: we never learned about love in school. As a result, we don't have the communication and relational skills to withstand the challenges of dating and relationships. Believe it or not, that person who ghosted you may be doing their best! Instead of addressing conflict, we run from it. We expect the people we date to be mind readers. There's a belief that they should just *know*, or the relationship isn't right. But that's so far from the truth. Every relationship has sources of contention–even in early stage dating. There's no way to avoid this unless you're dating a robot (please don't date a robot, we're begging you). Because when two people come together, they bring different perspectives, backgrounds, ways of thinking, and emotions.

When we talked to Dr. Alexandra Solomon on *Dateable*, she pointed out that conflict is inevitable in relationships. As a licensed clinical psychologist and the professor of the very popular Marriage 101 course at Northwestern University, she shared how the biggest dating mistake is jumping to someone new instead of trying to work through the challenges. When things don't go entirely our way, it's easy to swipe to the next person. We end up in an endless loop, and if we don't realize this trap, we'll go from person to person and bounce when sh*t gets hard–which will inevitably happen in every relationship.

To have the love lives we want, we need to get out of the mentality of expecting the right relationship to be effortless. While it should still feel relatively easy, it's not as simple as follow these thirty-five steps and you'll have the relationship of your dreams. It's all about honing your relational skills and being open and direct communicators. Contrary to popular dating advice, early stage dating is the best time to speak up and share your needs. Only then can you evaluate whether the person you're dating can meet them. Seeing how someone reacts when you're not totally aligned tells you so much more about the potential for this relationship than if you can have fun over a night of cocktails. So tell that person you're dating that you love a good-night text or that you want them to plan an evening out. See how they respond after sharing what you need. And instead of jumping ship at a single sign of contention, see how you can work through it together. You want to give people an opportunity to be a good partner to you, a crucial part of the getting-to-know-each-other stage. But if they aren't receptive? This is also valuable information that may make this person not the right partner for you. This is exactly the type of screening you should be doing early on!

In dating, we're all playing by unspoken rules and guidelines that aren't always authentic to who we are. These rules have not set us up for success—yet we continue to play by them. It's time to throw out the rules and start playing by our own.

Julie's Corner

I followed "the Rules" for years, thinking they would lead me to a partner. But all this did was give me anxiety and put me in a perpetual state of waiting to be chosen. I remember telling my married guy friend about a recent great date. He suggested texting my date to share how good of a time I had. I was shocked—he clearly knew nothing about dating! I couldn't text first or share my feelings like that! When that connection inevitably faded, I started to question why I was acting this way. As a naturally warm and friendly person, I wasn't showing my best traits—I was concealing them. So I stopped playing by the rules and started being more genuine. Not coincidentally that's when I started to get into actual relationships. Who would have guessed showing interest would also make people more interested in you?

YOU CAN'T HACK YOUR DATING LIFE

Our culture takes pride in being busy, so we look for easy solutions wherever possible. We want the latest tip, trick, or tactic to beeline to the finish line. We often see daters delete and reinstall the apps to trick the algorithm into prioritizing them as a new user. They change up their profiles weekly to gain traction. They'll A/B test their photos to see if that one with the half smirk will make people swipe more (you know, because of that air of mystery). We even see daters changing their age on their profile so they don't get cut off by other people's age filters (forever thirty-nine, huh?).

This mentality has been around long before dating apps, too. How many articles have you seen on the internet such as "Tricks to Make Women Like You" or "5 Time-Tested Ways to Get Him to Commit." People want the big secret–the big reveal of how to get the results you want. We're always looking for the latest methodology or a new way of doing–because we think that can explain why we're not meeting enough people or having the love life we've always wanted. One of the biggest questions we get from daters is where they can go to meet someone IRL. People are always looking for that magical place they'll walk into, and poof! their soulmate will be sitting right there. Spoiler alert: it's not the cryptocurrency meetup or your brother's cousin's holiday party (oh wait, isn't that your cousin, too?). Of course, you could meet someone at either of those places, but there's no magical moment where it'll just happen as it does in the movies (if there were, promise, we'd tell you).

If you've tried to hack dating, we get it; you want to get to your desired outcome ASAP. As humans, we love answers to our problems and a guarantee that we'll get what we want. We're always looking for ways to game the system . . . because dating is hard. But as we established earlier, these hacks tend to be shortsighted and cause us to spin our wheels more than set us up for a healthy relation-ship. When you're using hacks and tricks, you stop being yourself (cue the forever thirty-nine-year-old from earlier) while attracting people who are not looking for you . . . the real you. And that's never the best way to start a relationship. By focusing so much on how to hack the system, you lose track of what matters when dating. We get asked all the time why we haven't devoted episodes to talking about dating app algorithms and we always respond the same way: it's not worth anyone's time to agonize over. It's so much more fruitful to funnel your attention into building your relational skills–what you can control when dating. And then when the right person crosses your path (because they will, even without tricking an algorithm), the relationship will be on the right track from day one.

We get that it's challenging to make that real connection. It can feel draining to be on and off apps for years. But we need to remem-ber there is no formula for success in dating. Even if you're doing everything "right," you may not get instant results. The journey isn't always so linear. And if dating were so easy, finding that special someone wouldn't be so special. So, instead of trying to fast-track to the end, let's enjoy the process along the way. One day, when you find that great love, you'll see taking the long road was totally worth it.

> **BDE (Big Dateable Energy):**
> The only secret to finding your person
> is that there is no secret.

DEATH TO THE DATERVIEW

In today's busy world, where there are so many options, daters want to get all the information up front to make an informed decision as quickly as possible. We've seen daters do whatever they can to un-cover red flags early on, resorting to a daterview (you know, that date where it feels like you're more on a job interview than an actual date). And it makes sense why we turn to this type of tactic. We're told that dating is a numbers game and dating is like a job interview. You need to quickly cycle through all the people out there, because the worst thing you could do is waste time on the wrong person, right?

The problem is that we're not setting ourselves up for connection with this mentality. One of the daters we met, Maya, was the queen of the daterview and a Maverick to the core. As a busy professional in her midtwenties, Maya had a fulfilling life filled with trips around the world, a great job, and many single girlfriends with whom she partied on the weekends. Maya wanted the best in every aspect of her life—from the hottest new restaurant in New York City to the per-fect partner—and the last thing she wanted to do was settle. She had been single for the last four years, and while she'd rather be alone than with the wrong person, she still wanted to meet that special someone. Maya knew her type and had a clear vision of what she was looking for. So, like the best of us, she was on the apps, trying to find a match in the most efficient way possible.

Since she knew what she wanted, all she had to do was find him, right? Maya was guilty of relationshopping, swiping through her dat-ing apps like shopping for a new pair of shoes. She had her list of nonnegotiables—they had to be between the ages of twenty-eight and thirty-two, over six feet, live in Manhattan, and ideally work in tech or finance. These filters helped her narrow down her matches, but there was only so much she could infer from the profile. So she de-cided on a new system called "the five-minute date." She would vet the people briefly for the qualities she was looking for and then invite them to a coffee shop five minutes from her apartment. They'd both order drinks, and she'd decide within the first five minutes whether there was a connection. If not, she'd leave them money to cover the lattes and be on her merry way. If she felt that spark, she'd stay to finish her coffee and pull out her list (metaphorically, of course) of daterview-style questions: *Why are you still single? What do you do for work? Where did you go to school? Why did your last relationship end? What's your timeline for marriage and kids?*

We understand where Maya was coming from with this tactic. No one wants to be ghosted after a seemingly great four-hour date or after pouring their heart into a relationship that will only end in four months. So we do whatever we can to shield our hearts and have a strategy to optimize our time. But showing up with a checklist, needing to know immediately if this person is the one for you, doesn't make dating fun in the slightest! And it certainly doesn't make you someone open to a connection when the date feels like a job interview. Worst of all, it makes us focus on what the person *doesn't have* as opposed to getting to know the human being on the other side of the table.

We think these tactics are coming from a place of knowing what we want, but it's actually a form of self-protection. When we spoke with Nikki Novo, an intuitive and spiritual thought leader, on *Dateable,* she shared how a common misperception of using your intuition when dating is to get that quick yes or no. We do this because we tend to prioritize not feeling pain—even over experiencing love. Maybe we don't trust ourselves if we keep picking the wrong people or fear getting hurt. Or we struggle to sit in the ambiguity of not knowing if a relationship will pan out. But if we're really putting ourselves out there in a real way, we can't expect an instant answer. Dating today feels so transactional that we forget why we're dating in the first place. Love is soft and tender, yet we approach it with rigidity and judgment. Tactics like daterviews to suss out all the red flags or making ridiculous rules ("I'll never date someone whose first name starts with *J* again!") are driven more by our heads than our hearts.

Instead of resorting to the daterview or another hack you can use to know whether this person will be *your* person, get comfortable with the ambiguity of *not* knowing. You may find it challenging to relinquish this control (we sure as heck did), but this is what opens your heart. As Nikki mentioned, instead of looking for a yes or no on date number one, lean into the energy of curiosity. Instead of needing to know immediately, see if you're being drawn to this person. Sure, you may open yourself up to being hurt, but you'll also open yourself up to being loved. Instead of prioritizing speed, prioritize your energy levels when dating. Nikki shared that the best check-ins are *Do I still feel hopeful? Do I feel optimistic? Do I believe this is going to happen for me?* We lose ourselves if we get jaded. We think prioritizing speed protects us—but it actually hurts us.

There are no guarantees in love—but it's a risk we're pretty sure you want to take, or you wouldn't be reading this book. The first step is to recognize that these tactics are more about self-protection than anything else. Trusting the process may be scary. We're not telling you to wait years or invest in the wrong people (more on that later). But in early dating, you'll get your answer fairly quickly even if you give someone a little more time. Maybe you don't feel the spark immediately on date number one, but if you're attracted enough, go on that second date. By a couple of dates later you'll be able to tell whether the chemistry is growing or not. In the grand scheme of your journey, that extra time rarely makes a difference. But giving that person more of a chance instead of writing them off immediately could make all the difference in the world.

WHEN YOU KNOW, YOU KNOW ... OR DO YOU?

We've also been led to believe that the key to a good partner is that instant chemistry—or that elusive spark we all hear about. But we're here to tell you that this may be one of the worst indicators of whether someone is right for you. And it's not our fault: the rom-coms and society's portrayal of love have made us believe in this "when you know, you know" love-at-first-sight feeling.

Eli was a good-looking man in his early forties, an influencer who lived in LA. He had no problem meeting men, whether on the apps or IRL. He was an Energizer to the core—always on the go. Wherever Eli went, he thought he could meet his soulmate. And often, he did! The problem was that none of them could ever stick past the six-month mark. Eli was the ultimate spark chaser. He truly believed that *when you know, you know*. This usually led him to attractive and charismatic men who were not always the best for him. Eli was always judging the connection by the initial chemistry. He often dove headfirst (including when he moved to Argentina on a whim after meeting a hot bartender on vacation) because he believed that's how love worked. Then, like clockwork, when the six-month mark rolled around, he would inevitably realize their connection didn't have the legs to last.

Hear us out: it's rather alarming to believe that a strong connection on a first date indicates a future with this person. Back in the day (you know, before the internet and apps), people dated their neighbors, coworkers, classmates, and churchgoers. You got to know each other slowly—often before it became romantic. You could see how they interacted with others, dealt with adversity, and reacted when sh*t got hard. So why do we have this expectation today, that we must feel that electricity right away? Instead of focusing on the spark, see if there can be a slow burn.

Even if you meet on a dating app, you can let the relationship develop organically—if you drop this Expectation of Love on Demand. We think we meet people with potential, but we only have a glimpse into who they are. We need to determine whether they will have good follow-through, are trustworthy, share our values, or even want the same things we do. How could you glean all of that from one or two dates? Or even worse–a dating bio? Yet even so, the expectation is that you'll know right away, thanks to sayings such as *when you know, you know,* or the rom-com effect of believing in love at first sight. Because dating apps create an abundance of choice, it's quite common to go on a date thinking you need to decide if this is your soulmate by the end of the night. There's no way you'll know how you can ride out the waves of life with someone after an hour together. You don't have 99 percent of the info you need to determine whether this person would be a good life partner. We must accept that it's impossible to tell this early in the game.

Of course, we've all heard of a couple who meets, and *bam!* are engaged within a couple of months. But that's not the norm. Instead of prioritizing knowing immediately through the spark, we must change our expectations to appreciate the time it takes for a relationship to unfold. Instead of seeing this as a burden, see it as a gift. And when you think of it, would you even want to rob yourself of deepening a connection that comes with every stage? We may think we want a turbo relationship (i.e., one where you reach each milestone at an accelerated pace) because then we can be done, dammit! But a strong relationship doesn't work like that–there's no fast-forward button. And there's so much excitement in just getting to know each other; why would you want to rush through those initial feelings?

ARE THEY A GROWER OR A SHOW-ER?

By being more open to letting connections develop over time, you can also find the hidden gems out there (i.e., those emotionally available people who seem so rare today). Some of us are really good at dating. We're able to form a connection with anyone and everyone. But this comes more naturally to some of us than to others. Like *ahem* certain other things, some of us are show-ers, and others are growers. So many daters are naturally a bit shy and reserved—especially as dating is inherently awkward! Maybe this same person is outgoing with their friends, but it took years to build that rapport. Their dates don't even see that person because they decide within one hour (or even five minutes, if you're like Maya) whether they're someone they envision a life with. Not to say you'd fall madly in love with every single person after a few dates, but at least you'd start to uncover the many sides of them and see!

When we put that romantic pressure on a stranger, we're setting unrealistic expectations of someone we don't know well. A good relationship is built on a solid friendship. Build that friendship first. And remember that friendship takes time. When you think about your closest friends: were you immediate BFFs? Probably not. So don't expect an instant connection with your romantic prospects, either.

If you feel a hard no for someone, don't waste your time or theirs to keep seeing each other. But if you find yourself intrigued by someone, even if they aren't who you expected you'd end up with, keep exploring that intrigue. You may be thinking, *If I give everyone a chance, how will I be able to go on dates with* all *these people? How can I possibly give them* all *my time?* Well, friends, this is exactly what this book will help you with. It deserves repeating that dating is *not* a numbers game (yup, you heard us right), so rest assured we'll help you focus on the *right* people. There's no way to go out with everyone, but we aren't proposing that either. This book will help you know who to give your time and attention to—promise. And if you're getting a bad vibe, listen to that instinct. But if you're expecting to know that this person is right for you immediately, know that isn't realistic. That's just the Expectation of Love on Demand getting in your way.

Yue's Corner

I learned this lesson with my first significant relationship. On our first date, I decided he was not the one for me because I didn't feel a spark. However, I thought he was a great catch and wanted to introduce him to my best friend. So, I decided I'd get to know him platonically first before introducing them. Then when he went away for a week, I started to miss him! We had built such a strong friendship that I couldn't picture my life without him. And to my surprise, I found him more and more attractive. The connection grew strong, and I didn't even plan it that way. When he returned, I told him everything, and we quickly fell in love. That relationship lasted for five years!

THE ONLY WASTE OF TIME

In an effort not to waste time on the wrong people, we've seen daters clock dozens of unpaid hours, honing their detective skills as the Nancy Drew of dating apps. Before even matching with someone, they'll spend twenty minutes reviewing their profile and text their friends screenshots to get their take on the viability of someone's potential. Since we expect to know immediately if someone could be worth our time, we do whatever it takes to assess the situation.

Here's a perfect example of why this type of analysis doesn't work. Our podcast has an online community called Big Dateable Energy where members post their burning questions and help each other navigate modern dating. In one post, a member asked: "What does it mean when someone says, 'I like people who don't take life too seriously' in their profile?" It wasn't the question, per se, that was particularly interesting, but the interpretations of that one phrase were mind-blowing. We saw responses including:

"I don't like workaholics or people who are serious."

"I'm not looking to be tied down right away."

"I'm someone who enjoys life and can positively handle the rough times."

"I'm looking for someone who isn't rigid and can be flexible and open-minded."

"I'm looking for a casual relationship."

"I like to keep things superficial and not discuss serious topics."

"I don't want to be held to any expectations or standards."

Finally, one of our group members, Julia, chimed in as she used this language in her profile. Julia was shocked by the interpretations and never realized how people would view this statement to mean she wasn't looking for something serious when she meant "easygoing." She was very intentional about dating and sought a deeply connected relationship. It's a perfect example of how reading into one sentence could turn you away from someone looking for the same things as you. And not to mention how much time it took to decode something that didn't even end up being an indicator in any way!

While we don't believe the act of dating is ever a waste of time, getting hung up on the perfect opening line or what a phrase in their profile may or may not mean *is* a waste of time. No wonder people have dating app fatigue and burnout–they spend countless hours on interactions that don't even result in conversing with another human being! Especially for the Thinkers out there, the need to analyze every profile and message can send you into a state of analysis paralysis. We expect dating apps to be the silver bullet–to deliver our soulmate with the click of a button. But it doesn't work that way. It's nearly impossible to understand who someone is from a 2D photo and a couple of lines in a bio. Since dating apps give us the résumé of a potential match, we often fill in the blanks. But it's within the blanks that connection is formed.

The quicker we can all accept there's absolutely no way to know whether this person will be your person from their dating app profile or any other shortcut you're trying to take, the more you can focus on just seeing if you want to spend more time together. Call this a revolutionary idea: the only way to get to know someone is to *get to know someone*. Whether you're meeting them on apps or in the wild, it doesn't matter; you still need to have conversations, learn about each other, and see if this is a person who you want to spend time with. And dating is never a waste of time if you're getting to know another human being, figuring out what's important to you in a relationship, and understanding yourself better in the process.

Here's a hot tip: move the conversation off the app ASAP and get to the date! This is the one area we want you to fast-forward. So many connections fade when we spend weeks in a texting black hole. Get a Google Voice number if you don't want to give out your number yet. Have a phone or video call first to be more comfortable meeting them. Do whatever you need to do to move this process along. While the rest of falling in love takes time to unfold, this is the one part that should move quickly. We'll be going into this in much more depth in the second part of the book, don't you worry!

> **BDE (Big Dateable Energy):**
> Dating is never a waste of time if you're connecting.

TRUST IN YOUR TIMING

While it's natural to want this part of your life to fall into place, we need to trust our timing. We no longer live in a world where single people over thirty are outcasts (thanks, *Sex and the City*!). We're living longer than ever, so forty isn't even middle age. There are advances in science and technology that will help us reproduce later in life–if we even want to. People are constantly entering the dating pool after first, second, or third marriages. Younger generations are fluid, continuously exploring sexuality and gender identities, so why can't our love life take a similar form? While it's hard not to cling to societal tropes and stereotypes, remember you have time to let everything fall into place. Because you're meant for a great love–not just anyone. In the following chapters, we hope to alleviate some of the pressure you may be putting on yourself (as we experienced, too!). Dating is much more fun when you're not trying to rush to meet timelines. We're not saying you'll never feel stressed about time or wasting time (because some of it is only natural, especially when the biological clock is at play . . .). Still, it is a good perspective shift that not only can you find love and connection at any age, but it could be the best thing for your love life!

When we first spoke with former CNN anchor May Lee on *Dateable*, she shared how she had put love on the back burner for so long due to her career. May had her slew of dating experiences and relationships, but no one she pictured building a life with. At fifty-five, she was happy with her single life, but our conversation piqued her interest to get back on the apps–and to her surprise, she met someone wonderful. Two years later, she got engaged for the first time at age fifty-seven. Looking back, she believes all her relationships prepared her for this one, as she had never experienced a connection that was so open and communicative. She trusted her timing.

Who you spend your life with is a big decision. So it's good that our expectations are high (as long as we focus on the right things, something we'll discuss in the next chapter). It's a trap when we think it'll be an instant connection and we can fast-track to the end. Dating apps are meant to be introductions, not a way to skip through all the work of a relationship. The right person for you doesn't show up off the shelf. By understanding that building a partnership requires time and effort, we can reduce the significance placed on immediate "sparks," ultimately lifting ourselves out of the love crisis fueled by people giving up on each other too quickly.

KEY TAKEAWAYS

1. Give yourself the gift of time. While it may seem tempting to skip to the end, you rob yourself of the journey and experience of falling in love.
2. Unrealistic expectations of love keep us on the dating hamster wheel. Instead of running into a fictitious perfect relationship that doesn't exist, embrace the conflict and challenging conversations. Make sure you're living in reality, not a fantasy.
3. Opt for the long road of getting to know someone over the shortcut of inferring who they are. The only way to find something out is to see or hear it firsthand from the person you're trying to date.
4. The only waste of time in dating is when you're overanalyzing and ruminating. Stop trying to infer everything about someone through a dating profile and start having more conversations to get to know them as a human.
5. Chemistry and the spark are only a fraction of a relationship. We know that good on paper doesn't always equate to a good partner, so let's ditch the daterview and get to know each other!

Chapter 2:

The Settling Paradox

IT'S TIME TO BREAK UP WITH:

1. **Situationships:** Romantic relationships that lack clear labels and commitment, and are undefined, ambiguous, and uncertain by nature.
2. **Red-Flag Hunts:** Trying to discover anything and everything that could be a red flag—and often ignoring actual relationship deal-breakers.
3. **Finding "The One":** The concept that there's one perfect person out there with all the qualities you are looking for.

Drea called us in tears, frustrated over the guy she had been seeing for six months. She hadn't heard from him all week after they had an incredible time last Friday (and well into Saturday morning, if you know what we mean). Unfortunately, this wasn't unusual behavior for him. While it was great when they were together, he inconsistently popped in and out of her life, saying how much he missed her, only to not return her texts for a week. Drea had a hunch he was probably sleeping with other people, too (evidence: the hair tie she found at his place that was most certainly not hers). But despite blatantly telling her that he didn't want a girlfriend, she was determined to win him over (she was a Dreamer, after all). She hadn't met someone like him in ages: they had a classic "meet-cute" story when he approached her IRL during a SantaCon holiday bar crawl where they were dressed as Mr. and Mrs. Claus, respectively. So what if he had been so absolutely hammered that he didn't even remember her name the following day? He was six foot three, funny as hell, and made at least six figures. She told her friends she didn't want to settle for someone who didn't have these qualities, yet she was settling for a nonreciprocal, unpredictable, and uncommitted relationship (i.e., a situationship) instead.

Why would a smart woman like Drea want to be with a f*ck-boy like this? Because for years, society has told us what attributes to look for in a partner—mainly superficial qualities that look good on paper. They should be smart, successful, hot, and funny. But we never talk about how we want someone to make us feel. And when we do, we focus on the highs, not the consistent feeling we get from being with (and away from) this person. We're so scared of settling for someone who doesn't feel like our ideal partner that we end up swinging too far on the pendulum and settling for less-than-ideal treatment or unfulfilling relationships. Which brings us to the **Settling Paradox**, a phase where we tend to hyperfocus on surface-level qualities, often overlooking the qualities necessary for a healthy, long-term, emotionally fulfilling partnership. This fear of settling, ironically, leads us to settle for the wrong things, dismissing potentially suitable individuals while making space for those who are not. This cycle causes people to give up on finding genuine, meaningful connections, plunging us further into the love crisis. So why are we so afraid to settle, so much that we end up settling for the wrong relationships?

OUR IDEAL PARTNER PREFERENCES

We all have a vision of the type of partner we picture ourselves with. Whether it's from society's portrayal of what makes someone attractive or the kind of person our parents told us was "relationship material," an image in our mind has been reinforced over the years. Our preferences are based on mere exposure as well: whether it's from people we've seen in real life or through movies, television, and other media. The familiarity principle in social psychology (or the mere-exposure effect) shows that we're attracted to what is familiar to us, and that repeated exposure to certain people will increase our attraction toward them. So it's not our fault: our influences have made us believe a desirable partner is someone who is six feet tall, wears a size two, or has a hefty bank account—or whatever other traits you've been conditioned to believe are important.

But have you ever stopped to wonder why these traits even matter to you? It seems like everyone has a similar checklist that we've been regurgitating for generations. We tend to talk blindly about the characteristics we want because that's what we hear people say makes a desirable partner, and it's easy for us to wrap our heads around them. We gravitate toward the more surface-level, superficial characteristics of a person because they're simpler to quantify. When a friend asks you about your type, you don't try explaining that you're looking for someone with a kind heart, who gets you for the person you are, because how would she even know who to start looking for? So instead we say we like tall blonds who are funny and like to travel. We're all guilty of leaning into the superficial qualities first; it has been ingrained in our heads for years. No wonder we prioritize these aspects when discussing what we're looking for in a partner!

Daters also tell us they have a fear of "dating down"–especially if they've been single for a while and accomplished so much in their lives. We've seen daters list hundreds of qualities they're looking for (including us at one point–guilty!). If you're a triathlete, then of course you want someone to compete in races with you. If you've been to thirty-six countries (and counting!), you want someone well traveled. And if you're doing well in your career, you also want someone who earns at least six figures so you can enjoy twenty-dollar martinis. So what if you're eliminating 75 percent of the dating pool with height requirements alone?

We all have these aspirational qualities we use as a baseline of who would be good for us, some of which we don't even live up to ourselves. We've seen it all: from the woman with the laundry list of qualities representing less than 1 percent of the population, to the guy who wants someone fit when the only exercise he's done recently was walking from his fridge to the couch. We've seen plenty of people include photos of themselves at Machu Picchu (half of the people on Tinder, it feels!), hoping to attract an adventurous traveler, even when that photo was taken five years ago and they haven't been out of the country since. And remember the one time you ran a half marathon ten years ago? You totally need a fellow runner, right?

Settling gets a bad rap because it implies that you're sacrificing or accepting less than you deserve. The person you're seeing isn't enough: they're not hot enough, funny enough, successful enough, charismatic enough, and the list goes on and on. In hopes of finding the total package, we focus on specific surface-level traits or characteristics for people to measure up to. But in reality, we end up missing out on the big-picture view of how we feel around this person–you know, the *actual* total package. This feeling of needing "the best" or having all the boxes checked keeps us on a dating hamster wheel forever. All this does is make you feel like you're looking for a needle in a haystack. We're not telling you to date someone you're not attracted to or to throw away all your standards (more on that later). But we need to redefine what qualities matter to us and recognize when we're sacrificing fundamentals for some vision of a partner that may not even be what we truly need.

REMEMBER YOUR DATING ARCHETYPE!

Using this lens will help you connect the dots to see how you may fall for the Settling Paradox.

- **Achievers:** How can you prioritize being in the *right* relationship, not any relationship?
- **Dreamers:** How can you take situations at face value instead of seeing the potential?
- **Energizers:** How can you be more discerning of who you go on dates with?
- **Mavericks:** How can you expand outside of your typical type?
- **Thinkers:** How can you focus on what feels good for you even if it's not always logical?

WE'RE FILTERING ALL WRONG

Dating apps perpetuate our fixation with more superficial traits because we can't filter for the qualities that actually matter. You can learn someone's height, occupation, or sun sign from a profile, but you can't tell whether they will be loyal or run when times get tough. Dating apps have reduced people to profile pics, so it's only natural to judge a book by its cover. According to a study by NYU, our average attention span gives us seven seconds to form an impression. So, of course we'll be swayed by superficial qualities!

Dating apps give us an easy way to check all the boxes. And with the abundance of choice dating apps provide, it's easy to swipe past someone who may not hit all the marks. The irony is that the one thing that you don't need in a relationship is a dating profile. With all the technological advances, it's incredible we're still vetting partners this way. People struggle with dating apps because your life partner can't be reduced to a list of qualities. Humans are much more dynamic than that! There are the intangibles that can't be summed up by where someone went to school or if they're in your Uber radius. So it's never surprising when we hear another story of how someone would have passed over their partner on an app if they hadn't met IRL. What ended up attracting them in the first place (like their positive energy or caring personality, for instance) would have never come through in this two-dimensional space.

As we know, it's nearly impossible to tell from a dating app whether someone will be your person from just the information given on the screen. Dating apps give us a feeling of endless options, an illusion of trading up for some ideal we hold in our minds. And the qualities we're fixating on may not even be an accurate representation of who they really are! We've heard countless stories of when someone looks way different from their profile pic IRL (for better or for worse). That's not to say we can't use dating apps and technology effectively because we certainly believe you can. And we will get to that in a later chapter, revealing ways to make the apps work *for* you. But first, we need to understand the limitations of the data and information we're presented with–and how this affects the dateability of potential partners, whether we meet them online or in the wild.

THERE'S NO CHECKLIST FOR COMPATIBILITY

When we're so focused on superficial traits, the problem is that we often minimize crucial qualities that make us compatible for the long haul. We conflate compatibility with similarity: "We both play tennis" or "We both grew up on the East Coast." While it's always nice to have something in common, it's just happenstance, and it says nothing about how you'd operate in a relationship. For example, even if you both play tennis, that's not a sign of compatibility, per se. Compatibility is someone's attitude and behaviors in relation to yours; it's so much more important that someone is excited to support your interests while they develop their own—which may or may not be tennis! The actual definition of compatibility, according to the *Cambridge English Dictionary*, is being able to exist, live, or work successfully with something or someone else. There's evidence that the happiest couples end up being more complementary, where they can round out each other's personalities. Of course, we want to share similar values and aspects of our lifestyle, but we must stop expecting our partners to be carbon copies of ourselves and thinking we're with the wrong person because we aren't 100 percent aligned on every last thing.

When we met Tori, we knew she was a Thinker to the core when we saw the list of qualities she was looking for in a partner. She had really thought hard about her list, making it as exhaustive as she possibly could . . . or so she thought. Her list was quite logical: Tori had lived in San Francisco for the last decade and wanted someone equally committed to staying in the city. She had been an avid skier since she was ten and wanted a fellow snow bunny she could spend weekends in Tahoe with, cuddled up by the fire after a long day on the slopes. And as a software engineer, she wanted another STEM professional who could relate to her challenges as a woman in tech.

This list wasn't wrong. You can even argue that it made sense to focus on compatible lifestyles. But Tori's list was coming from her head, not her heart. These were not qualities that would sustain a relationship, yet she held on to relationships because someone matched these qualities. And most importantly, they weren't grounded in what would make a compatible partner *for her*. Tori wasn't in tune with what qualities she needed for both romantic chemistry and long-term compatibility. When she stayed in the Settling Paradox, she did not feel anything for any of the women she dated. And often, she went on that second, third, and fourth date because they had what she was looking for on paper. She continued to date one woman for a month despite not actually even *liking* her as a person.

When Tori finally realized that she was drawn to certain qualities at the expense of mutual respect, trust, good communication, and emotional connection—you know, what matters for the long haul—she realized something needed to change. When she started to refocus her list on compatibility, she realized what she wanted and what she needed were two very different things. Tori also noticed that many of the women she met who were fellow STEM professionals ended up being *too* similar to her. Their conversations often fell flat, and she wondered whether someone more extroverted would better balance her out. Eventually Tori realized she didn't need someone in her professional field; she just wanted someone who could listen and support her dreams and aspirations. She needed someone who wanted to spend time with her—and whose company she equally enjoyed. Someone who understood her, loved her, and just wanted to be with her. You would think: "Yeah, isn't that every relationship?" Well, not when you're in the Settling Paradox, overemphasizing qualities that don't matter and settling for less than what is needed for a fulfilling relationship.

We want you to think long and hard about what qualities are essential to you in a partner and how to prioritize ones that matter more. We'll dive into our Perfect Partner Equation in chapter 6 to help you with this. But for now, stop thinking compatibility equals similarity. Instead, focus on what's a measure of compatibility for you. Think back to your closest friends' qualities (or even ex-partners!) that just worked for you. What made you trust someone? What made you feel good in their presence? What made you work well together? Like we said, we'll go into this in much more detail. But for now, we want you to start putting these qualities at the forefront when evaluating potential partners. As Tori realized, she still wanted someone who shared the same lifestyle and values. But it didn't necessarily have to show up in the way she once thought. After all, Tori could easily find someone who would happily go to Tahoe even if they weren't skiing black diamonds. But finding someone with the integrity, loyalty, and accountability she needed was much more important.

> **BDE (Big Dateable Energy):**
> You're looking for your complement, not your clone.

WE'RE IGNORING THE REAL RED FLAGS

In an effort not to settle, we want to look out for the red flags. But we see daters nitpicking every slight interaction or ick instead of paying attention to the actual issues that become detrimental to a relationship. They suggested going for a walk on a date? Next. They don't have a social media presence? Suspect. They've been single for over a year? Something must be wrong. Have a pet chinchilla? WTF. While these may not be our ideal preferences, there's a line between an incompatibility or annoyance and something that could be a red flag or deal-breaker.

So, what is an actual red flag? We like this definition by the self-help expert Dr. Wendy Walsh: "In relationships, red flags are signs that the person probably can't have a healthy relationship, and proceeding down the road together would be emotionally dangerous." Let's take one of the above red flags. Maybe they've been single for a while because something is fundamentally wrong with them to make them undateable. Or perhaps it's just that dating is hard and they haven't found the right person yet (PS: aren't you single, too?). We make so many assumptions and judgments right off the bat that we could take this as an opportunity to learn more. By throwing up "red flags" at every ick, it minimizes *actual* red flags, such as not being respectful, not having emotional intimacy, or being abusive. You know, the actual red flags that wreak havoc on your relationships.

Let's really think about the term "red flag" when using it. As we mentioned earlier, no one will meet every criterion on your list. No one has every aspect of their life together. Yet, we expect perfection and stay endlessly on the dating hamster wheel, uninstalling and reinstalling our dating apps in search of "the One" (which we know doesn't exist). Or we settle for unrequited love, unfulfilling relationships, or, worse, bad treatment. Especially the Energizers out there, you may be guilty of getting so caught up in the spark that you miss the real red flags. The feeling that it's better to be with someone than no one really prevents you from recognizing a good partner when you meet one.

So, how do you know if something is a red flag that could become a deal-breaker (i.e., a reason you end a relationship)? Let's take a look at some examples:

Assumed Red Flags	Actual Red Flags (Maybe Even Deal-Breakers)
They text too much, even throwing a double text here and there.	You're the only one texting.
You aren't instantly crazy about them.	They make you feel crazy (gaslighting at its finest).
They haven't said they love you yet (mind you, it's only been a couple of months).	They love bomb you (which later leads to manipulation).
They ask you out again on a date within the same week (not so fast, buddy!).	They never actually ask you out on a real date (is this going anywhere?).
They don't like to go out and party.	The only time you see them is after two in the morning when they've been partying.
They don't have a lot of sexual experience.	They only have sexual experience.
They want to put a label on it within the first couple of months.	The only label they want is f*ck buddy.
They want to hang out a lot.	You never know when you're going to hang out next.
The spark isn't immediately there.	All that's there is the initial spark.

Again, it comes back to: are you vetting for the right things? The best part of a relationship is being with someone you feel secure enough with to be your true self. You're working toward similar goals in life and see your future together. Maybe you aren't together 24/7 yet, but you know you are an essential part of each other's lives, and you see your relationship continuing to grow. You're aligned with what kind of life you want to create together. You welcome each other's baggage and commit to unpacking and healing together. If these building blocks aren't there, what's the point when you really think about it? By understanding the real red flags and the actual deal-breakers, you can save yourself from settling for the wrong people. And who knows, that person with the pet chinchilla may end up being a fabulous partner.

STOP SETTLING FOR SITUATIONSHIPS

So now that we've examined what red flags to really look out for, we're hoping it becomes abundantly clear when you find yourself settling for situationships: the ambiguous relationship that has you wondering "What are we?" Situationships lack the definition and commitment of a real relationship—and can keep us on the hook with people who can never give us what we truly want. While this may sound all well and good (It's cool, it's casual! We'll just see where this goes!), situationships tend to be full of anxiety, confusion, and uncertainty because you never know where you stand. They lack the trust, intimacy, communication, and support one ultimately needs from a relationship. We don't know about you, but feeling emotionally distraught doesn't seem like a healthy situation. Yet many daters stay in situationships long past their expiration date (including both of us, guilty as charged).

So, have you found yourself settling in a situationship? Let's do a quick gut check:

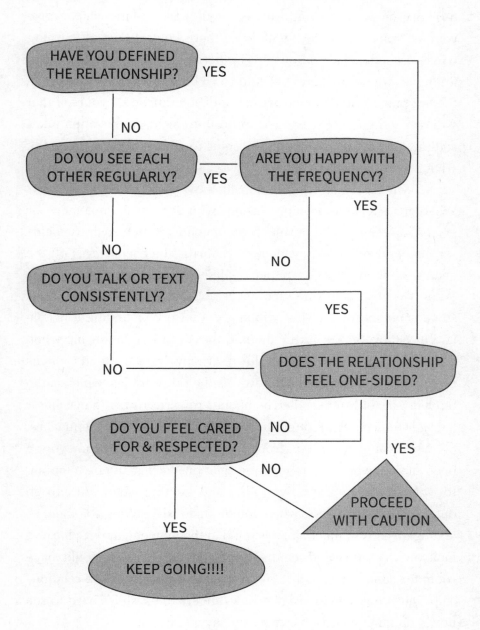

If you're finding your latest fling falling into more situationship territory or seeing a pattern over your past "relationships," give yourself some grace. We've all been there before! Part of learning what's essential in a relationship is experiencing what you *don't* want firsthand. Your mom may have told you a hundred times not to touch the hot pan, but it probably wasn't until you touched it yourself that you realized you never wanted to do that again. And it often takes settling for one too many situationships to change your definition of what settling actually is.

So why do we stay in relationships we know aren't serving us? Whether it's a situationship, a friends with benefits arrangement, or even a one-sided relationship, it often comes from a scarcity mindset that we won't find anyone better. Maybe the chemistry is off the charts, or their good-on-paper qualities are too hard to pass up. When we meet someone who checks all the boxes on our list, it's some accomplishment—like winning the lottery or finding a needle in a haystack. So, we justify the bad parts of the relationship when strong feelings of lust (or even love!) are involved. We tend to focus on the now, a phenomenon known as the present bias, which is the tendency to settle for smaller, immediate rewards rather than wait for a larger future payoff, often undervaluing long-term consequences. So, when you get that text from your toxic ex or that person you've been seeing (who "isn't ready for a relationship"), it can be tempting to want to meet up. It's always fun and exciting when you two go out. But that next week when you're anxiously waiting for them to text again—not so much. It feels good in the moment, and it's hard to look into the future and see that letting go of this person could make room for someone equally open to a committed long-term relationship. Our future selves are almost strangers to us, so it's hard to see how stopping one action today may pay off later.

But there's always an opportunity cost. The only way to make room for the right person is to stop settling for people who aren't treating you the way you want to be treated. The next time you find yourself holding on to a situationship, take a step back and see if this person has the qualities you want—you know, the ones that correlate with chemistry *and* long-term compatibility. And if they don't, remember your future self will thank you someday if you let them go. Even if it means being on your own for a bit. So, if you're at a crossroads where deep down you know you're holding on to someone who isn't right, the best decision can be to end the relationship (even if the other person still wants to be with you on their terms).

Believing there is someone better out there is going to take a leap of faith. It will require that you reframe what matters and develop an abundance mindset. When you start to believe that there are many great people out there, you won't have that crippling anxiety of losing "the One" or getting rejected because you'll know there's someone better suited for you. You may be thinking, easier said than done, but we guarantee you'll have a different outlook on it all by the end of this book. We know this type of partner and relationship is out there, and soon you will, too. And then you'll be able to look back and wonder why you ever settled for anything less.

> **BDE (Big Dateable Energy):**
> Why settle for crumbs when you can have the whole damn cake?

THE PROBLEM WITH BANKING ON POTENTIAL

One of the biggest reasons we stay in situationships or relationships that aren't serving us is that we're hoping for change. Cue the sunk-cost fallacy, where we've already invested so much time and energy, the last thing we want to do is walk away. So often, we get caught up in who we want someone to be that we overlook the person they are.

We become their inadvertent PR agents, rationalizing their every action—or inaction. Didn't text back for a week? It's been busy at work. They aren't ready to DTR (define the relationship)? It's okay; it'll happen once they finally get over their ex. We may know deep down that this person isn't showing up the way we want, but when our beliefs clash with our actions (cognitive dissonance, as psychologists call it), we tend to justify behaviors that may not align with our true desires. This is the true definition of settling—when we aren't being honest with our wants and needs. Instead of having actual conversations or walking away, we bank on the potential instead of recognizing the current situation. We say that things will work out when they change jobs, or when they deal with their depression, or when they finally realize they *should* be in a relationship. Our minds can justify any behavior if it supports our narrative. Especially for the Dreamers out there, we need to stop convincing ourselves that love will conquer all while settling for less-than treatment, gray areas, and situationships.

As your typical Dreamer, Drea continued to hold on to the f*ckboy she met at SantaCon despite knowing he wasn't treating her well. Unfortunately, she had a pattern of doing this: many of her relationships were highly one-sided. From her "ex," who would only refer to her as his "friend," to her friend with benefits who made out with someone else in front of her face, Drea had a slew of unhealthy relationships. She was guilty of getting caught up in her ideal vision of the person, and the SantaCon f*ckboy was no different. Even though they hadn't gone on an actual date for months after they met, Drea hung on to their first night out together. It was Christmas; they bonded over sushi and their Jewish upbringings. He was attractive and successful—the type of guy Drea always envisioned for herself!

But after the holidays (and conveniently when she started to catch feelings), he never seemed to have the time to meet up anymore. He was too busy working. Whenever one project was done, another quickly occupied his time. Their dinners turned into texts that eventually turned into emails (why he had time to send emails all day while he was so busy at work is still a mystery). She tried to rationalize why he could never meet up because she was so wrapped up in what *could* be. So what if he lived and worked two blocks away from her? He was busy with work. He was good on paper, but not in practice.

In her mind, they were in a relationship for close to a year but all they really had was a textlationship (you know, when all your interactions are over text only). This is the danger of banking on potential. His crumbs of attention validated this was *something*, but was it really a relationship or a fulfilling dating situation? Absolutely not! This is a dynamic we see all too often in situationships, where you get a dopamine hit from those occasional spikes of relationship-like behavior, keeping you hooked. Eventually, Drea expressed her need for a real relationship, where they were exclusive and saw each other at least once a week (ummmm . . . the bare minimum, in our opinion). As expected, he told her he didn't have the time or energy to devote to a relationship.

Despite getting rejected, this was the best thing that could have happened to Drea. She finally removed the rose-colored glasses and could stop expending energy on someone who was only giving her breadcrumbs. The only way to ensure you aren't settling is to be realistic with how the person you're dating shows up *today*. While your friends with benefits *could* turn into something more, the odds aren't on your side here (in fact, a study showed only 15 percent of friends with benefits relationships became romantic partners). If you're looking for a committed monogamous relationship, the best thing you can do is focus on others looking for the same thing as you *right now*.

So next time you have a situation where you're always wondering what could be, ask yourself: *Do I like the person they are today or who I want them to be in the future? Am I happy with the relationship as is, or am I banking on it to change?* And the only way to know all this is to communicate your needs, set boundaries, and stop settling for this half-in, half-out mentality.

Yue's Corner

My "great New York love" was a guy who texted me once a week and who I saw maybe twice a month. His nickname was the Tin Man, from The Wizard of Oz, as he lacked any real emotions—or at least didn't show them to me. I was hooked on him because the few times we got together, it was sexy, exciting, and he made my knees weak. For almost two years, I obsessed over the potential of this guy until finally my mom had enough of my pining and asked, "Can you imagine a relationship where he treats you the same way he does right now? Would you find that acceptable?" It finally dawned on me that I was longing for a man who did not display the characteristics of the type of partner I wanted. I was ignoring the reality that he would never prioritize me or our relationship. I learned to recognize the signs early and prioritize my own needs—because you're never settling if you're staying true to yourself.

MAYBE YOUR TYPE ISN'T YOUR TYPE

Everyone has certain qualities that are important to them, but have you ever thought maybe your type isn't working out so well for you? We're not saying to throw all your preferences out the window, but we're encouraging you to challenge your assumptions. We'll go into this in way more depth when we look at your Perfect Partner Equation in chapter 6. But for now, at least be open to expanding the type of people you may be attracted to. Because what if we told you there's evidence that who you *think* you want most likely isn't who you'll end up with anyway?

When we spoke with Dr. Paul Eastwick on *Dateable* about his work at the UC Davis Attraction Lab, he shared that while everyone has their ideal partner preferences, they are not predictive of who we ultimately find attractive. As he learned from his research, we're often good at describing the traits we want that are indicative of a whole population's preference (of course you want someone warm over someone moody!), but it's hard to understand how important an individual trait is to you (even if you say you want someone adventurous, is that actually going to be the standout trait of the person you fall for?). Dr. Eastwick also shared that what appeals to us on paper isn't what is always attractive to us in person. For example, if you were to look at two groups of people on dating apps—one where you extensively looked through people's profiles vetting for your ideal partner preferences, and one where you just swiped on people you found attractive enough—there would be equal odds of liking someone you picked from either group when you actually meet in person. So in short: you're just as likely to fall for someone who doesn't have the specific attributes you're seeking as you are for someone who possesses them. This all comes down to the fact that we don't correctly predict what traits matter to us.

These findings are in line with a prominent theme we noticed when talking to people who did meet their special someone: they never ended up being exactly the person they imagined. They didn't necessarily do a one-eighty and go for the opposite, but they did tweak the qualities they prioritized and let go of the ones that proved not to matter. Especially for you Mavericks, who may think you know exactly what you want and pride yourself on knowing right away whether someone's a good fit or not. It's not about abandoning all qualities you once deemed necessary in a partner; it's about seeing how these qualities can show up differently. Let's say you have a history of going for the stand-up comedian type or the loud extrovert because you want to be with someone funny. You can still find that person who makes you laugh, even if they're quieter or have more of a low-key sense of humor. By expanding how you view these criteria, you're not confined to your type–because this may not even be your most critical desired traits, as we just found out!

Yes, this may seem overwhelming. You're probably wondering where you should start if you're expanding your type. Chapter 6 will provide you with exactly this framework! Just remember: having a "type" only limits who you can meet. When you meet someone you connect with on a deeper level–emotionally, physically, and intimately–the last thing you do is settle. All the things you thought were essential suddenly become inconsequential. So instead of holding on to an exact image of who you want your partner to be, stay open to the package they show up in. The next time you meet someone who doesn't fit your typical "type" but you're attracted to and curious about, remember, this could be a good thing! Because maybe they could be different–in the best way possible.

> **BDE (Big Dateable Energy):**
> Instead of focusing on your type,
> focus on finding someone good for you.

"NICE" SHOULD BE THE BARE MINIMUM

On the opposite end of the spectrum is when you compromise on the qualities you're looking for just because someone is "nice." They may be doing all the right things, but what if the connection is not there? It's only natural to overcorrect–especially when you've had a slew of relationships that felt more one-sided. Achievers, especially, may be prone to staying in "good enough" relationships out of fear of starting over again. With specific milestones in mind, it's easy to overlook how you feel around someone. But this, friends, is also selling yourself short and depriving you of the great love story you deeply desire. We don't want you to settle for a relationship that isn't full of love and emotional connection, either.

This was something our Achiever-in-residence, Andrew, had to remember. Sure, dating was hard, but being with the wrong person was even more difficult. He knew this because he had been in a year-long relationship with Ann, who checked all the boxes except the biggest one of all: his heart. When they first met, it felt like Andrew hit the jackpot. Ann did everything he could imagine a partner doing. She'd make him care packages before he left on work trips and she even threw him a big surprise birthday party with all his friends and family.

But as the months progressed, their relationship became stagnant. They spent most of their nights watching TV, and very rarely did they have meaningful conversations. Andrew had a hard time connecting with Ann on a deeper level, despite his best efforts. He always said how nice she was, but deep down, he knew that wasn't enough. Their relationship seemed good on the outside (his parents were shocked when they eventually parted ways), but Andrew knew it lacked depth on the inside. As an Achiever, it was hard to let this relationship go—but once he did, he knew it was the right choice.

We bring up this example because it's not only about settling for mistreatment. If you aren't feeling love and connection, that's also settling. Because while companionship is nice, it's not enough. Nice should be the baseline. It shouldn't be the primary trait holding the relationship together. So, really examine why you're in a relationship. Is it that you can't imagine doing life without this person, or do they feel like the safe choice? Do you have other fears seeping in, like you don't know who else is out there, or you're getting older and afraid it's getting too late? Do you know what your needs are in a relationship? And can you recognize a good relationship if you were in one?

We often don't want to let something go because we don't know what's on the other side. But, again, it goes back to the present bias. The future is unknown, and it's hard to see whether there will be someone out there who is better suited for you. It can be a difficult balance: when do you end a relationship because it feels like something is off, and when do you accept that it'll never be 100 percent perfect? We get it; it can feel like, *Omg, how am I ever going to find this person?* Don't worry; we'll help you gain clarity in the second part of this book. But making way for the right people is a big part of finding your person.

> **BDE (Big Dateable Energy):**
> You can't find the right person if you're with the wrong one.

THE DIFFERENCE BETWEEN
HAVING STANDARDS AND BEING PICKY

We often hear from daters: "What's the difference between having standards and being picky?" Having standards means knowing you're a catch and deserve to be treated well. It's knowing your values and ensuring you're aligned with someone who shares them. It's knowing that life's too short not to laugh until your stomach hurts, have good sex, and be madly in love—or whatever your dream relationship looks like. Having standards means being discerning of who you let in and out of your life. You're thoughtful about making choices and intentional about your love life.

When you're being picky, you're evaluating if someone measures up. It's the difference between writing someone off because they mispronounce a word occasionally (picky) and being with someone who keeps you intellectually stimulated (standards). Maybe they drive a car you don't like. They're not aware of the hottest new restaurants in your city. They're not well traveled. The list goes on and on. When you're in the picky mindset, it feels like no one is good enough or "right for you." Know that being too picky is actually a huge red flag. It means all you see are people's faults and shortcomings instead of what they can bring to your life. If you were to turn it around, would you want to date someone with this deficit mindset? Would you like someone critiquing and assessing your worth based on what TV shows you watch? Nope, we wouldn't, either.

You absolutely should be selective about who you spend your time with and give your heart to. It's okay to have a list of nonnegotiables. Holding on to your core values is essential. Being with someone who wants the same things in life is fundamental. But try reexamining where you may have rigid requirements. Striking a balance between having reasonable standards and being open-minded is exactly what you need to meet someone wonderful.

CHOOSING THE UNFAMILIAR

The key to escaping the Settling Paradox is choosing differently. You've probably heard the age-old expression "Your picker is broken," suggesting a pattern of making poor choices when selecting romantic partners. When we talked to the psychotherapist Marc Sholes, author of *Reset Your Romantic GPS*, on *Dateable*, he shared that we're not necessarily picking the wrong people, but rather, we're picking what's comfortable to us. Early in life, depending on the security or insecurity of our caregivers, we learn a language around connections that's laid down as a GPS in our psyches. For example, if your needs were inconsistently met or neglected, you may have internalized that your needs are not that important because they aren't being responded to. Instead of focusing on your needs, you concentrated on the needs of your caregivers instead. Your emphasis was on figuring out what *they* need, so they can be more available to you. As Marc explained, this preoccupation with others becomes the learned language. And now, in your adult romantic life, you're drawn to the people who are less attuned to your needs because that's what feels familiar. We're not picking the wrong people; we're picking what we know. So, that situationship where they show spurts of interest only to withdraw a day later may be what connection feels like to you.

Knowing this can help you pause before falling into your default behavior. Instead of assuming you met "the One" the next time you have butterflies in your stomach (which is more likely to be anxiety!), you can recognize that chemistry comes from what you know. And when there aren't fireworks with that person who shows up and responds consistently, you can evaluate whether there's genuinely no romantic connection or if it's just uncomfortable because it feels different. Take this as our invitation to finally end that situationship, because you now know that it's keeping you stuck in a familiar place.

By assuming your picker is broken, you're playing a much too passive role in your dating life. The most significant shift you can make is to move from a reflex to a choice. You're in control of the type of person you choose. You have the power to decide who you give your time to. You get to determine whether you're going to prioritize being treated well. And you get to choose when it's time to change your criteria of what makes a great partner. When we talked to the dating coach Evan Marc Katz on *Dateable*, he said something that has stayed with us: *You don't attract the wrong people; you accept the wrong people.* The narcissists don't flock to you; you choose them over and over again. Other people don't have it easier in dating: they just choose better. It may feel like a fantasy to find a relationship where you know exactly where you stand, with a person you're attracted to who also treats you well. But we're here to tell you that is entirely possible—and that's what we should all strive for. And when you start prioritizing how you feel in a relationship, it becomes a lot easier to sift out the right people (more on that later!).

Julie's Corner

For years, I stayed in an on-again, off-again relationship with a person I believed was the "the One"—despite our relationship not having the levels of commitment I so deeply desired. This made sense though: undefined relationships with this type of push-pull dynamic were the norm for me. I had a history of situationships and one-sided loves. Once I finally let my ex go (for real this time), I started choosing differently. I wanted someone who would show up consistently and fully commit to a relationship. When I met my current partner, there were no games and his intentions were clear from the start. This allowed us to focus on our connection and our whole dating experience felt refreshingly simple—something I had never experienced before.

REIMAGINING "THE ONE"

It's time for us to proclaim this loud and proud: there is no "the One." This concept that there's one perfect person out there for you is what keeps you fixated on the laundry list of requirements you need in a partner. No one person has everything you are looking for. It's up to you to deem what's essential and what isn't in a relationship. It's less about finding someone who has all the attributes you think you need, and more about finding someone who is willing to build the type of relationship you both want. Everyone will have a flaw or two (or ten!)–including you. Ultimately, you need to find a relationship where you can fully embrace each other–the good, the bad, the weird.

Our partner will f*ck up from time to time–it's called being human. There's a difference between two people committed to making it work and a situation where one person is holding together the whole damn relationship. As Dr. Eastwick shared from his research, having a good relationship is less indicative of having picked the right person but more about how you build a relationship over time–together. Good relationships happen when you grow and create your microculture in partnership.

Chances are they won't have some stuff on your metaphorical (or, in some cases, physical) list. It won't matter because they'll be perfectly imperfect for you. And most importantly, they'll treat you with the respect and love you deserve. As we learned from chapter 1, we need time to reveal whether someone is a good fit. Your partner doesn't come off the rack with a predefined checklist of what makes them dateable. When we stop looking at "settling" as being with someone who doesn't check all the boxes, it opens up the possibilities of finding an incredible partner–and appreciating people for what they bring to the table. This is what gets us out of the love crisis because it allows us to focus on like-minded people ready for a relationship instead of trying to convince those who aren't. One of our favorite quotes is from a guest on *Dateable*, the writer Heidi Isern: "Hunting for a single person to be your 'one'–the ballerina, the poet, the bank account, and the parent is all too much pressure for someone you don't know yet. But 'the One' is created over time by slowly undressing who they are, not what they should be." Rest assured, we'll go into our Perfect Partner Equation in the second half of this book. But what you can change today is your expectations of what makes a good partner–and see that you deserve someone who will treat you like the total package you are.

KEY TAKEAWAYS

1. We often focus on more superficial qualities because they are easier to quantify and are what have been reinforced through society. These traits are not the true measure of compatibility and distract us from what actually matters.

2. It's time we stop living in the fantasy of who we want someone to be and start focusing on who they are today. No more acting as their PR agent, justifying bad behavior. Take their actions at face value and start choosing differently.

3. The only time you *are* settling is if you aren't being treated the way you want to be treated, if you're unhappy, or if you are not fulfilled in your relationship. Every second you're with the wrong person is preventing you from being with the right one.

4. Expanding your type can expand your possibilities. Question whether you're only gravitating toward what's familiar and ask yourself if it would better serve you to try something different.

5. You're not settling if someone doesn't have every quality you once imagined. No one is going to be perfect, not even you. Remember, "the One" doesn't exist. But there are many incredible partners out there who could be perfectly imperfect for you.

Chapter 3:

The Validation Trap

IT'S TIME TO BREAK UP WITH:

1. **The Bachelor Vortex:** The need to progress to the next round of dating, whether you like the person or not.
2. **Vanity Swipes:** Racking up matches and likes to feel better about oneself, oftentimes never moving to an actual date.
3. **Being a Dating Chameleon:** The date version of yourself, the one that tries to appeal to the masses, instead of showing who you really are.

As you may remember, Andrew was convinced he had a third-date curse. At the age of thirty-four, he was back into the dating scene after breaking up with his girlfriend of three years. Most of his friends were coupled up and starting to have children, and he felt the pressure to find someone to hit these milestones with. For whatever reason, dating was difficult for Andrew. The first couple of dates were generally fine; it was early, so the stakes were low. But around that third date, when things would get real, it would all start to crumble. He'd get ghosted, or the person he was seeing was suddenly not ready for a relationship.

As an Achiever, you can imagine how personally he took this when it kept happening time and time again. If you get ghosted once or twice, it's not a huge deal. But compound this ten times over (maybe even in the same month!), and it'll make the best of us question if we're worthy of a relationship. This line of thinking is what's causing so many daters to retreat from love–adding fuel to the love crisis.

The trouble begins when we use dating to measure whether we're good enough. We seek approval from others and wonder what's wrong with us when we can't get to that next date. When all your friends start settling down, and you're struggling with dating, it's easy to ask yourself: Why can *they* find someone when I can't? What's so wrong with *me* that I'm unable to keep someone interested for the long haul? We see dating as a reflection of ourselves, which brings us to the **Validation Trap**: letting dating define our worth instead of using it to find a good match. As a result, we end up feeling unlovable, unworthy, and discouraged when things don't work out–which undoubtedly leaves us to cling to relationships that aren't suitable for us. So how did we get here?

THE ULTIMATE MEASURE OF SUCCESS

In our society, there's a constant reinforcement that romantic love is the ultimate measure of personal success and happiness. There's something "wrong" if you're single, and we treat it as a problem that needs to be fixed. Whether through the media, our Instagram feeds, or in daily conversation with our friends and family, you've probably had one too many people ask if you've met someone special or, even worse, why you're still single. Maybe your parents are all up in your business asking when they can expect grandkids or you just feel this self-induced pressure that you need to check all the life milestones–and by a certain age, nonetheless.

Why do we think like this in the first place? There's a perception that being in a relationship makes you "better" than someone single, as you've now unlocked a new status and are on the way to achieving these milestones. We tend to treat milestones like adding items in our shopping cart. We judge ourselves based on what we have: a career, a house, a partner; and then we compare our shopping carts to other people's shopping carts. Our culture thrives on the need to always keep progressing and gaining more, whether that's getting into a relationship, getting engaged, getting married, having kids, the list goes on and on. We place value on what we can get and earn, and since being single is seen as a default status (or something we are trying to get out of), it doesn't validate our self-worth.

It's easy to fall into this way of thinking as our society makes it black-and-white: if you're in a relationship, you've succeeded, and if you're not, you've failed. This could not be further from the truth, but it's the narrative that many of us hold on to, either consciously or unconsciously. When this part of life isn't falling into place, it feels like something is wrong with us. So repeat after us: your relationship status does not define your worth. The fact that society places being in a relationship on a pedestal doesn't mean you're any less than if you're not in one.

We're told that love will "fix" us and if we can get this part of our life in order, then we'll be happy. On *Dateable*, we spoke about this misbelief with Dr. Jenny Taitz, psychologist and author of *How to Be Single and Happy*. She has observed how many of us think that finding the right person will mean a permanently happier mood and elevated life. While happiness may increase after a great date or decline after a breakup, eventually it comes back to our baseline. It's what psychologists call the set-point theory of happiness, where our level of well-being remains relatively constant, influenced by heredity and what's ingrained in us. Happiness can fluctuate in the short term, but the change is not sustained. In fact, Dr. Taitz referenced a study by Michigan State University professor Richard Lucas of how on average, people only got a one-tenth of a point bump in happiness on an eleven-point scale when they got married (that's less than 1 percent for any math nerds out there). The study also found that just as many people reported being less happy post-marriage as reported being more content after they tied the knot. In short: marriage made the same number of people happier as it did less happy.

It's not to say that relationships and marriage won't bring you happiness (especially when you're with the *right* partner, not just any partner), but it's up to us to increase our happiness baselines through our own self-worth–instead of external factors such as dating. We're social creatures and crave some level of validation from others after all! But when this becomes the goal of dating, the balance of seeking outside validation from others throws things off-kilter. It's near impossible to form the type of love relationship we know you actually want.

> **BDE (Big Dateable Energy):**
> Relationships won't save you and being single won't destroy you.

REMEMBER YOUR DATING ARCHETYPE!

Using this lens will help you connect the dots to see how you may fall for the Validation Trap.

- **Achievers:** How can you prioritize connection over progression?
- **Dreamers:** How can you see your value beyond being in a relationship?
- **Energizers:** How can you give yourself the attention and recognition you seek?
- **Mavericks:** How can you recognize when it's your ego talking?
- **Thinkers:** How can you find assurance within yourself instead of others?

DATING AS A MIRROR

While we know logically that dating doesn't define our worth, it's easier said than done not to look for validation. When you put yourself out there in the dating world, by default, you're opening yourself in the most vulnerable way. In what other context would someone look at your photo for seven seconds (yes, that's all it takes to form an impression) and decide yes or no? Or for someone to determine within an hour of mini golf whether they can envision a life with you? At the core of it, you're asking someone to love you. To choose you. To be with you. And if they don't, of course, that will sting. It's no wonder your insecurities are front and center when you engage in the comparison game or experience rejection.

Even for the most confident of us, it can hit hard when someone says they don't want to go on another date or pursue a relationship. And the worst is when someone you *didn't even like* says they aren't interested. It's easy to go down the rabbit hole of thinking if someone like this doesn't want me, no one will. The logical brain knows this is not true, but your ego says otherwise. When we have insecurities (as we all do), they come to the surface when dating. We start going down the spiral of whether we're attractive enough, interesting enough, or just enough, leading to self-doubt. As a result, this takes away from the actual purpose of dating: finding a compatible partner. When we face rejection, our mind tends to wander to everything wrong with us instead of just realizing this person wasn't a fit.

Dating holds up a mirror to reflect all our unresolved issues. When we talked to the marriage and family therapist Vienna Pharaon on *Dateable* about her book *The Origins of You*, she explained that we all have wounds from our childhood and formative years–and our past is the present if they remain unresolved. For instance, if you grew up in a family that puts conditions around love (e.g., being the straight-A student, varsity athlete, comic relief, or peacemaker of the family), you learn that your value comes from an external source rather than who you inherently are. This may result in a worthiness wound and belief that you only deserve someone's love, attention, or affection if you've earned it. So, of course, this manifests as seeking validation from the people you date.

You can see how every little interaction in dating can bring up more than meets the eye. When that person you're dating doesn't text back or cancels plans at the last minute, this may trigger your prioritization wound if, for instance, your parents were always working and didn't make enough time for you growing up. You may start to conjure up all the more important things this person had to do (Was it another date? Would they rather be with friends?) that took precedence over you. No wonder this leads to obsessing over their every interaction–and even trying tactics like not texting first–to prove that you're still desirable. The point of discovering these wounds is not to blame our parents, but to highlight how dating can trigger so much of what's going on underneath.

When dating isn't going your way, it's crucial to consider the larger picture of what is happening to you. Instead of putting so much emphasis on that person who ghosted you, get to the root of why this bothers you. When you can identify where this pain is coming from internally, you can shift the focus from other people and the need for external validation. We're not going to say dating isn't personal because it *is* personal! But that doesn't mean we let others dictate how we feel about ourselves. We'll go into more tactics later in the book, but for now, let's recognize dating is a reflection of how we view ourselves, not necessarily how others view us.

WILL YOU ACCEPT THIS ROSE?

Blame it on dating culture or reality TV; we've been programmed to "win" at dating. We're so focused on proceeding to that next date, defining the relationship, and even locking it down through marriage. And when these milestones don't happen—or don't happen at the pace we expect—our worthiness wound flares up. But dating isn't another achievement. It's not a degree or a promotion you earn. And this certainly isn't *The Bachelor*, where the goal is to progress to the next round (although sometimes it feels like it!).

The problem is when we have this mentality, we get sucked into what we like to call the Bachelor Vortex, where we become more concerned with moving the relationship along rather than determining if we even *like* this person. Every time you get a rose to progress to the next round (literally or metaphorically), there's a dopamine hit from being chosen. When we fall for the Validation Trap, even people we have no interest in dating can make or break us. Let's be real:

not all thirty-two girls on *The Bachelor* want to marry this one dude. They want to win. We need to escape this vortex, though, because by being in some invisible race, we're losing sight of why we date in the first place.

As a high-functioning Achiever, Andrew was fixated on moving past the third date. He wanted to prove to his friends (and himself) that he could be successful in dating. His confidence was so heavily tied to whether he got that next date or text message back. Because if someone was willing to keep going out with him, it meant he was lovable, right? The more Andrew got in his head, the more it became a self-fulfilling prophecy that he couldn't get past date number three. So, on his most recent date, he found himself asking reassuring questions such as:

"Do you like me?"

"Do you think there will be another date?"

"Am I what you're looking for?"

Once again, his date told him there wasn't any chemistry. By going into the date with this "pick me" mentality, Andrew came off as seeking approval, not a connection. Not once did Andrew ask:

"Do I like this person?"

"Do I want to have another date?"

"Is this what I'm looking for?"

Look, we all have a little "pick-me" in us. We all want to be liked and chosen. But when you're so focused on moving forward, you tend to bend over backward—more focused on being a good match for everyone else than on finding a good match for yourself. You start obsessing over every interaction—whether they'll text again or ask you on another date—letting others control your emotions and determine your value. It's hard to stay present and evaluate who is right for *you* when your emphasis is on being right for them. And it's nearly impossible to enjoy dating when you're focused on hitting milestones and worried about how you're measuring up. The question is: do you want to be in the driver's seat of your love life or the anxious hitchhiker waiting to be picked up?

Reality check: most dates *don't* work out. If you can accept that 99 percent of people aren't going to be matches for the long term, it'll be a lot easier to accept that it has nothing to do with your value as a person when it's not a fit. You'll never be everyone's cup of tea—because nobody is. And this is a good thing! It's what makes dating so *exciting*. If everyone were a fit, there would be no magic when you finally meet that special someone. Every rejection or disappointment doesn't define your worth—all it's doing is making room for the right person.

It's hard not to take it personally when someone doesn't want to continue to see you, but it's often not as personal as we make it. Most relationships are not meant to last forever. It doesn't mean there's something wrong with you. It just wasn't a match for whatever reason. More often than not, you won't move to that next date or relationship marker. This is not to be pessimistic by any means but rather to set realistic expectations. Instead of taking part in some invisible race you think you must win, you can start to see various stages of dating as a state of being. Eventually, you'll get to your desired destination, but for now, enjoy the ride.

Yue's Corner

I used to be so focused on relationships moving on a predetermined timeline—meeting friends by the second month, or moving in together within the first year—with emphasis on the progression over the connection. However, when I moved to Beijing on a whim, I adopted a "dating on vacation" mindset, free from rules and expectations, since I didn't know how long I'd be in the country. This expat mentality led to an intense month-and-a-half relationship, where we just wanted to maximize our time together. Reflecting on this, I realized arbitrary markers don't define success; it's the depth of connection that matters. Whether a relationship lasts for days or decades, what truly counts is the quality of time spent together. And the best connections happen when we're present, just trying to get to know each other.

DATING IS *NOT* A NUMBERS GAME

The reason you don't need to be chosen by everyone is that you don't need a room full of people vying for your attention at all times, like on *The Bachelor*. Because realistically, you're not going to date all those people anyway. Contrary to popular belief, we're here to tell you dating is *not* a numbers game. Sure, there's some truth to the phrase (if you go on one date a year, the odds of meeting someone you click with is clearly a lot lower), and of course, when a romantic prospect doesn't pan out it's helpful to know there are others around the corner. But at a certain point, it makes it hard to have a deeper, more substantial relationship when you're spreading yourself too thin. It's time to stop with the vanity swipes and back-to-back dates, where we focus more on the number of matches or dates instead of forming actual connections.

Back to Eli, our Energizer serial dater who was constantly on the hunt for love, whether online, in the club, or at the grocery store. Eli always had two or three men in rotation and was always out on the town, meeting new people IRL. And that's not even including his dating app queue! When Eli showed us how many prospects he had, we asked why he kept swiping if he already had some eligible people lined up. He genuinely believed that dating was a numbers game and that he had to meet as many people as possible. The problem was that he was racking up a bunch of superficial connections instead of prioritizing finding a compatible partner. And to be frank, Eli liked the attention. He was guilty of swiping on anyone and everyone in order to prove to himself that he was desirable.

With his fan-club mentality, Eli attracted other f*ckboys looking for attention. The type of guys who thrived off this energy but didn't want to be in monogamous relationships. And those who did want a relationship found his attention-seeking antics unattractive. Your dates can feel it when you're chasing validation—and it doesn't create a strong foundation for a relationship. Not to mention, Eli was completely burned-out from dating. It was exhausting to constantly meet new people and deal with the fallout every time a date didn't work out. Eventually, Eli had to pause and ask himself: am I seeking connection or attention?

You may think going out with more people will increase the odds of meeting your person. But the truth is quite counterintuitive. We want to shift your focus from quantity to quality. Dating isn't a popularity contest, and it sure as hell isn't a pageant or a campaign for office. Daters tell us they want to optimize their dating profiles to appeal to as many people as possible. As any Marketing 101 course can tell you, when you try to appeal to everyone, you end up appealing to no one. After all, there's a reason targeted marketing has a much higher conversion rate than awareness campaigns. It's the same for dating: going on fewer dates with more viable prospects ends up being more fruitful in the end. Only then can you invest the time and effort necessary to get to know someone instead of always moving on to the next person.

We see so many daters hung up on the fact that they don't have enough matches or dates lined up. Don't let this discourage you or make you think you're not worthy of finding love. It's just a vanity metric. Start shifting your intention toward attracting one special person–your ideal partner. We'd so much rather you go on fewer–but better–dates where you're really connecting and being your authentic self. Because all it takes is one (or a few if you're poly).

BDE (Big Dateable Energy):
Dating isn't a numbers game; it's about
finding your number one partner.

A WORD ABOUT SEX

We'd be remiss not to bring sex into the equation when talking about validation. Sex can be a beautiful thing shared by consenting human beings. It can be a form of pleasure and connection. But when it becomes a form of validation, and you only feel worthy if someone is willing to have sex with you, that's when it becomes problematic.

We are often asked if there's a right time to sleep together. But the question should be a matter of why, not when. Are you having sex because the two of you have a connection? Or are you doing it because you want this person to like you, feel like they may leave you if you don't, or think it's your only way of gauging compatibility?

While it may feel good in the moment, it impacts your self-esteem in the long run if you only see your value through sex. You bring so much more to a relationship than just that! And the last thing we want you to do is hang on to unhealthy or even exploitative relationships because you're so reliant on the sex.

We're not trying to sound like your middle school sex ed teacher, but it's vital to enter into sexual relationships when you feel secure with yourself outside of sex. Having the mentality of "I like who I am, and that won't change whether we have sex or not" is vital. Even if you think there's a connection, you always run the risk of the person bailing after the deed is done. And if someone doesn't want to sleep with you, this doesn't reflect your attractiveness or desirability.

We understand that there's some validation when it comes to sex. You are putting yourself out there in the most intimate way possible. So tell the person you slept with it was fantastic (if it was!). Accept their compliments when they tell you how sexy or attractive you are. But also know you are more than just what you bring to the bedroom. Recognizing your own self-worth—whether you have sex or not—is the sexiest form of love.

THE DANGER OF HAVING
SOMEBODY OVER NOBODY

It's important to note that the desire to be chosen is natural. In a re-lationship, we want someone to choose us—to love, cherish, and be by our side. But when you want to be chosen at all costs, this is when we stay in unhealthy patterns or toxic relationships. It can feel better to have *somebody*. Because if we're single without any prospects, it would confirm that we're destined to be alone. At least there's a per-ception of being in a relationship—even if it's not good—which gives you validation.

Staying in these unhealthy situations can create a cycle of mis-treatment that eats at your self-esteem. When we feel unworthy, we settle for less than we deserve or put up with behaviors that aren't aligned with our values—and, even worse, get deeply invested in the wrong people. You may know this person isn't good for you (as do your friends, therapist, and even the barista at your local coffee shop), yet you stay. Especially for the Dreamers, it may be challeng-ing to establish and maintain healthy boundaries when it comes to pleasing others and gaining approval. This makes it all too easy to fall into a dynamic where one person seeks constant approval, and the other holds the power to provide or withhold validation.

You may think it's love, but you may have actually developed a trauma bond. Dr. Patrick Carnes, a leading sex addiction expert, de-veloped the term "trauma bond" to describe the emotional bonds with an individual that arise from a recurring, cyclical pattern of abuse perpetrated by intermittent reinforcement through rewards and punishments. And this can be your situationship, on-again, off-again relationship, or any other arrangement that lacks consistency and respect. Picture the mental and emotional toll it takes when you never know where you stand; one minute, someone tells you how wonderful you are, and the next, they say they don't want to commit. That is traumatic—yet we normalize this type of behavior. Instead of finding someone who treats us well, we double down on proving ourselves to this person (who doesn't deserve our time!).

We think we need to try a little harder. Be a little more flexible. Be a little more chill. Or withdraw so they can chase. They'll soon see what you bring to the table, right? When you find yourself trying to win someone over or prove you are worthy, ask yourself: why do I want to be with someone so badly who doesn't want to be with me? While it feels hard to let go because you're tied to this person (or the trauma bond you've created), you need to look objectively at why you're hanging on to a relationship (or situationship) you know isn't serving you. Is it out of fear of being alone? Is it an addiction to the other person? Is it that you don't think you'll find someone else? Or is this creating a level of false intimacy that, in a way, feels safer than actually putting yourself out there?

We were intrigued by our conversation on *Dateable* with the best-selling author Mark Manson about his work with *Love Is Not Enough*, an audio series that followed five daters over six months as they navigated their f*cked-up dating situations. He shared that many people stay in unhealthy dynamics because it allows both parties to feel intimacy without exposing themselves. For instance, with the common runner-chaser dynamic (where one person repeatedly ends the relationship while the other strives to maintain it), both individuals feel validated: the runner when they are pursued, and the chaser when they succeed. However, neither ultimately has their needs met nor are they exhibiting the levels of vulnerability required in a healthy relationship.

By seeing a relationship for what it is—seeking validation—you can take a step back and do the necessary work. No longer will you be auditioning for the role; the right person doesn't need to be convinced you're right for them. You'll start paying attention to whether this person is a compatible partner and if you feel like your best self around them. When you can find that validation within yourself instead of relying on others, you will no longer attract the type of people who may be more susceptible to manipulation and toxic behavior. You're now the chooser, not someone waiting to be chosen. And if someone falls short of meeting your needs, you choose yourself. How much more validating is that?

Julie's Corner

I had a pattern of staying on the hook with people who either couldn't fully commit or outright said they didn't want to be in a relationship. As a Dreamer-Achiever, it felt like the ultimate romantic conquest to try to change their mind to prove my worthiness. But all this did was further the cycle of not getting the validation I desperately craved. I can see now I chose these partners because I wasn't ready for a real relationship. It was safer to be in situations where it would never work and I could always blame them when the "relationship" inevitably fell apart. When I did finally go to therapy, I put the attention I was giving to others back onto myself. At times it was confronting, but it was ultimately what I needed to be ready for the reciprocal partnership I always wanted but was afraid of not finding.

IS IT LOVE OR YOUR EGO?

We often stay on the hook for the wrong people because the conquest can feel validating. When you have to work to get someone's interest, it feels like you're achieving some victory (oh hey, Achievers, we see you). But the challenge of winning someone over is exhausting and, quite candidly, overrated. And when that rejection inevitably happens, that worthiness wound will flare up yet again. Can you recognize when you're pursuing someone to validate your ego? It's time to not let our pride get the best of us.

We talked to a dater who admitted that she stayed with a friend with benefits who treated her incredibly poorly because she was determined to change his mind about being in a relationship. They were in the same group of friends, and one day, out of nowhere, he confessed he liked her. She was unsure if she felt the same way, but after countless group texts and internal debates, she decided to go all in. By then, though, he decided he no longer wanted to be in a relationship. This should have been a sign to end things right then and there. But her ego kicked in, and she didn't like that he turned the tables. Why did he change his mind? Was she no longer good enough for him? This "relationship" continued for two and a half years as she tried to prove her worth. Spoiler alert: he still didn't want a relationship in the end. But it was for the best: her focus on validation made her believe she was in love with this person, who did not share the sentiment.

As humans, we are designed to protect our egos. Gaining validation or approval (especially from our romantic partners) makes us feel good, but being in a relationship just for validation will ultimately lead to disappointment. So, is it love or ego? Let's check ourselves for a minute.

Leading with Your Ego	Leading with Your Heart
You think you can change someone's mind about what they want in a relationship (or whether they want one at all).	You accept what they say at face value and see if what they want aligns with what you want.
You play games to act uninterested or try to get the upper hand to make this person fight for you.	You're honest and up-front about what you're looking for and see whether someone is also on the same page.
You pull back by not texting or accepting plans, in order to test how dedicated they are to you.	You are communicative and put forward effort to see each other. You also trust their feelings for you.
You're with someone you know isn't good for you because you don't want to be the only single person in your friend group.	You're with someone because you feel good around them, and they are additive to your life.
You sleep with them because you want to boost your self-esteem and validate your attractiveness.	You sleep with them because there's a genuine connection.
You're more concerned with how your relationship looks on social media.	You're more concerned with how your relationship feels between you and your partner.

The shift is to approach dating with a love-first mentality where you constantly ask yourself, "How would I act/respond if it's coming from a place of love?" This may seem the opposite of what you've been told in the past by other dating books and experts: love is a battlefield, and you must keep your armor up and do whatever it takes to protect yourself. But this is the exact reason dating feels so combative—and the opposite of the love and connection we want. When we spoke to the happiness expert and positive psychologist Rob Mack on *Dateable*, he shared how relationships end up being ego-driven experiences when two people are more obsessed about power plays than having a loving experience. A good relationship isn't built on the foundation of proving your value to someone else— or to yourself. There's no one to win over when a relationship is built on mutual respect, trust, and love. And if that's the type of relationship you want, why would you date any other way?

Embracing this love-first, heart-centered approach may be as simple as saying: I desire a long-term committed relationship. They're unable to give that to me, so I wish them well on their journey, and I'll continue on mine. No longer are you trying to change someone and get their validation. You can be open with your feelings but not wait around, pining over someone who doesn't choose you back. And at the other end of the spectrum, your ego may lead you to leave a promising relationship to protect yourself. Let's say you get some critical feedback from the person you're dating. When you lead with the ego, every conflict or perceived criticism signals your relationship is failing. Mavericks, especially, may be out the door at the first sign of a challenge, thinking "I deserve better than this!" Leading with your heart, on the other hand, will help you see that the conflict is not a personal attack but rather an opportunity to strengthen your relationship. If someone is willing to work through a conflict with you—in a way that's love-first—this can be the most validating feeling in the world! It means they want to put in the work to be with you. Look how different these two perspectives can be!

Needing validation in relationships isn't inherently problematic. We all want to feel acknowledged, understood, and accepted. Part of what keeps us seeking validation is that we don't validate each other enough in dating. It's no wonder words of affirmation is the most common love language. Everyone is craving the validation that we so stingily dole out. To break the Validation Trap, let people know that you choose to be with them, that you enjoy spending time with them, and that you adore them. Know that when you're acting from a place of authenticity, not ego, what's meant for you will surface, and what's not will wash away. The more you can view dating from a place of love, the less outcome-driven you'll be. You don't need to fight for someone's attention and affection. You don't need to convince someone to choose you. You don't need to play games in order to receive someone's affections. It becomes much clearer who you should be pursuing—because they are also pursuing you. There's no need to prove your value: you are inherently worthy, and the right person will see that.

BDE (Big Dateable Energy):
The sexiest layer you can shed is your ego.

IF THEY WANTED TO, THEY WANTED—
OR WOULD THEY?

Even if you come from a place of love, you may inevitably hit a point where someone doesn't want to pursue a relationship. It can be easy to take this personally, even when it's not personal. While we are completely supportive of having a partner who will do whatever it takes for your relationship to work, statements such as "if they wanted to, they would" leave you feeling like you weren't enough to make that effort. The reality is that after two hours of talking to someone over cocktails, we have no idea what's going on in their life. We don't know someone's whole story even a few months in. Maybe they are struggling with their mental health. Or they are further into the dating process with someone else. Or they are debating a move across the country. Or simply not feeling ready to commit to another person. The reason almost doesn't matter because it's not a reflection of your value.

We need to shut down those thoughts that you're not good enough for them. You not being the right fit is very different from not being good enough. Thinkers tend to dwell on those reasons for something not working out, replaying every interaction and every conversation. It's never a bad thing to reflect on patterns of how you're showing up on dates, but it's important to remember that you're one piece of the puzzle. It's so easy to assume it didn't work out because of something you did, because you only have visibility into yourself.

Here's a hard lesson we had to learn: it's not always about you. Relationships are complex and require multiple factors to align to work. Reducing why a relationship didn't work to a simple "if-then" statement oversimplifies the intricacies involved. It goes back to the Expectation of Love on Demand, where we believe that when two people like each other, everything will fall into place, and that someone will move mountains to make it work if they genuinely want to be with you. But it's not always that simple. Just because someone likes you doesn't mean they have the capacity to be with you, or the ability to meet your needs. That's not a reflection of you but rather a reflection of your compatibility.

Someone can most certainly like you but not be willing (or able) to put in the work required for a relationship. They may not be ready to confront their hang-ups and personal challenges to be there for another person. It's hard not to take these situations personally but think of them as a way to course correct for the right person. Sometimes, relationships don't work out. All it means is that the person is no longer right for you, making room for someone who is.

THERE'S A LID FOR EVERY POT

One of our favorite sayings (that you may have heard us say repeatedly on the podcast) is that there's a lid for every pot, because we strongly believe the world contains a fitting romantic partner for everyone. Your pot certainly doesn't need a lid, but there's one out there that would be the perfect fit for you. Actually, there are many lids that would fit your pot. When we fall victim to the Validation Trap, we morph into someone to be "liked," and move farther and farther from our true selves. It's important not to turn into a dating chameleon by presenting as a version of yourself that you believe will appeal to others.

If you have people-pleaser tendencies, you may sacrifice yourself to make others like you. As a Thinker, Tori often second-guessed herself quite a bit while dating. It felt validating when some-one thought they both had a lot in common. She found herself telling her dates "Oh yeah, I love hiking" when she hadn't hit a trail in over a year. There was this one time when she told her hipster date that her favorite musician was an up-and-coming indie band instead of admitting her most played artist was Taylor Swift. She was morphing herself into someone she wasn't, hoping to be liked at the expense of her authentic self.

We do this because the need for validation is normal. We feel good when people like us. But when it dominates your search for love, this is how you end up with the wrong people. The right per-son wouldn't care if your interests aren't totally aligned, and they'd welcome the opportunity to share a new experience with you. If they would end things because you are a Swiftie, would you even want to be with that person anyway? When you hide aspects of yourself, you miss the chance of finding someone who genuinely appreciates and values you for who you are. The right lid will like you *because* of all your pot's quirks and imperfections. Everyone has insecurities when it comes to dating. But it's usually our im-perfections that make us unique. Show them your weird and quirky side! Tell them about your hobby that isn't run-of-the-mill. The last thing you want to do is compromise who you are. And to Tori's sur-prise, when she stopped trying to mold herself into the type of per-son she thought her date wanted, she started having more dating success. People found Tori's pottery-making hobby super fascinat-ing, even though she didn't find anyone with the same passion. It's not about the pottery (again, you're not looking for a carbon copy); it's about Tori feeling confident and free to be her unique self. And it felt good for Tori to openly talk about her interests instead of hiding them. The true measure of success on a date is: *Am I showing up as my authentic self? Can I be comfortable in my own skin around this person?* If you're dating to meet someone with relationship potential, this is the best—and only—way.

BDE (Big Dateable Energy):
The only thing you need to be is yourself.

YOU COMPLETE YOURSELF

Blame Tom Cruise's iconic line in the movie *Jerry Maguire* where he declares his love to Renée Zellweger by saying those three words: you complete me. No, you're not a half-person trying to meet your other half. And you certainly don't need someone to complete you. Yes, you want a partner who balances you, supports you, and is there for you through thick and thin, but it doesn't mean you'll crumble when they're not around. The right partner adds to your life, but they don't save you.

Society wants you to believe you must be coupled up to be whole. It's on us to defy this myth. Your happiness and worth are not contingent on someone asking you for another date or whether they want to commit to a relationship with you. So send out that holiday card on your own! Take yourself on an extravagant date! Live your life to the fullest! Focus on everything you have to celebrate in your personal life. What are some ways to recognize that you complete yourself? Let's take a look:

Ways Others Complete You	Ways You Complete Yourself
You see yourself as inadequate if someone says they don't want to be in a relationship with you.	You realize that just because this person didn't want a relationship with you, it's not an indication of if someone else will—in fact, you know someone great is just around the corner.
You are bummed when you don't have a date on a Friday night and think you're a loser with no plans.	You love every second of your night with two great loves: Netflix and DoorDash.
You are down in the dumps because there are no romantic prospects in your life.	You see all the love in your life, whether it's from your friends, family, or pets.
You see your time being single as a waiting period before a relationship.	You enjoy the single stage of life just as much as you'll enjoy the next stage when you are in a committed, loving relationship.
You skip your friend's wedding because you don't have a plus-one and don't want to be the only single one there.	You get down on the dance floor and fifth-wheel it with all your coupled-up friends. Who cares when you're having fun!
You keep fighting for a relationship you know isn't working because you don't want to be single again.	You realize it's better to be alone than be with the wrong person.

It may seem counterintuitive to be okay with being single in order to find a relationship, but trust us (and psychology), it takes the pressure off! Being single isn't always a layover on the way to being in a relationship, nor will it be forever. In fact, you're most ready for a relationship when you're least dependent on having one. There are so many privileges of enjoying your time alone and fully getting to know yourself. Get to the point where you think: *If this is what it means to be single for the rest of my life, it's pretty darn good.* It's not giving up or succumbing to a life alone. After all, the one relationship we'll have forever is with ourselves—whether in a partnership or not. If you can see the full life you already have, then a relationship begins to feel additive. When you are comfortable being alone, you stop needing people to pick you. Suddenly, the stakes don't feel as high, and the anxiety goes away—because you no longer view dating as a reflection of yourself. This is what frees us from the love crisis and makes dating a lot more enjoyable! By feeling more confident and at ease, you trust that the right person will recognize a good thing when they see it. When you know you're freaking dateable, the question becomes: are *they* up to par or not?

KEY TAKEAWAYS

1. Relationships do not define us and love is not the ultimate measure of success. There's a difference between *wanting* a relationship and *needing* one to feel whole.
2. Dating is *not* a numbers game or a popularity contest. You're never going to be everyone's cup of tea, so any rejection or disappointment that may happen is not a reflection of who you are as a person.
3. When relationships aren't progressing at the pace you want, it doesn't mean you're not measuring up. It's important to lead with love, not ego. Sometimes relationships just don't work out. And that's okay. Longevity isn't the only success metric.
4. You can only meet the right person by showing your true, authentic self. If someone doesn't like you for who you are, it's much better to move on to find someone who does. And yes, that person does exist!
5. Remember, you complete yourself. A relationship is just the cherry on top.

Chapter 4:

Relationship Chicken

IT'S TIME TO BREAK UP WITH:

1. **Cool Girl/Nice Guy Syndrome:** The act of playing it cool or being overly accommodating in an effort to not rock the boat, meaning you never state your needs.
2. **The Lowest Common Denominator:** Accepting bad dating behavior as the norm—and exhibiting the same behaviors you despise—to play at the same level as everyone else.
3. **The Dating ATM:** Treating dating transactionally, tallying up every interaction and exchange.

We were chatting with Tori when she asked the million-dollar question: when should you define the relationship? She had been seeing Leslie for the last three months, and they hadn't had the "talk" yet. As your typical Thinker, she was overanalyzing every scenario: Was it too soon? What if Leslie didn't feel the same way? What if Tori scared her away? She didn't want to be the one to broach the topic first. It was almost easier to stay in this undefined space than to put her heart on the line. And despite wanting to define the relationship (DTR) with Leslie, Tori was also dating a few people at the same time. She had no idea whether Leslie was seeing other people, and the last thing she wanted to do was put all her eggs in one basket.

As she was telling us this, Leslie texted her. Instead of responding, Tori decided to leave the message on read. She'd reply in a couple of hours—she didn't want to seem thirsty, after all! Plus, she had to maintain this appearance of "being busy." Maybe Leslie would think Tori was on another date, which would be great because that would mean the power was back on her side.

Despite all these games, Tori wanted a relationship—and wanted to explore one with Leslie. A major problem with modern dating is that people do the exact opposite of what they want from a relationship in order to get into one. If you were in a healthy, committed relationship, you'd never wait to text back your partner so that you could have the upper hand. You'd tell them that you love spending time together, and you wouldn't be afraid it would scare them off. So why would you act this way to *get into* a relationship, yet would never be this way while *in* a relationship? We like to call this **Relationship Chicken**: when you don't want to be the one to show your cards first, acting in the exact opposite way you would in a relationship in order to protect your heart. Like the game of chicken, both people try to avoid being the one to surrender first, only to both end up resisting love. But this game of chicken isn't serving anyone—and only puts us deeper into a love crisis. So why do we do this?

THE WIN-LOSE MENTALITY

The irony is that a relationship is a partnership, but in dating, we're pitted against each other like we're in *The Hunger Games*. As we touched upon in chapter 1, bad dating books such as *The Game* or *The Rules* taught us to neg each other or play hard to get to "win" in this game called love. And it makes sense: our culture depicts dating as a competitive pursuit. How many movies or TV shows have you watched where the romantic leads try to make each other jealous or play "hot and cold" to win the other's affection? The media portrays courtship as manipulating each other in order to maximize our chances of being liked. No wonder we internalize this mindset!

While dating has always been a game, dating apps make it a battlefield. Outside of the obvious gamification of apps, there's a feeling of anonymity that keeps us removed from the person on the other side of the screen. And with so many options, it's nearly impossible to treat every match with respect and integrity. Dating apps have become a war zone where bad dating behavior is normalized, with terms such as breadcrumbing, ghosting, zombieing, roaching, and love bombing. All these tactics do, though, is keep us trapped in dating hell.

Some of us may have fallen for these dynamics along the way (or been guilty of doing them ourselves), but did they pave the way for a healthy, sustainable relationship? *Hell no.* All they did was teach us how to master indifference and, quite frankly, be an a**hole. Yet, for whatever reason, we think we still need to play these games—consciously or unconsciously (we see you, person who still hasn't texted back). Especially for the Thinkers out there, you may be prone to thinking of dating like chess, pondering your every move. We're afraid to "lose" because it equates to getting hurt—and we want to protect our fragile hearts. It's easier to say "I didn't try that hard" or "I have others in the pipeline" than to avoid the reality of someone saying no to us.

You may be thinking: I don't play games. Maybe you don't even realize you're playing them after years and years of conditioning. If you're even withholding just a little bit (that text, your feelings, whatever), you may be partaking more than you think. As you can see, maintaining our pride gets us nowhere. That's no way to date if you actually want to find love!

> **BDE (Big Dateable Energy):**
> There are no losers if there isn't a game.

REMEMBER YOUR DATING ARCHETYPE!

Using this lens will help you connect the dots to see how you may fall for Relationship Chicken.

- **Achievers:** How can you not keep score while you're dating?
- **Dreamers:** How can you be more confident in asking for what you want?
- **Energizers:** How do you start dating with a relationship lens?
- **Mavericks:** How can you make sure you're *actually* putting yourself out there?
- **Thinkers:** How can you act with more conviction even without all the information?

PLAYING IT COOL
IS RUINING YOUR DATING LIFE

A big part of why we play these games is to make people like us and not come off as desperate. We're told the worst thing we can do for our dating lives is to be "too needy" so we don't text back immediately or accept a date too soon. Instead of telling our dates we had a great time and can't wait to see them again, we act like it's just another Tuesday and we could care less if they reached out again. They don't see us frantically checking our phones every five minutes hoping for a text! Especially for hetero women, we've been conditioned to do whatever we can to appear easygoing and low-maintenance.

That appearance of coming off so chill is exactly what's sacrificing your own needs. There's a big difference between being needy and having needs. If you have a pulse, you have needs! We've seen the most confident daters out there start to exhibit symptoms of CGS, aka Cool Girl/Nice Guy Syndrome, the act of playing it cool so you don't come off thirsty. You'll be so easygoing and accommodating to others, even at your own expense. They didn't call back? It's cool! Had to cancel a date at the last minute? No problem! Seeing other people? Well, we never said we're exclusive, so it's all good.

When you play it cool, you end up bottling up all your emotions, never talking to the other person, and then one day you *explode*! Maybe you've been upset that they haven't been making enough effort for weeks, so you send a text message telling them it's over once and for all. Or you say that you're cool with casual relationships and hookups but go into a dark spiral when nothing ever seems to turn into more. For the Mavericks out there, by trying to maintain your independence, you go out of your way to be nonchalant in dating, even when you *really* like someone. But if you don't show your cards, how can people know that you are relationship material? And for the Dreamers, you may play it cool out of fear of rocking the boat and scaring away any prospects. But all that's doing is depriving yourself of the relationship you want.

Don't worry, it's not just limited to these archetypes. CGS can affect any dater who doesn't want to share how they really feel. We think that playing it cool allows us to maintain a level of control of the relationship. Because if you never showed your true feelings and needs, you can't get hurt, right? But unfortunately, it doesn't work that way. As we'll explain in detail later, it's much better to put yourself out there to get rejected than to hold back and settle for the wrong person. The right person will return the sentiment when you *aren't* playing it cool, as they'll know what you want, and that is damn sexy.

Yue's Corner

I used to be super confident with people I wasn't interested in but cold to people I liked. I would ignore texts for hours, turn down dates, and not say nice things to them on purpose. I thought all these tactics would make me seem less available and give me the upper hand. If this sounds confusing, imagine how the people I dated felt. Once, when I tried to have a DTR conversation with a guy I really liked, he didn't even know I was into him. The conversation came out like verbal diarrhea, sharing all my pent-up feelings and emotions. As I shared, he looked more and more perplexed. While my feelings grew, he saw me as a fading fling. In hindsight, no surprise there. I did everything to drive him away, thinking it would make him want me more. I thought I was winning when he didn't even know he was in the game.

DO YOU WANT A SOULMATE OR A STALEMATE?

When both parties show as little interest as possible or don't put in enough effort, nothing happens. Zip. Zilch. Nada. We start to enter a dating stalemate. And this is exactly why we hear so many daters complaining that nobody wants to meet up. Nobody wants to initiate.

Nobody wants to return texts. It's because when we're one-upping each other in disinterest, we spend more effort holding back our actions than actually acting.

We have this long-running joke that Relationship Chicken is a competition of who can do the least. This scenario could be a self-fulfilling prophecy for many:

> You match with someone on a dating app.
> They text, "hey."
> You message, "hey."
> They wait three days to message again with, "Hey, how's your day?"
> Since they waited three days, you wait five days to message back with, "Good, how's your day?"
> A week later, they message back, "Hey, sorry been busy. How are you?"
> In an effort to win this game, you wait two weeks and reply with, "I've been busy, too! I'm good. What's new?"
> And a year later, you miiiight meet up.

As you can see, this is a vicious cycle. Instead of leading with an open heart, we protect ourselves at all costs. We may think we're trying to make ourselves more desirable to our potential suitors, but we're afraid of being vulnerable and exposing ourselves to hurt. So, inaction becomes the norm, and we, as daters, start to succumb to the lowest common denominator (LCD). As our dear friend Sonica put so eloquently on our podcast, when we sink to the LCD, we accept (and participate in!) the worst behavior driven by dating culture. We need to stop this toxic cycle where bad dating behavior begets worse and worse dating behavior—and dating becomes a standoff.

When Maya first started using apps, she was bright-eyed and bushy-tailed, eager to meet the love of her life. She'd spend hours crafting individualized openers based on the profiles of her matches.

Maya asked plenty of questions and made herself readily available. But she soon realized that her actions were unmet, and her friends advised her she was *too available* and *too open*. So, she took it down a notch. And down a notch. And down a few more notches. She soon became standoffish, fading from conversations and even ghosting a person or two. As a Maverick, the last thing Maya wanted to do was invest in people who weren't investing in her. She didn't want to look like a fool, so bringing her effort down to their level felt safer. Since she felt like a low priority, she started giving less and less of her time and energy—often writing people off quickly and resorting to her infamous five-minute date.

The thing was, in other aspects of life, Maya wasn't like this. She was a girl boss who went after what she wanted. When Maya had plans with friends, she made it a point never to flake and always gave them her undivided attention. If she got an intro to a new professional contact, she'd put time on the calendar and make it a priority to meet right away. But dating seemed to be a whole different story. And we get it; when everyone is ghosting one another, and bad behavior feels like the norm, it's hard to bring your whole self. You don't want to get your hopes up and set yourself up for disappointment. But by succumbing to the lowest common denominator, Maya closed herself off from love.

To find great love, vulnerability is the key, even if that means experiencing disappointment. We think putting ourselves "out there" is getting on the apps, going out to meet new people, and so on. But opening yourself up, even when you're not entirely sure what you'll get in return, is actually what putting yourself out there means. At the end of the day, the only person you can control is yourself. You get to choose whether you're acting in a way that brings you closer to love.

Let others rise to your level instead of allowing the worst behaviors drag you down. Lead by example and invite others to put themselves out there. And if they don't? Then this is the perfect filtering system to put your time and attention into others who are at your level. If you're the type of person who makes plans and is proactive, have the confidence to seek someone who is proactive, too, or who is at least respectful of your proactiveness. If someone gives you 10 percent effort, instead of giving them 9 percent, give them zero. Only then can you move on to someone who shows up the way you do.

Ultimately, you can't force anyone else to rise to your level, but you can hold yourself accountable. People who are not playing Relationship Chicken will find your way refreshing. And the ones who don't—well, that's their loss. Let people who want to play games play. You don't need to be part of the game. Even if your efforts go unreturned, it may be momentarily disappointing, but in the grand scheme of things, it will be a blip in your great love story. As we established with the Validation Trap, when someone doesn't return your sentiments, it doesn't define your worth. It means nothing. It's simply that this person isn't meeting you where you're at. When you stay true to your values and have integrity in how you act, that's the only way you'll know who is—or isn't—a fit for you.

> **BDE (Big Dateable Energy):**
> Always choose action over inaction.

THE STANDSTILL DILEMMA

Note: This section may be a little more heteronormative. If that's not you, feel free to bypass!

We certainly don't want to go back to the days of even *more* toxic masculinity, but there's a fascinating phenomenon that's unique to post-#MeToo dating: the straddling of old versus new gender roles that are contradictory to each other. For hetero men, the last thing you want to do is come on too strong or be a harasser or anything in that vein. So we're caught at a standstill, complete immobility.

If we had a dollar for every time someone said "I wish I could just meet someone in real life," we'd be frolicking around on a private island right now, giving away this book for free like we're Oprah. We've witnessed daters see someone they want to approach IRL, but instead try to find this mysterious person (who is literally five feet away) on a dating app. How much easier would it have been to say hello? Either (a) the person would have loved it or (b) you would have gotten your answer and been able to move on. Instead, they've become the "one that got away" into the sea of dating apps, never to be found again. You may be thinking: WTF? Why would someone do this? But being more passive when it comes to dating has become the norm. It's easier to hide behind a screen. Wait for the other person to initiate. But all it has done is put us in a place where we're stilted, and no action is being taken at all. So how did we get here?

The Old Way: let the man initiate. For anyone who is a Millennial or older, you've received so much gendered messaging it's hard to unlearn it all. Our societal expectations about how men and women behave go deep—it's even affected how we're socialized growing up. Think back to grade school. If a boy made a girl cry, chances are that some adult would say, "Oh, it's because he likes her." Little boys are often told by their relatives that they're "heartbreakers" because they're so cute and will probably have multiple girlfriends when they grow up. And as we grow up and start to date, men are told to be the pursuers and woman are told to "lean back." Whether it came from *Cosmopolitan* magazine, *The Rules*, or other dating advice, women were told the cardinal sin of dating was to make the first move. So . . . women became sitting ducks, waiting to be chosen by our Disney Princes or whoever else would give attention (no wonder the Validation Trap impacts us!). And if he didn't pursue you, then it meant he just wasn't into you—no questions asked. Think *Bridget Jones's Diary, My Best Friend's Wedding, 10 Things I Hate About You* . . . the list goes on and on. Traditional gender roles were the basis for every romantic interaction, with men being seen as the providers and protectors while women were damsels in distress.

The New Way: let empowered women initiate. The strong female character was born during the rise of mainstream feminism. Think of Samantha Jones from *Sex and the City, Buffy the Vampire Slayer,* and Kate Hudson's character in *How to Lose a Guy in 10 Days.* This woman would *never* wait for a guy to approach her at the bar. She would walk right up to a stranger and say, "Hey, you're cute. Let's get dinner on Tuesday, seven p.m." Men are attracted to this woman's confidence and take-charge attitude, making it hard to turn her down. She's also a career woman who slays everything she does, so if this guy doesn't work out, no problem; she has a very fulfilling life. *She don't need no man.* This woman completely crushes the old gender roles and believes in initiating; it's the empowered feminist thing to do.

The problem here is this trope isn't necessarily realistic or progressive. We're now just encouraging women to behave like men. Being the one to make the move felt unnatural for most women (because how can we expect instant change after years and years of conditioning!). And the "dating like a man" or "having sex like a man" tropes became power plays, removing the human emotions associated with dating and sex. All the behaviors that bothered women about men were suddenly what women emulated. While we don't want to take for granted the gains of the feminist movement, we need to ask ourselves how this is helping us or hindering us from having relationships. And all this does is minimize men, too, putting them into a stereotype that compounds the challenges of seeing each other as human beings.

The New New Way: nobody initiates. In recent years, while women have been told to lean in, hetero men have been told to lean out. As a result of #MeToo, a hetero man doesn't feel comfortable initiating romantically the way he used to. The workplace used to be one of the top places to meet your life partner. But now you're not just risking being rejected; you're risking becoming a sexual harasser—and losing your job. When we talked to Christine Emba, the *Washington Post* columnist and author of *Rethinking Sex*, on *Dateable*, she told us how she met a man in San Francisco who said, "I'd never ask out a woman at work. That's like handing someone a loaded shotgun." This may seem dramatic, but many men we talk with feel the same way. The Harvey Weinstein case is clear: of course, you can't use your power to force people to have sex with you! But the unintended fallout of #MeToo is that it has made good-natured straight men much more timid.

We've had so many male daters tell us they're unsure what to do in today's climate. Do they go in for the first kiss or wait for the woman? Is a light touch on the elbow okay, or should there be no flirting until the woman starts first? Should a man pay for the first date, or will that be offensive to an equal partner? As you read this, you may be tensing up, playing back all the times you've been in limbo about what to do. And that is precisely why so many people end up doing nothing at all.

One of the shocking revelations we've had by hosting *Dateable* is that straight men and women have a lot of the *same* challenges: it feels like everyone is in a waiting game. The lack of initiative by hetero men has also made women initiate less. It's no fun to be the one taking charge and initiating plans constantly. Apps such as Bumble that put the work entirely on women are not the answer. The fact that Bumble stepped away from their "women make the first move" strategy already proves the point. Dating only works if all parties give it their all. And when they don't? *Nobody* initiates, and everyone sits around complaining about how nobody initiates.

The Solution: we all lean in. While we debate who should make the first move or initiate, we're missing the big picture. In the ten-thousand-foot view of your entire relationship, this is all so irrelevant! Who cares who sends the message or says hi first? By focusing on it so much, you miss the chance to experience a heartfelt connection where you'll be happy that *one of you* made the move. In today's world, it's so easy to miss someone amazing or swipe right past them. Everyone needs to f*cking lean in.

Maybe one day—one day—we'll reach the point where neither party puts as much weight on this aspect of dating. While progress has been made in challenging and reshaping gender roles, it is gradual and ongoing. But for now, let's look at each other as humans above everything else.

If you're still clinging on to power dynamics, you're not looking for a relationship, despite what you may say. You're playing games. If you're serious about finding someone, you will approach someone you find attractive. You will text the person you're interested in. And you will want to tell that person you like spending time with them. It's about showing genuine interest. Especially in a time of blended generations, it's nearly impossible to know which gender-role beliefs someone subscribes to. In later chapters, we'll go into more detail about how to change your mindset with all these dating games and prescribed rules, but for now, let's acknowledge where we've been so we can evolve from it.

Julie's Corner

In early dating, I found myself passively waiting for men to make the first move. Eventually I got to a place where I said f*ck it and started messaging first on dating apps. I'd suggest moving the conversation to text or even meeting in person. My dates appreciated this proactive approach, with so many other stagnant conversations. I found that when I gave an inch, they went a mile. I wasn't overthinking gender roles; just reaching out if I saw someone interesting, knowing that I had nothing to lose. My current partner gave me the perfect opportunity. On his dating profile, he had photos of his friends' faces covered by smiley-face emojis. I commented, "It looks like your friends are really happy to be with you," as I would joke with a friend. This was enough to get the conversation going and for him to ask me out.

IT SHOULDN'T BE THIS TRANSACTIONAL

The real problem is greater than gender roles: it's that we're thinking about dating transactionally. These interactions (or lack thereof) come from a place of fear, not a mindset conducive to connection. When we're so petty about everything—who texted first, who planned the last date, etc., etc.—we start to view the budding relationship as an exchange, not an emotional connection. We must stop looking at dating as a Dating ATM where we keep making withdrawals (wanting results) without putting anything in. Dating is not built on debits and credits.

For many of you, especially Achievers, if a date doesn't meet your expectations (e.g., you ask them out and expect them to ask you for the next date), you start playing chicken by pulling back or prematurely deciding this relationship isn't worth pursuing. You should not be the only one initiating, but when you're constantly calculating your return on investment (ROI) with your dates, it's not setting you up for success in love. And it's not sustainable, as we learned when we interviewed the couple Nate and Kaley Klemp, who wrote the book *The 80/80 Marriage: A New Model for a Happier, Stronger Relationship*, on *Dateable*. Nate and Kaley did not believe that a relationship was fifty-fifty; there is no such thing as an equal partnership. They believed if you did what's more than expected of you in a relationship, you would inspire your partner to do the same, and therefore both parties would want to be doing more than the bare minimum.

What if you could apply the same mindset to dating? You can't control what others do, but if you can take away this transactional mentality, you do what's authentic to you without expecting reciprocity. It goes back to everyone leaning in instead of succumbing to the lowest common denominator. Lean into initiating a text conversation. Lean into planning out your next date. Lean into expressing your appreciation for someone's time. You are not "losing" when you make that extra effort. You are a wonderful human desiring a genuine connection, and you'll inspire the right person to do the same. And if they don't, then they weren't the right partner anyway! By leading more with your heart, you'll stop with the calculated thinking, paving the way for a meaningful relationship.

> **BDE (Big Dateable Energy):**
> The only calculation you need is you + me.

THE DANGER: LONELINESS

At the epicenter of the love crisis is the loneliness epidemic. This is what happens when we don't lean in and take chances in love. In a *Psychology Today* article titled "What's behind the Rise of Lonely, Single Men," Dr. Greg Matos ruffled some feathers by calling out exactly what has been happening–the alarming increase in men who've given up on dating. So we knew we had to get him on *Dateable*. Dr. Matos highlighted that with blurred gender roles and numerous dating fails, there are more single men than ever due to lack of relational skills. This trend has been detrimental to mental health and has fueled extremist groups such as the incel communities (men blaming women for their involuntary celibacy) and red-pillers (the online community where men share their toxic views on women). In short, it seems like many men have given up on love. We've heard young men say, "I'd much rather play video games with my roommates than make an effort with a woman who most likely won't like me back." We fear this is the outcome if we keep ruminating on gender roles. No one can win in this scenario if we keep blaming the "other" for not doing what we expect them to do.

It isn't just lonely single men that are on the rise. It's lonely single people in general. According to a recent Pew Research report, more than half of US adults said dating is not going well for them. And half of single adults report that they're not dating at all. Moreover, when asked why they chose not to date, 61 percent of this group cited having "more important priorities" as the main reason. This forever-single mentality is not just in America. Population decline is a major issue in Asia. Take Japan, for example, currently witnessing the biggest-ever natural decline in population. To curb the decline, the Japanese government is considering AI matchmaking to help heterosexual singles date. Singapore is another country to have government-sponsored dating events. In China, the government has also stepped in to set up blind date drives to help disinterested singles. In Beijing, there are even "dating parks" where parents of single young adults hold up signs of their children's qualifications (e.g., height, education, assets) in hopes of matchmaking with other parents doing the same.

People have given up on love because dating and relationships are hard. But most of this comes from fear. Fear of being hurt. Fear of being misunderstood. Fear of rejection. We love the saying "choose your hard" because it puts in perspective that every decision you make in life comes with its own set of challenges and difficulties. No path is entirely smooth or effortless. Dating is hard. Relationships are hard. But also, being on your own is hard. *Every* action (or inaction) takes effort. Instead of viewing challenges as obstacles, we can view them as an inherent part of any path we choose, and an opportunity for growth and fulfillment. So the next time dating feels challenging, instead of just deleting all the apps or shutting out the world, recognize that it's part of the process. Lean in however you can. Because whatever happens, at least you'll know you're giving it your all instead of defaulting to what may momentarily feel easier.

> **BDE (Big Dateable Energy):**
> Love might be a battlefield, but not trying
> is just surrendering to defeat.

THE END OF DATING PURGATORY

The other fallout of Relationship Chicken is that so many of us stay in limbo, unsure of how to progress a relationship. It's often easier to do nothing than to run the risk of getting hurt. Because no one wants to get rejected or invest in the wrong person! But when we don't have the necessary conversations to gain clarity of our situations, eventually they will fizzle out.

Take the example of Tori. She and Leslie continued to see each other for another three months, having a full-blown situationship where neither of them ever talked about where they saw this relationship going or what they wanted. Whenever Tori started to muster up the courage to have a conversation, she started "hesidating," unsure if she wanted to pursue something serious. While she liked Leslie, how did she know whether she was the right person for her? What if they were a good match now but wouldn't be in the future? With her Thinker ways, Tori was all in her head, in a state of analysis paralysis, pulling away when she got confused. Leslie started feeling like Tori was playing games so she started to pull away, too. You can see how this put their "relationship" into a state of ambiguity, even though Tori did like Leslie and wanted this to be something more. Eventually, they started seeing each other less frequently, and their "relationship" finally ended before they even had the chance to build one.

The reality is that the only way to know if someone is right for you is to invest in the relationship, even if you're not 100 percent sure—because you'll never be. We know you want to make the most informed decision possible (talking to you, Thinkers), always considering the various scenarios. The fear of making the wrong decision is causing you to stay in dating purgatory, which is an anxiety-induced place causing you to play chicken. We encourage everyone to start getting into relationships, even if you aren't sure whether they're your forever person. A DTR or exclusivity conversation doesn't mean you must now get married. We like this idea of doing a thirty-day test run. For a month, you give the relationship your all, seeing each other exclusively (and regularly!) and having the types of conversations necessary to move the relationship forward. At the end of the month, you can evaluate how you're feeling and decide whether you want to continue or part ways. It's not leading the other person on, especially if you're having these conversations together. You're simply trying to figure out if you two could work! We have such an all-or-nothing approach to dating these days and that's what makes it so daunting. This shorter-term approach can help you take smaller, more incremental steps to get off situationship slope or wherever else you find yourself in purgatory mode.

There's so much fear seeping into dating these days: fear of rejection, fear of missing out, fear of commitment, fear of making the wrong choice; the list goes on and on. But if you want to be in a relationship, you need to be willing to take some chances–even if they don't work out. We need not fear the "what are we" convos and what this means for our ego/pride if we don't get our desired answer, as that will just put us at a standstill, contributing to the love crisis. And as we shared with the Validation Trap, you are not a failure if it doesn't work out. And who knows: when you stop playing Relationship Chicken, you may find yourself in the relationship you've always imagined.

> **BDE (Big Dateable Energy):**
> When you're overthinking, you're underdoing.

ARE YOU DATING TO DATE—
OR TO BE IN A RELATIONSHIP?

We often stay in dating limbo for so long because being good at dating doesn't always translate to being good at a relationship. When you have an active dating life, it doesn't necessarily mean you're looking for a real relationship–or capable of being vulnerable enough to be in one. Often, the serial daters are just as guilty of Relationship Chicken as the ones holding back and not making any moves. As your typical Energizer, Eli started dating when he was seventeen. In his early forties, he realized he'd probably been on more than a thousand first dates. Eli had no trouble attracting men in real life and on dating apps. On the first date, he'd be fun and playful and would always get that second date. But scheduling him for that next date was a nightmare! He recently met a guy he was interested in at a masquerade yacht party, but when they tried to schedule a date, his first available night was in three weeks! By then, in dating terms, the ship had sailed.

People often think that they have to be good at dating by going on as many dates as possible and packing their social calendar. But all this does is give off the vibe that you're not looking for a relationship. How can someone think you're ready for a relationship when you're constantly out, and it's nearly impossible to schedule time with you? While you think you're just broadening your opportunities and not coming off as thirsty, people looking for a relationship won't see you as a viable option. People often want to get into a relationship so they don't have to pack their social calendars! If you're unwilling to show a side of you that's more settled, how can someone imagine settling down with you?

When you're a pro dater, you're driving away (or ignoring) the people looking for a genuine partnership. With this Relationship Chicken behavior, you will only attract people who want the game playing and the butterflies but not an actual relationship. Take a look at some of the ways you may be pushing away a relationship despite constantly dating:

Only focusing on fun activities: We often see daters place more importance on the date experience than on getting to know their date. If you spend more time telling your friends about the concert you took your date to than what you like about the person, you may be guilty of overemphasizing the date and de-emphasizing the relationship.

Short-term planning: If planning a date for more than a week out is difficult, how can you imagine building your lives together? If you can't commit until the day of, or your social calendar is just that jam-packed, it doesn't seem like you'll be able to integrate someone into your life.

Dating multiple people at once: It's common to hedge your bets by dating a few people in the beginning stages. But at some point, if you're serious about ever having a relationship, you need to double down on one person so you can start to deepen the connection, be more vulnerable, and take chances—you know, what you do in a relationship.

Engaging in casual hookups: If your physical needs are met elsewhere, you're not bringing your entire self to someone who could be a real partner. Even if you say you can compartmentalize the two, there tends to be spillover, making things a bit murky. Everyone you're involved with takes up some mental real estate, whether they're a partner contender or not. If you engage in more casual hookups and FWB arrangements, you may feel inclined to default to them instead of putting your energy into a person with relationship potential.

Limited emotional investment: You can show up for all your dates and make all the right moves, but if your heart isn't in it, you might as well not be there. If you keep the conversations surface-level and shy away from ever talking about your feelings or anything deeper, you may be keeping a wall up that protects you from something more serious.

There's an important question to ask yourself: am I dating to date, or am I dating to be in a relationship? If it's the latter, instead of "just getting out there," date in an intentional way that's centered around getting into a relationship. Show you have the capacity and necessary skills to be a great date *and* partner. So, what are some skills that make you more relationship material? Take a look and circle which ones you have:

Skills to Be a Great Date	Skills to Be a Great Partner
Attentiveness (the ability to make someone feel comfortable)	Communication (not just talking, but actually communicating, especially when there's a disconnect or sign of friction)
Being an engaging conversationalist	Empathy and compassion
Active listening	Emotional availability
Authenticity (being yourself and showing genuine interest)	Vulnerability
Positivity	Being supportive
Respectfulness and kindness	Trustworthiness
Being punctual	Consistency and reliability
Lightheartedness and the ability to have fun!	Willingness to work together as a team

Now be real: are you also bringing these to early dating? Cross off any that you may not be showing on the first few dates. If you find that one column outweighs the other, it's time to bring more balance into the equation. Dating skills are imperative because they set the baseline as the necessary prelude to a relationship. They're what make you attractive to the other person in the first place! More often than not, though, we tend to fall short on "partner skills." We've been told for so long to hide these skills on dates so we don't scare people away. Or we shouldn't act like a partner until someone earns that right. But this mentality isn't getting us into relationships; instead, it's keeping us stuck in date mode indefinitely. What if you were to look at everyone you dated as a partner—even if it's for one hour, one week, or one month? Yes, that feels scary because trust and security aren't always there when dating someone new. The ambiguity alone is often why we resort to putting our guard up and going into self-protection mode. But if you recognize this is just the ego talking, you'll see that by dating this way, you'll grow those muscles to become a great partner no matter what happens. Even if you aren't sure what the future holds with this specific person, eventually, the right partner will recognize a good thing when they see it.

> **BDE (Big Dateable Energy):**
> Being a great date is being a great partner.

END THE CYCLE OF SELF-SABOTAGE

Another downside of playing Relationship Chicken is you may self-sabotage a great relationship because you're so used to putting up walls and partaking in chicken-like behaviors. When you're going on red-flag hunts, always getting the ick or bouncing over something seemingly trivial, you must stop and ask yourself: *Why do I say I want a relationship but chicken out once it could be more serious?*

When we talked with the self-sabotage researcher Dr. Raquel Peel on *Dateable*, she shared how certain attitudes and behaviors we employ–knowingly or unknowingly–inevitably damage the relation-ship, justify the outcomes, and lead us to withdraw. When we have learned narratives such as "relationships don't work" or "men will cheat," we look for that confirmation bias. And as humans, we love being right. There's something gratifying about saying "I knew it" or "This person wasn't good for me anyway." As a recovering romantic saboteur herself, Dr. Peel had to counter her urges to leave when things got hard. This was her trigger due to the deep-seated belief that her partners would get sick of her and end the relationship, so she wanted to be the one to leave! If you identify with any of this, especially Mavericks who are known for running away when they're challenged, recognize that this stuff can run deep. And you may have a different trigger. For example, if you feel emotionally vulnerable, you may shut down or even cheat! It goes back to playing Relation-ship Chicken to protect yourself. When you're more focused on win-ning and proving yourself right, you lose the chance of deepening an emotional connection.

So, do you want to be right, or do you want to be in a relation-ship? We're not saying it's Relationship Chicken if you end a rela-tionship that isn't working (if it's not good, get out!). But as Dr. Peel shared, if you have a pattern of cycling through people quickly and tend to have quick justifications for why your relationships aren't working–especially if you put the reason on the other person–it may be time to realize you're the common denominator here. The heal-ing starts when you can look at yourself in the mirror and confront the actions that keep you in this cycle. Are you choosing the wrong people from the start to justify the failure? Are you nitpicking people apart, looking for faults that aren't there so you're the one to break it off? When we're so focused on being right that we sabotage a good relationship, it becomes a self-fulfilling prophecy.

We can also use our mindset to break the cycle. Our minds can influence powerful beliefs that feed our actions. How much better would it be to believe your relationship will work out instead of not? How much more rewarding would it be to think that you deserve a relationship instead of thinking there is no one out there for you? If you find a self-sabotaging thought popping up, start to question its accuracy. Even if it happened before, it doesn't mean it'll happen again. You don't need to prove it right; instead, you get to choose whether you believe it or challenge it entirely.

CONTRIBUTE TO YOUR RELATIONSHIP JAR

Now is a good time to reexamine your behaviors to see whether they align with how you'd want to behave in a relationship. When you're getting to know someone or have been on a few dates with them, check your actions against Relationship Chicken behaviors. Try our relationship jar exercise:

You can have imaginary or real jars, one marked RELATIONSHIP and the other marked NON-RELATIONSHIP. For every action you take, determine if the action contributes to relationship-building behavior or not. Toss a coin in the relevant jar for visual checks and balances of your behaviors. This will keep you accountable for each action you take so you don't revert to your default setting. To get you started, here is a Chicken Check you can use to identify your behaviors. See which jar your behaviors fall into.

Instead of This Chicken Behavior	Try This Relationship Behavior
Waiting to text someone back because you don't want to come off as too interested.	Text back as soon as you see the message even if it's just acknowledging receipt.
Not telling someone you had a great time even though you did.	Tell them you had a great time as soon as the thought pops into your head.
Withholding your desire for a committed relationship, fearing it would scare them away.	Share that a committed relationship is part of your core values.
Being okay with a situationship even though it is not serving you.	Be transparent about how you feel (even if it's vulnerable) and ask them for more. If they can't, you have your answer.
Constantly playing it cool with a "no big deal" attitude even though their behavior does bother you (e.g., rescheduling a date last minute).	Be honest with yourself and the other person about your discomfort and insecurities.

This is just a sample of the many chicken-like behaviors you could exhibit while dating, so feel free to keep thinking about these as you date and add more to your jars now that you're aware of them. We must not lose sight of the fact that we want connection. We don't want to play Relationship Chicken. We're accustomed to playing chicken because it's easier to blame the apps or the other people in our city instead of looking at ourselves. When we act in alignment with having a relationship, that's when the magic starts to happen. In the second part of the book, we'll dive into all that and how to get crystal clear on what you want. But for now, you know what traps to watch out for, which we're all so susceptible to falling for in modern dating.

You're not alone in exhibiting these chicken-like behaviors (we all have!). The key is gaining that awareness so you can make the necessary changes. The only way out of the love crisis is to become our own agents of change. We need to remember that dating is not a war zone. There are no winners, and there are no losers. The person on the other side is not the enemy or the opponent. It's not a game of me versus you. Instead of expecting others to perform their roles, how can you take control of your actions and look for ways to deepen this connection? As long as you're both f*cking leaning in, you'll avoid playing Relationship Chicken and finally start creating a life with someone.

KEY TAKEAWAYS

1. How you would behave *in* a relationship should not differ from how you would act to *get into* a relationship. Stop playing Relationship Chicken if you actually want a relationship.

2. There is no winning or losing in dating. If someone's trying to win, they're wrong for you.

3. Make the move. If you take action, it gives the other person the opportunity to meet you. And if they don't? You have your answer!

4. The only way to know whether you're compatible for a long-term relationship is to have a relationship. It doesn't have to be all-or-nothing, and it's okay to do a trial run, especially if you openly communicate with each other.

5. Start filling your relationship jar. Even if you haven't defined the relationship yet, give to it like you have. And if you find the other person isn't contributing to their relationship jar, then you can also find someone who will.

PART 2:

The Path to Finding Love

Prelude:

Let's Raise the Bar

Whoa! That was a lot. No wonder we're all struggling with modern dating and this impending love crisis. But by now, we hope we've made it abundantly clear that the current dating landscape is setting us up to fail. You, and every other dater, have become prisoners to these traps. It is not your fault. However, it's imperative to understand where you've been, because only then can you shape where you want to go. As we mentioned, these are just traps. They are not the way dating has to be. There is a way to break free, if you choose to do so. Remember, this book is not about trying to adapt to dating culture—which will inevitably trap you time and time again. We're going to rise above it. The second part of this book is about escaping these traps so you can finally have the joyful, fulfilling dating life you so deeply desire.

Over the next five chapters, we'll take you through the framework that was a game-changer for us and the thousands of daters we've helped throughout our time at *Dateable*. This blueprint is an accumulation of what we've learned over the last almost decade by looking at all the steps and missteps, the time well spent versus wasted, and what made people joyful versus miserable while dating. Here are the five components of this framework:

1. **Letting go:** Release the baggage and beliefs that are holding you back.
2. **Gaining clarity:** Uncover what you truly want and need.
3. **Showing up:** Give to dating what you want to get out of dating.

4. **Investing appropriately:** Prioritize your time, energy, and emotions into what matters.
5. **Persevering through it all:** Stay resilient despite the inevitable challenges and setbacks.

This framework will lead us to the dating utopia we described in the beginning. You can have authentic connections, seamless communication, and feel empowered to express your true self. No more guesswork. No more gamification. No more fearing being "too soon," "too much," or "not enough." In this utopia, the pursuit of love is both rewarding and fun! This framework is about creating sustainable relationships with others–and yourself. Remember, the way we're currently approaching dating is sending us into a downward spiral and into a love crisis. So if you catch yourself thinking, *Well, that's not how dating works . . .* or *But isn't that going to scare them away?*–stop. It's time to throw out all preconceived notions and approach dating differently.

Inevitably, we all have certain aspects of dating that are more challenging for us than others. Since we're all coming from different backgrounds, life experiences, and ways of thinking, some chapters or sections within a chapter may resonate more than others. There may be some sections that confirm what you may already be doing (go you!) and others that make you stop and say: *I've never thought about it that way before.* To help personalize your experience as you continue reading, keep this **one question** in mind for your archetype:

Achievers, can you surrender the desire to control every aspect of the dating process?
Dating is not a predetermined formula where A plus B inevitably leads to C. By releasing your attachment to specific outcomes, you

open yourself up to more pleasure in the process itself. Let go of the incessant need to plan every future milestone. Instead, immerse yourself fully in the experience, connecting with your date on a deeper level, appreciating their presence, and savoring the moment for what it truly is.

Dreamers, how can you balance being realistic *and* optimistic?

Love is not a rom-com and does not conquer all. While we don't want you to lose your loving, supportive nature, we want to put you in the driver's seat. If you can start acting in ways that best align with your needs (and recognize when they aren't being met!), you can start living your actual love story, not just the fantasy of it. Start prioritizing yourself—not just the person you're dating—and recognize that you deserve the whole damn pie, not just a sliver of it.

Energizers, what could it mean to slow down your search for love?

Sometimes, you need to slow down to speed up. By spending more time reflecting, you'll understand what's right for the long term instead of only acting on that fleeting feeling. While dating can still be a priority, it doesn't need to be all-consuming. You don't need to sacrifice yourself and the other areas of your life. Think about all the things you *get to do* because you are single. These moments are what bring you fulfillment and happiness—and what will ultimately attract the right person anyway!

Mavericks, what would it look like to truly let someone in?

Relationships are partnerships, and you need to shift your energy from "me" to "we." In order to build deeper connections, reveal more about yourself—even if it means showing your flaws and insecurities—and embrace difficult conversations. Allow yourself to be vulnerable and take risks even with the possiblity of disappointment or heartbreak. Don't be afraid to knock down those walls! Remember that growth requires courage, so if you're scared to have the conversation or put yourself out there, it's a strong sign that you should attempt it.

Thinkers, can you catch yourself *right before* you spiral?

Love is not a problem to solve. While it's tempting to think through all the possibilities and scenarios, it's imperative to let dating situations play out how they are meant to. Instead of seeking certainty and control, accept that love is an inherently uncertain process. Stop worrying about making the wrong decision or getting hurt because all that does is lead you to overanalyze every move and avoid taking risks. Challenge the worst-case scenario, consider alternative perspectives, and give yourself permission to lead with your heart, not your head.

As you can see, it all starts with you. So are you ready to start falling in love?

Chapter 5:

Letting Go

IT'S TIME TO DISCOVER:

1. **Rejection Therapy:** Actively seeking out and putting yourself through a series of rejections, in an effort to desensitize your feeling of devastation each time.
2. **Limitless Beliefs:** The idea that anything is possible, and that you aren't confined to your past thoughts or experiences.
3. **The 1 Percent Rule:** Taking a small step every day to look for new opportunities to heal and grow.

We believe we constantly need to be acquiring: going on more dates, getting more matches, always doing more. But as we've discovered from our own experiences (and those daters who are now in happy, healthy relationships), a more critical act is letting go of what's no longer serving you. Letting go of those thoughts of *The last time I fell in love, I got my heart broken into a million pieces,* or *Every time I open myself up to love, they leave.* Letting go of the unresolved grievances or emotional distress from all the past heartbreaks or rejections. Letting go of the expectations and pressure of societal constructs–the plus-ones on invitations, family gatherings where your aunt grills you about being single, or the feeling like something is wrong with you if you haven't been in a serious relationship by a certain age. Oof, no wonder we're all so fatigued while dating!

Maybe you're well aware of some of what's holding you back (hello, lingering ex who couldn't commit yet won't go away), but others may be more below the surface. When Maya first came to us about her dating struggles, she was most concerned with getting higher-quality matches on the apps. As your typical Maverick, she struggled to connect with people she wanted to date, as no one was up to her standards. But as we started peeling back the layers, we saw that Maya was still holding on to a lot of past anger and trust issues. During her senior year of college, she had met Dan. He was everything she wanted in a partner, and they continued dating after they graduated. She thought their relationship was headed for marriage, but he abruptly broke up with her one day, saying he wanted to explore other types of women. This ate at her self-esteem, which was already not the best due to her extremely critical mother, who would always make remarks about her not being thin enough, her hair not being straight enough, the list goes on and on! When Dan broke up with her, it confirmed everything her mother had said. Because she hadn't healed from this experience, it continued to manifest while dating. Her pickiness on the apps and her five-minute dates were the perfect defense mechanism. By discounting people quickly, she could reject others before they rejected her. See how deep-rooted this can be?

Our dating lives can be impacted by both significant trauma *and* a culmination of lowercase-*t* traumas such as a breakup, a series of rejections, or other bad dating behaviors. As you can see with Maya's example, the beliefs and thought patterns imprinted on us in our formative years continue to mess with our love lives (and mental health!). When you don't heal from your past, it follows you into your future, creeping into all your relationships. So, in this chapter, we will help you start letting go. That doesn't mean you will forget what may have happened (or even be over it, especially if it was traumatic!). But no longer will you let your past define your present. You'll better understand yourself and be able to apply the lessons you learned to your dating life instead of being hindered by the past.

So take a deep breath: it's time to release the roadblocks getting in your way. Letting go is essential, so take your time with this chapter. You can always come back to it again if needed. Don't be surprised if this brings up some emotions, but feeling the pain is part of your healing journey. People often bypass this step, but doing this hard work now will set you up for a fulfilling partnership later. So, how do you start to let go of what's holding you back?

REWRITING THE STORIES WE TELL OURSELVES

We build stories in our heads based on our beliefs, patterns, and experiences. And it makes sense: we need to comprehend everything happening in our lives–especially when we need to manage our emotions and the complexities of dating. We're also seeking answers to why our love lives aren't unfolding the way we want. For whatever reason, people insist on asking single people why they are still single like it's some case to be cracked. So you start to come up with stories: *I always go for the emotionally unavailable kind*, or *Toxic people are drawn to me*, or *I'm just not the relationship type*. These stories become detrimental to your love life because they become your reality if you don't let them go. Suddenly, all you're seeing are the emotionally unavailable or toxic people out there instead of the many dateable people who exist. And even worse, they shape our identities as the "forever single" person or the "one who attracts broken people."

Many of these stories may not even reflect who you are today or the person you're becoming. There's comfort in staying in the same cocoon and living in the past, but your memories are often an idealized version that never existed. Part of why letting go is challenging for many of us is that we cling to our old identities—that's typically where our stories come from. The beautiful thing about dating is that it helps you learn who you are and who you want to be. As with the rest of life, we're constantly evolving, so why do we have to create narratives about ourselves based on our past? If you're known as the party animal, yet want to be seen as serious-relationship material, can you be open to shedding that part of yourself? If you made a mistake and cheated in a past relationship, can you recognize what you learned in the process instead of believing "once a cheater, always a cheater"? If you don't have much relationship experience, can you be open to being "someone without substantial relational experience" or "someone who has not been tainted by dating"? There's always an evolution of your old identity that will move you forward.

Stories are only problematic when they impact our ability to have healthy relationships. If we turn them into tales of self-love or resilience, they can help us. It's easy to go to a dark place, though, especially when your love life isn't working out the way you want it to be. So, how do you get out of this mindset and rewrite your story?

Take Inventory

The first step is compiling and understanding the stories that live rent-free in your head. Which ones are getting in the way of your love life? Where are they coming from? You can unpack them on your own or even talk to your therapist if you have one, as Andrew did. He was sitting at his therapist's office, recalling the four first dates he had been on that week, and how none of them progressed into more (as an Achiever, you know how much that destroyed him!). While he felt rejected, his despair went much deeper than these women he had met on the apps. He feared being left behind. All his friends were getting married, and Andrew was the only single one in the group. He wondered whether he had made a mistake ending things last year with his ex, Ann. Though the relationship had stagnated, had that been his one shot at love? Was he not the "relationship type" and destined to be alone?

His therapist stopped him in his tracks. Why did he believe he wasn't the "relationship type"? Andrew explained that growing up, he struggled with dating. He vividly remembers missing his high school prom because he got rejected by the girl who he asked to be his date. Even well beyond college, his experiences always seemed more one-sided or unrequited. Current-day dating wasn't working well either: this third-date curse confirmed nothing had changed. He just wasn't the type of guy who got the girl. By the end of this session, Andrew realized that he had two dominant stories getting in the way of his love life: he was not relationship material and he would be left behind.

What stories are you telling yourself? If you stop and think now, even for a moment, a few will likely pop up from your subconscious. Jot them down as they surface. See if you can identify where these stories may be coming from. Once you can identify the patterns that emerge, you can deconstruct these stories and change the narrative once and for all!

Become a Myth-Buster

Now that you've taken inventory of what you tell yourself, ask whether it's even true. We often seek evidence to confirm a belief, but can you try to be a myth-buster instead? Can you think of counterexamples that disprove your theory that this *always* happens? Recalling both your positive and negative experiences is crucial to see the entire picture. We've seen daters speak in absolutes:

- I *never* go on good dates.
- I *never* get matches.
- I *never* meet anyone out and about.

We recently talked to a dater who went on for thirty minutes about how he struggled with dating in the past year. He shared how three of his relationships didn't work out. Before he went on, we stopped him and pointed out the fact that he'd had three relationships! It was something worth celebrating even if they didn't last! This simple reframe helped him see all the positives that were happening instead of fixating on what wasn't working.

Same for our Achiever, Andrew. When he talked to his therapist, she pressed him to look at his life over the past decade. So what if he didn't have a lot of relationship experience? Was Andrew incapable of being in one, or was it not a priority in his life? He finished at the top of his high school class and went to college on a full-ride scholarship. All Andrew wanted to do postcollege was to get a good job at a consulting firm and live close to his dearest friends. Andrew prioritized his career and building a life in Chicago. His therapist pointed out that he wasn't incapable of being in a relationship; he just didn't start prioritizing finding one until recently. By reframing the facts, Andrew believed that he was, in fact, capable of being a relationship person. Dates didn't always have to progress, and relationships didn't have to last forever to be successful. Andrew would never be left behind because he was still progressing–with dating and all aspects of life (cue the recent promotion he got!). Even if the date didn't work out, he was learning more about himself and what he wanted. Instead of bringing his "unable to connect" identity to every new date, he started finding evidence that contradicted it. He knew he was able to hold down long-term relationships (proof: his friends for over a decade!) and slowly he started to believe it was only a matter of time before he met someone who matched his energy and appreciated him for who he was romantically.

Whatever story you're grappling with, zoom out and see where you can poke holes in the narrative. For every example of it being true, find another where it's false. You'll prove to yourself that your past doesn't define you. Remove the terms *always* and *never* and see each instance as a moment, not the entire picture. Only then can you realize that this chapter is just part of your ongoing story of resilience and growth.

Control the Narrative

Even if there is some ounce of truth here, it doesn't mean it has to be your full narrative. On our podcast, the expert storyteller Corey Rosen told us that the heart of a story is *change*. If nothing changes, then it's just an anecdote. A story has three parts: it was like this, something happened, and now it's like this. We often get so caught up in "how it was," instead of seeing how we can evolve from our experiences. Let's say you always go for the emotionally unavailable kind. Look at why that is. Maybe it's that you have struggled to believe you deserve an emotionally available partner. Your more empowered story could be: "I have lacked confidence in the past, staying with people I knew weren't right for me. But I've done a lot of work to understand what I bring to the table, so I can open myself up to someone who has also done the work." That's an entirely different narrative that highlights profound change.

There's always an opportunity to own your story. Has anyone ever asked you the dreaded question of why you're still single or why your last relationship didn't work out? Or maybe you've tried to withhold information about yourself, such as being in recovery for an addiction or having a dysfunctional family. You can own your story and tell it in a way that shows how you've evolved as a person, and if that scares someone away, they're not the right fit for you. For example, you could share how you're divorced and then go on a tirade about your ex for an hour, disclosing your financial problems and lack of sex life. Or you could share that you and your ex weren't aligned on core values and felt it best to part ways. See how different these two stories sound? One feels like a pity party while the latter exudes confidence and direction. Instead of looking at your past experiences as hindrances, find that pivotal moment of change: one that turns your story into a learning experience, a gratitude narrative, or an empowerment tale. So, how are you going to tell your story?

> **BDE (Big Dateable Energy):**
> You're the writer, director, producer, and lead of your great love story.

CHANGING YOUR DEFINITION OF LOVE

Often, what's fueling our narratives are the toxic definitions of love we're holding on to and the people we let into our lives. Many of us have never seen a good role model for a relationship. Maybe your parents are divorced or seem disconnected despite many years together. If one of your parents is always fighting for the other one's attention, this may be a relationship pattern you bring into your love life. Our definitions of love can explain why so many of us are accepting one-sided relationships and normalizing the "lows" as part of the process. Even if your parents had a great relationship, it still may not be the model of love that works for you.

Society's portrayal of love also idealizes romance in an unhealthy way. It doesn't need to be so dramatic, filled with ups and downs. If you look at popular TV shows, love is like an emotional roller coaster (Carrie and Mr. Big, Rachel and Ross, we're looking at you!). Love shouldn't feel obsessive, conflicted, or troublesome. It's often uneventful and at times–dare we say–boring. But this can be a good thing! It means you feel safe and secure with no drama to report to your friends. If you put it that way, we love boring! Because it means that your relationship is peaceful and happy.

To let go of unrealistic images of love that aren't helping you, find as many positive examples of relationships in your life as you can. Maybe you notice the way your coworker talks about his wife. You can tell that they're still in love twenty years into their relationship, but you also see that their relationship isn't all passion and hot-and-heavy declarations of love. They must coordinate school pickups for their children, plan weeknight dinners, and operate as a team. But even through the mundane tasks, you can see that they built a beautiful, harmonious life together and respect the heck out of each other. Make that your new model for love! Dreamers especially: seeing all dimensions of love–the sexy and the unsexy–can bring you back to the reality of what's important for a relationship that can withstand the test of time.

Another technique you can use is to observe what you admire about your friends' relationships with their partners. See how they show up together for social events, how they talk to each other, and how they talk *about* each other. While it's great to get dating advice from your single friends who are in the dating trenches with you, your married friends (or ones in solid partnerships) can be great untapped resources. You can cherry-pick from different people of different generations to piece together a 360-degree view of what love means to you. Who knows, maybe you'll even start to appreciate the qualities of your parents' relationship in ways you never thought you could! Doing this allows you to establish a gold standard of what healthy love looks like to you.

Julie's Corner

Looking back, I realized why I struggled to find the right partner for so long. I was defining love by the passion I saw in the movies. There's no doubt I shared a deep connection with my ex, but it wasn't the type of love conducive to a life partnership. The relationship was filled with extreme highs and lows: one day he'd be telling me he loved me, and the next, he'd be saying he couldn't be in a serious relationship. By doing Dateable *and seeing examples of healthy couples in my life, I was able to redefine my ideal love—valuing safety, security, and consistency in a way I never did in the past. It wasn't until I let go of my ex—and my old definition of love—that I could find a partner to give to a relationship the way I needed.*

DETACHING FROM YOUR ATTACHMENT STYLE

If you've turned to your trusty friend Google to understand why relationships don't seem to go your way, you've probably stumbled upon attachment theory, which suggests that the early bonds we form with our primary caregivers (usually parent-child) influence our romantic relationships and attachments throughout life. Part of why attachment theory is so popular is that it gives us an explanation for why our love lives aren't going the way we want. It was our childhood, dammit! Our parents messed us up by being too responsive or not being responsive enough. And now, this is why dating is so hard as an adult.

Daters everywhere turn to the book *Attached*, by Amir Levine and Rachel S. F. Heller, which connected earlier theories from the psychologists John Bowlby and Mary Ainsworth to show how understanding the four attachment styles (secure, anxious, avoidant, and fearful-avoidant) could help you find—and keep—love. Attachment theory helps us understand ourselves and our patterns. It gives context to why we do what we do and how our background, upbringing, and thought processes shape our actions. While we believe attachment theory helps us to understand some of our dating woes, we can't just blame our parents—they are human, too. We must act on the information, not simply say, "I'm anxiously attached; therefore, I'm doomed." That doesn't get us anywhere.

To detach from our attachment styles, we need to dig into how they're impacting our dating patterns. Maya knew she had a habit of playing games when dating. As a Maverick, she would act cold and disinterested when she liked the person. She wanted the guy to pursue her, to pull out all the stops. Maya was often "busy," partly due to her lifestyle but mostly because she wanted to intentionally make it difficult to win her over. But the problem was that her avoidant tendencies caused people to pull away, which triggered her anxiety . . . because she would see them pulling away! She was testing them, but they thought she was disinterested or aloof.

The way she dated came from her worthiness wound, as we learned from talking to the therapist Vienna Pharaon about her book *The Origins of You*, which we mentioned in chapter 3. Maya's wound resulted from growing up in a family that placed conditions around love. Her mom ingrained the idea that she would only be loved if she looked a certain way. Being raised in a highly critical household, Maya felt she needed to constantly prove herself and perform in a certain way to be loved. And this carried over to her adult dating life. She knew someone could hurt her by not sending a text or saying they didn't want to see her again. So Maya tried to get ahead of it by being the one who was disinterested first, which is something she also did in her childhood. When her parents got mad at her, she'd close her door and avoid them. She remembers vividly when she was seven, her dad caught her playing with toys instead of doing homework. Full of anger and rage, he slammed the door so hard it knocked a few books off her bookshelf. Maya stayed in her room for the rest of the night and didn't come out for dinner. Her parents never addressed the incident with her, nor did her father explain why he was so angry. They went about the following day as if nothing happened. Maya felt loved again. From then, her inner child learned that if she avoided the conflict, the problem would go away, and everything would be fine.

This mindset stayed with her while dating and became her default approach to love. It wasn't until recently that Maya connected this root wound to her avoidant attachment style. She's learning to let go of the past by asking "Is this the seven-year-old me right now?" whenever she feels the instinct to run, hide, or keep quiet. Maya realized that staying in the confines of her attachment style was what kept her from forming more meaningful connections.

By understanding and acknowledging your upbringing and childhood wounds, you can start to heal from them. When we don't do this, it causes us to behave in ways that don't ultimately serve us. But we can't let our attachment style define our worth as daters. We don't need to be completely secure to be a viable partner. We are human, and becoming more secure is a work in progress. There will always be a little anxiety from your past. Instead of hiding it, you can share your journey with the people you date. It doesn't need to be needy or accusatory (you didn't text me back fast enough!), but rather, you can do it in a vulnerable way that comes from the heart. For example, share your past experiences of waiting for that text back and how anxiety-inducing it is. The person you're dating will be conscious of this now, and the right person will want to do whatever they can to make you feel secure.

So when you see a symptom of your attachment style creep in, how can you get in front of it? For instance, if someone doesn't text you for two hours, could you consider texting them? Or could you list out the many reasons why they may not be getting back to you that have nothing to do with you? Or try a walk around the neighborhood to quiet your mind? Do whatever you need to do to name what you're experiencing but not let it take over. You can even say, "I see you, anxious attachment!" The goal isn't to be 100 percent secure, because you may be anxious or avoidant in specific ways but not others. It's not so binary! You may feel no insecurities about your partner going out with friends but feel massive anxiety if you don't hear from them for a few hours. Someone else could feel the exact opposite and still be anxiously attached. And let's address the obvious here: *everyone* feels a level of anxiety in today's modern dating world, where you never know if you'll be ghosted or if you'll ever see this person again. There's nothing wrong with you if you have any of the attachment styles; they simply provide valuable information for you to acknowledge and address, empowering you to discover the most beneficial way to navigate your relationships.

BDE (Big Dateable Energy):
Become secure in your insecurities.

HEALING YOUR DATING CUTS
AND RELATIONSHIP SCARS

Outside of her upbringing, part of why Maya put up a shield of armor was that she had been hurt in the past. Her infamous five-minute dates were a way to protect her heart. As we mentioned, Maya was devastated after her breakup with Dan when she had to restart her life completely. As she reentered the dating scene, she was trying to spot as many red flags as possible to avoid the potential pain of heartbreak again. Many of you Mavericks may find this relatable: on the surface, she presented herself as someone who couldn't find a viable prospect, thus choosing to stay single. But deep down, she was scared to put herself out there again. Whether it's a big breakup like Maya experienced or a series of mini heartbreaks you've encountered, the result is a fear of getting hurt again.

If the negative experiences we encounter from dating and relationships go unchecked for too long, they can travel with us from date to date or relationship to relationship. It's like not acknowledging ants in your apartment. You see them out of the corner of your eye, but you choose to deny their existence? Good luck with that! Recognizing failures, disappointments, and heartbreaking moments is perfectly healthy and therapeutic. When we minimize these experiences, we keep them bottled up, and they keep seeping into our dating experiences. Let's look a bit deeper into how these show up and what we can do to heal them:

Dating Cuts

If you've been dating long enough, you're bound to experience dating trauma, which could look like a series of slights and painful micro-interactions. It may not hurt to get ghosted once, but when compounded twenty times over, it starts to eat away at your self-confidence and self-worth. It also doesn't help that we're often told to get over or minimize these experiences (hey, it was only a three-month fling, right?), which makes them worse. We agree that it's not a good use of your time to dwell on these people or moments, but let's take a second to acknowledge that this does still hurt. Energizers especially may find that when you are in this release period after all the go-go-go, the past pain you've been suppressing may suddenly come up to the surface. We are meant to feel feelings because that's how our body processes them. Not allowing this natural processing can result in emotions being bottled up, hindering your overall well-being.

Relationship Scars

These are the emotional issues, negative experiences, and unre-solved conflicts from our past relationships, which can manifest as distrust, jealousy, fear of commitment, or poor communication skills. They go deeper than dating cuts because they imprint how you think relationships will play out. Maya feeling blindsided by her relation-ship is a prime example. Maybe you're over your ex in the sense that you'd never want to date them again, but is something they said still affecting you? If you weren't the one to end the relationship, are you scared that someone will leave you again? What happened in the past isn't indicative of the future. If your past partner cheated on you, it doesn't mean your next one will. If your ex couldn't commit, it doesn't mean that you aren't long-term-relationship material. Espe-cially if your last relationship was abusive or toxic, there may be per-sisting scars that make you feel undeserving of love (which is most certainly not the case).

Whether you're frustrated, sad, or angry, your feelings are valid and shouldn't be ignored. You don't need to minimize your one-week relationship where you thought you met "the One" (only for them to tell you there wasn't any chemistry!). This can feel devastating, and you are absolutely entitled to feel that way. The quicker you can get to "That feels really sh*tty. I'm sad that this promising prospect didn't work out," the quicker you can come to terms with what you want instead. And when you start addressing your emotions, you can learn to move through the pain because *the only way out is through.*

Once you've recognized past pain, the path forward is to take care of yourself. Yes, that can be trips to the spa or a silent retreat, but it doesn't have to be so elaborate. It can be anything that helps you show yourself compassion, connect with your feelings, and ded-icate time to yourself. Sometimes, addressing your dating cuts and relationship scars means taking a break from dating. While we aren't proponents of uninstalling the apps only to reinstall them one week later, we do think an occasional, good, healthy break is in order. In our professional lives, we take a vacation–or even a sabbatical if we're lucky. The same goes for dating: sometimes, you need to slow down to speed up. But it has to be an *intentional* break. Use this time to process your past and find a path forward. That could mean reflecting on past relationships and envisioning what you want to change for a future one. A hard reset may be what you need to truly be on your own for once–no straggling friends with benefits, no situationships, no random app convos–so you can stop distracting yourself with a busy social life. And if you feel like you don't want to go through this process alone, we highly recommend professional guidance. Your therapist can act as a supportive guide, standing by your side as you navigate and process through past pains.

Whatever you do to reset, remember what's happened to you in the past is not indicative of who you are and what value you bring to this world. And it's certainly not a sign that you will be alone forever. One day when you meet someone special, you'll realize that persevering through these dating experiences helped make you who you are today. Let the pain be a positive force for change.

Yue's Corner

When I found the incriminating text messages confirming my partner's infidelity, my world crumbled. For the next month, I made a point to sit with all that hurt—oftentimes in a dark closet where I observed my emotions like I was watching some plotless movie. Slowly I started to see the betrayal was no reflection of my worth. I was with the wrong person and how lucky was I to be freed from that! I celebrated that epiphany with a romantic solo trip to Greece. One day in Mykonos, I thought to myself: I wish him the best. That's when I knew I had moved on. I thanked the universe for showing me what wasn't right for me and putting me exactly where I was supposed to be. Taking the time to process that traumatic breakup lessened the pain, and made space for love, compassion, and hope to enter my life again.

REJECTION IS REDIRECTION

As you know, Andrew was stuck on this third-date curse. We were intrigued, so we convinced Andrew to have us call up a few of his past dates to hear what may have gone wrong:

- "I thought we were having a great time, but when the waiter came to ask if we wanted a second drink, he said no. I assumed he wasn't interested. When I never heard from him again, I wasn't surprised."
- "We were leaving the bar, and before we could fully say goodbye, he left quickly to catch the L train in a rush. I was having fun, but this made me second-guess the whole night."

- "I was attracted to Andrew, but he didn't indicate he was super into me. Normally I'd follow up after a date if we had a good time and I hadn't heard from them, but I just let this one go since he didn't seem that interested."

We were confused. These were all women who Andrew thought had rejected him. When we shared the feedback, he was utterly shocked. As an Achiever, Andrew was deeply disappointed that these dates didn't progress. He couldn't face getting another "there wasn't an emotional connection" text, so he bolted before that could happen. Had he been so afraid of rejection that he unknowingly rejected all of them first?

The fear of rejection prevents many of us from making a move, putting ourselves out there, and asking for what we want. But rejection is part of everyday life. Without rejection, we would find ourselves in all sorts of bad situations. Think of rejection as redirection; it's not a no; it's a "not for me." If you feel like you're getting rejected often, this could be a good thing! It means you're putting yourself out there and are that much closer to the yes. Many of us forget that *most people we meet will not be a match for us.* The whole point of dating is that we're getting through the non-matches to get to the right ones. As we established with the Validation Trap, dating is not pageantry. There is no contest. There are no judges. You are just trying to find someone compatible with you. And we have rejection to thank for guiding us through this dating journey.

This revelation is what finally freed Andrew from this third-date curse. He realized that when a date doesn't progress into more, it's not that he's a failure or there's something wrong with him. It simply means it wasn't the right fit. We need to give ourselves more grace when things don't work out. Would you ever tell your friend they were a flawed person if someone didn't ask them out for a second date? No. You'd say to them that someone amazing is right around the corner. Someone who is a much better match for them. So why can't we say these kinds of affirmations to ourselves?

We are huge fans of Rejection Therapy, a practice the best-selling author Jia Jiang coined in his book *Rejection Proof*, where he sought out rejection every day for a hundred days straight to build resilience. The less we look at rejection as negative, the better equipped we will be to find love. We challenge you to take on your own Rejection Therapy experiment by listing out some dares where rejection is likely. There are three rules as set out by Jia: (1) ethical, (2) legal, and (3) doesn't defy the laws of physics. And then spend a dedicated amount of time (two weeks to a month is recommended) crossing off the items on this list. Think of it as a rejection scavenger hunt. You can totally gamify this with your friends, too! Some ideas are:

- Ask for a free drink at a bar.
- Ask a stranger for gum.
- Ask a stranger for a piggyback ride.
- Ask a store manager to see their break room.
- Ask to be upgraded.
- Ask to be interviewed on camera when you see a news film crew.
- Ask for a side of steak at a vegetarian restaurant.
- Ask for a discount . . . anywhere.

You can download our 30-Day Dating Rejection Therapy checklist at www.howtobedateable.com.

The point is to take yourself out of your comfort zone. We had Andrew spend a week making ridiculous requests, and by the end of this challenge, he could see that rejections were trivial in the grand scheme of things. Not only will this toughen you up for romantic rejections, it'll also help you craft your "ask." You'd be surprised what you actually get if you ask for it in the right way. And if you don't, you'll realize after a day or two (or even a couple of hours!) that it wasn't that big of a deal.

Just like in dating, the rejection may sting, but it won't feel like the end of the world. And when you meet someone who chooses you back, all those rejections will be a distant memory (what were their names again?). Remember this as you let go of the fear of rejection.

> **BDE (Big Dateable Energy):**
> Beyond fear lies everything you've ever desired.

ENDING THE RUMINATION CYCLES

It's hard to let go of anything if these thoughts keep coming up over and over again. In psychology, rumination refers to the repetitive and unproductive dwelling on negative thoughts—usually about past experiences or uncertainties of the future. When we focus on the "what if" scenarios—the causes or consequences of problems—and not the actions we can take to solve the problem, it's like spinning your wheels in mud. You're expending energy, making a mess, but not making any progress. Take Tori, our resident Thinker. When Tori was waiting for a promising date to text her back, she started replaying the conversations in her mind. She began to spiral: What if she did something off-putting on the date she wasn't aware of? What if she missed the signs her date wasn't interested? Did she scare her away?! But as Tori ran through all the possible scenarios, it drove her insane. She didn't uncover the secret to this mystery; she only engaged in repetitive negative thoughts that looped continuously in her mind, like a bad trip. She eventually felt sick to her stomach and convinced herself that she was getting ghosted. Only then did her date, Aimee, text her back, saying that she was back from a long work meeting. Tori had put herself into a tizzy for no reason at all!

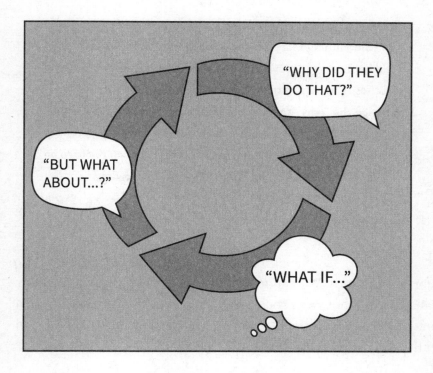

So many of us experience dating anxiety because rumination leads us into a vicious cycle of overanalyzing and trying to find answers that are out of our control. And that's because rumination usually involves the stories we make up in our heads. It is often an automatic response; it's natural to make this our default state. So, how do we start moving from rumination to reflection, which is a more constructive, conscious, and intentional process that can help solve your dating challenges? The shift begins when we look inward and gain insight into what we're experiencing. When we spoke to the therapist Dr. Jenny Taitz about being single and happy, she said the most influential exercise she recommends to her clients is a process to end these rumination cycles:

1. **Acknowledge that you're doing it.** If your mind starts to wander into a series of questions and what-ifs, take a beat and

acknowledge what you're doing. For Tori, it helped to use the 4-7-8 breathing technique, where she inhaled for four seconds, held her breath for seven seconds, and then exhaled for eight seconds. This helped take her out of her head and into her body.

2. **Change the "why" to "how."** Dr. Taitz believes this is a great way to reframe rumination as reflection. For example, if someone is thinking, *Why can't I find someone who likes me when I've been on hundreds of dates?* You can flip that by asking: *How can I not let my self-worth be tainted by other people's opinions?* This gives you an opportunity for introspection and growth.

Reframing, as difficult as it is, is a key part of using the past to move us forward. We cannot control other people's actions. All we can control is how we process them and what we can learn from all our trials and tribulations. Learning to relinquish control may be one of the biggest gifts of letting go.

FROM LIMITING BELIEFS TO LIMITLESS BELIEFS

A major part of this purging process is recalibrating your belief system. Our beliefs are built when we are children, stemming from our upbringing and formative years. We can believe all sorts of things, but the difference between a belief and a limiting belief is that the latter holds us back from who we are meant to be and what we really want. Just like on Instagram, we see the world through various filters. We sometimes have the filter of "you aren't worthy of love" or "you're too old to date." Much like a photo filter, these thoughts selectively screen out evidence that might reveal a different perspective. We often struggle to shake our limiting beliefs even if we know they don't make sense logically. They tend to be heavily influenced by cultural and societal norms and perpetuated by our surroundings—

from our friends to social media—and seep into how we date. Let's say you have a friend who is very pessimistic about dating and believes that modern dating is a hellscape. Just being in their presence brings up some limiting beliefs, such as you're destined to be alone (which is certainly not true, but you can see how your environment can start to mess with your head!). Our limiting beliefs can also play into our self-confidence. So often, we hear daters say they believe that they need to look a certain way or be at a certain weight/height to attract a partner. Why do you think so many people lie about these stats on their dating profiles? This ends up being a belief they carry as to why their love lives aren't falling into place. But it's simply not true! People of all shapes and sizes have relationships every day. Getting bogged down by these types of beliefs ends up not serving us in the slightest.

It's hard to undo years and years of conditioning. We all have limiting beliefs in some way or another. No one is immune to them. We can't expect them to magically go away tomorrow; however, we can learn to manage them. The big mistake many of us make is not admitting to these beliefs. How can you start to make space for these beliefs to surface, so we can turn them into *limitless* beliefs?

Think about your limitless beliefs as the idea that anything is possible without being confined to your past thoughts and experiences. Here are a few common ones we've both experienced that you can flip into *limitless* beliefs:

Limiting Belief	Limitless Belief
I'm too old to date.	Dating gets better with age. With age comes wisdom.
There's no one good on the apps/my city/wherever I'm looking for love.	There are tons of great people everywhere! I just haven't met them yet.
I'll never find love again after my ex who I thought was "the One."	I will be able to love again, and there isn't just one person out there for me, but many great loves.
I'm not thin enough/tall enough/attractive enough.	The right person will love me just the way I am in whatever shape or size.
I'm not man enough/masculine enough/feminine enough.	There are all types of men and women out there, of course I'm enough! And in today's world, gender and gender roles aren't so binary anyway.
Love isn't something that's meant for me.	I already have an abundance of love in my life, and one day I'll experience the romantic love I've always wanted. It's not a matter of if but when.

See how different these sound? Limiting beliefs make us feel defeated, sad, out of control, and confined. But limitless beliefs can make us feel empowered and hopeful. To start your limitless beliefs transformation, try this technique:

1. Jot down as many limiting beliefs as possible.
2. Write down "not the truth" on your list to acknowledge that these limiting beliefs are getting in your way and are not backed by any evidence.

3. Circle the three most prominent limiting beliefs and translate them into beliefs you'd rather have (i.e., your limitless beliefs).
4. Start to look for evidence of these new limitless beliefs. For example, you may have friends who are happier that they got married later in life. It may be a good thing to settle down at a later stage. Keep finding evidence that supports these new beliefs.
5. Mentally associate a limitless belief with a physical object. For example, you can tie it your favorite mug, so you think of your new limitless belief every time you see it.

Beliefs can take some time to unlearn. While they can't be changed overnight, they can be transformed over time. All we ask is that you start with "I'm open to believing . . ." with the list of your limitless beliefs. For example, I'm open to believing that dating gets better with age. Or, I'm open to believing there's a more compatible partner for me around the corner. Being open is the first step to considering all that is possible. Even just saying you're open makes these beliefs feel more attainable.

This transformation to limitless beliefs won't happen immediately and the old limiting beliefs will make cameos here and there. Take inventory when they pop up. What are the triggers? While they may not go away completely, you can lessen their impact and know they don't hold the amount of truth you once thought. By addressing your limiting beliefs and staying open to changing them into limitless ones, you can feel more empowered knowing you are in the driver's seat. We know you are worthy of having an incredible love life. The question is, do you think so, too?

FROM VICTIM TO HERO

Part of why letting go is so hard is that we get stuck on "Why me?" We think everything terrible has happened *to us* and that nothing is in our control. It's easy to blame dating apps. It's easy to blame your ex, who screwed you over. But if you're constantly in victim mode, things will happen *to* you instead of *for* you. You're the main character, the superhero of your movie. Instead of asking, "Why is this happening to me?" ask, "What can I do about it?"

After a year and a half into her marriage, the author Gabrielle Stone left her husband after finding out that he was having an affair with a nineteen-year-old for the previous six months. Two weeks later, she met a man she fell madly in love with—only for him to break up with her right before they were to get on a plane to Italy together. She could have crumbled right there, but she decided to go on the trip anyway and have her own *Eat Pray Love* experience, which inspired her to write the book *Eat, Pray, #FML* about her story. Despite the series of heartbreaks she retold on *Dateable*, we admired her main character attitude. She explained that when you hit a fork in the road, you can decide if you will let this experience define you. She accepted this as part of her story and could use what happened to better herself. She still experienced the lowest of lows, but Gabrielle maintained a vision that she would use these experiences to propel herself forward.

While not everyone will turn their tragedies into a book or a screenplay (but more power to you if you do!), we can all learn from Gabrielle's hero mentality. While you certainly don't deserve to keep getting screwed by f*ckboys or toxic relationships, there is likely something unhealed within you that causes you to attract these types of people or situations. When you go from victim to hero, you take accountability to do the work and begin your healing journey. Through all of Gabrielle's painful experiences, she realized there was an unhealed abandonment wound that she needed to tend to. While on her trip, she saw her strength in getting through this challenging period on her own. She could see that she could never be abandoned because she wouldn't abandon herself. Once she changed her core belief, she started attracting people who wouldn't leave her.

As discussed earlier in this chapter, it's up to you to show up for yourself and write your story. You're the main character who decides how your life will play out—not someone else. We think we need closure with others, but that closure comes within ourselves. You'll start to be grateful for everything you have going for you. Hey, aren't you grateful you got your hands on this book?! We are grateful that you're here, that's for sure!

This victim-to-hero mentality shift doesn't have to happen immediately. All we ask is that you try to have a growth mindset of 1 percent at a time. While it's easy to fixate on what you lost because of a failed relationship or dating experience, look at what you've gained— whether a new hobby, better relational skills, or increased knowledge about yourself. That's when you can start to view every experience as an opportunity! It's incredible what progress you make if you grow 1 percent more each day from the challenges you experience.

YOUR LETTING-GO CEREMONY

One of our favorite ways to physically and emotionally experience change is to ceremonialize it!! There's a reason why people have ceremonies; it's to put intentionality behind what they're committing to. This can be as simple as writing down everything you want to let go and then tearing up the piece of paper while listening to "Let It Go." Or you can make a whole production out of it—print photos, write words, bring out objects, invite people, play drums, and scream into the woods. We've seen it all, and you can do what your heart desires. Whatever you do, make this a regular thing; we believe in letting go on a regular basis.

As part of your letting-go ceremony, keep in mind that you're making room for what will better serve you:

- Are there physical belongings you are emotionally attached to that keep you stuck in the past? It's time to get rid of these items. Consider donating so you feel good about letting them go. It's also an excellent opportunity to declutter your space! If a certain nightstand reminds you of your toxic ex who got it for you, it's time to replace it with something new you love.

- Evaluate your relationship with social media and see whether it's triggering you to revert to the past. Consider ways to control social media exposure (some apps limit your time, for instance), or unfollow any triggering accounts and replace them with new, uplifting, empowering ones.

- Take inventory of any thoughts that you ruminate on. For one week, jot down the repetitive thoughts that may be negative. How can you consciously replace these thoughts with something that serves you better? For example, if your old thought is, *I'm not worthy of love because my exes have chosen other people over me*, change this thought to *I am worthy of love, and I am ready for the right person who will appreciate my love*.

- Look at the people in your life who may be weighing you down. For example, are you still talking to an ex? Do you have a toxic friend or family member? Limit your exposure to these people. Spend more time around people who truly want the best for you.

Remember, the healing journey takes time. It's not about forgetting or invalidating past experiences but, rather, living in the present and defining the future you want. Letting go can be a freeing exercise—you get to shake off all those expectations, past grievances, emotional baggage, or whatever you're holding on to. Don't be surprised if it suddenly feels like a heavy weight has been lifted, because this stuff can bog you down! This work isn't one-and-done, though. It's a continual process, and this first cleanse will change how you approach dating, a crucial step in transcending modern dating!

KEY TAKEAWAYS

1. Our past experiences shape who we are today but don't define our future. The stories we tell ourselves, our definitions of love, attachment issues, and past dating and relationship experiences all contribute to the weights holding us back. The best we can do is learn and evolve from these experiences.

2. Rejection is redirection. Instead of adding past rejections to your dating scars, see them as your path forward. Embrace Rejection Therapy to lessen the blow.

3. Turn rumination into reflection. Get out of the endless cycle by asking "how," not "why." This gives you an opportunity for introspection and growth.

4. Turn your limiting beliefs into limitless ones! Our culture, society, friends, and family all play into how we see the world, and many of our beliefs are not serving us.

5. Healing is a continuous process that doesn't happen overnight. Embrace the 1 percent rule and express gratitude for the progress you're making.

Chapter 6:

Gaining Clarity

> ### IT'S TIME TO DISCOVER:
>
> 1. **Your Dating Why:** What's really driving you to date in the first place.
> 2. **Your Dating North Star:** Your guiding principles for how you want to date and who you choose to date.
> 3. **The Perfect Partner Equation:** The factors that help determine who would make an ideal partner for you.

With so much choice in modern dating, we lack focus and direction. There isn't a single script to follow, and we can't assume that everyone's goal is to meet someone, get married, move to the burbs, and have 2.5 kids (how is that even possible anyway?). Maybe you've already been there, done that, or you know this more traditional path isn't for you. And even if you do want these things, you probably want them with the *right person*, in the type of relationship that's right *for you*. But how do you even know what that looks like?

Remember Eli, our Energizer serial dater? Despite his countless dates and strings of mini relationships, he never paused to think about why he was even dating and what he wanted out of a relationship until the day he was stranded on the island of Crete at the start of the pandemic. What was supposed to be a vacation turned into forced alone time. As the world shut down, Eli got a flashback of all the thousands of first dates, the microwave relationships that burned out, and the pure exhaustion from it all. *Had he been so wrapped up in dating that he lost himself in the process? What was he even looking for anymore?*

When you date without clarity and intentionality, you get lost. It's like trying to hike without a map: you end up wandering aimlessly and spending too much time in the woods. Of course, you will start to get tired, discouraged, and wonder if you even want to keep hiking–or how you can even survive! When you don't have a compass to guide you, that's when you end up feeling fatigued by modern dating.

Through this chapter, we'll help you find your "Dating North Star," consisting of *why* you date and your core needs. As you may remember from your middle school science class, the North Star is famous for holding nearly still while the entire northern sky moves around it. Think of your dating life just like that. By connecting to your needs, you'll get less caught up in modern dating culture and how others date (ahem, the person who ghosted you last week) and more focused on what you want from dating. The North Star helps to ground you in what matters most to design a love life that works for you. When you go on date after date without this clarity, you're just staying on this dating hamster wheel. If you've gotten this far in our book, we know that is *not* what you want. Our goal is for you to be more intentional about your love life and reduce the time you're putting into dating (yes, we know this sounds like the dream, and we promise we will get there!). So how do you gain this clarity to feel empowered by all the choices and options available?

WHAT'S YOUR DATING WHY?

With everything we do in life, there must be an underlying reason for *why* we're doing what we're doing. When we polled our *Dateable* community about their reasons for dating, we got answers such as:

- Find a life partner.
- Build a family.
- Have companionship.
- Not die alone.
- Meet my soulmate.
- Do life with someone.
- Find a genuine connection.

While these are legitimate reasons, they are also very future-focused and disconnected from why you're dating *right now*. So often, we use broad terms and sweeping generalizations such as "to be in a relationship" or "to have companionship." But what does that even mean for you? It's hard not to get derailed by the "shoulds." You *should* want to be in a monogamous relationship. You *should* date for marriage. You *should* want to build a family. But for many of us, these preconceived reasons don't feel entirely right. It often doesn't feel like our own words, but more of a reiteration of what others have told us all our lives. Most of us have never taken a minute to think about what a relationship means to us; it's more than just something you do once you get to a certain age, and dating is a means to an end. **The irony is that we spend so much effort and energy trying to define a relationship with others, but we haven't defined what a relationship means to us.**

One of our most popular *Dateable* episodes was "Relationships,

Are You Sure You Want One?" with the authors and coaches Simone Milasas and Brendon Watt, who wrote the book by the same title while actively uncoupling from a decade-long relationship. In their episode, they discussed how we often gloss over why we want to be in a relationship. It's almost an automatic response that, obviously, we date to be in a relationship. We also think relationships will change our life trajectory. Somehow we'll be happier, healthier, and more fulfilled. The truth is a relationship is only additive. It does not fill your gaps, make you whole, or magically make you happy. With that in mind, ask yourself what you really want out of relationships. Do you even want one? If you did not have the option of being in a relationship, what would you be missing out on? Really asking yourself these questions will make you think more deeply about *why* you want a relationship at all.

The first step to gaining clarity is to establish your Dating Why: what's really driving you to date in the first place. When we talked to Eli over Zoom (he was stranded in Crete, remember!), we began unpacking his Dating Why. He liked the attention from others. Eli was the middle child, with six other siblings. His Jamaican immigrant parents worked frequently, and he felt like he was always fighting for attention. The attention he received from dating validated his need. Since we didn't want him to stay stuck in the Validation Trap, we decided to dig in a little deeper.

Why is getting attention important to you?
Because I want to feel seen and heard.

Why do you want to feel seen and heard?
Because I want to feel understood.

Why do you want to feel understood?
I want to be prioritized by someone who just gets me.

Now that's a Dating Why! If you're struggling to think of your own, ask yourself some of the following questions. Don't overthink this and simply write down the first thoughts that come to mind.

- What gets you excited about dating?
- When you're feeling down about dating, what motivates you to keep going?
- When thinking about the near future, what do you want to get out of dating?
- When zooming out and thinking of the big picture, what do you want to get out of dating?
- What do you think will be the most rewarding thing about dating?
- Why do you think you want to date in the first place?
- Why do you want love?

Once you have a general idea of what motivates and inspires you, take a step back and ask yourself, *What am I looking for?* Bonus points if you can answer without using the words "relationship," "love," "companionship," or "partner." Next, ask yourself: *Why is this important to me?* This is your Dating Why.

WHY, WHY, WHY?

You may have noticed from Eli's example that we asked him "Why?" two more times after his initial answer. This tactic comes from a method called the 5 Whys, which helps get to the real root cause (originally from Sakichi Toyoda of the Toyota Motor Corporation). It's as straightforward as the name suggests: you ask "Why?" five times. Each level of abstraction allows you to go beyond the symptoms of the problem into what is really happening. Over the years, others have taken on this approach, reducing the number of questions, especially when they can guide the Whys a bit. When talking to guests on *Dateable*, we love using this technique as it always reveals more than what's on the surface. If you want to push your "Why," ask yourself this three to five times to see how much more you can uncover. No need to go more than that, though, as that's when we get into overthinking territory!

IDENTIFYING YOUR CORE NEEDS

Do you know the worst dating advice ever uttered? Don't be needy. Because if you're a breathing, living human being, you have needs. And you will also have needs in a relationship! If you're not sharing them, you're suppressing them. Meeting each other's needs is a crucial aspect of a successful relationship: you're giving your partner a blueprint of how they can love and care for you. The strength of your bond is, in fact, dependent upon meeting each other's needs. But for whatever reason, we think we can't share our needs while dating because we don't want to scare the other person away. We make excuses such as *I don't know them well enough*, or *We're not at that stage yet*. This is complete BS. Dating can do one of two things for you: (1) help you heal your wounds or (2) deepen your wounds. If you don't express your needs, then you're doing the latter. Dating is the best opportunity to express what you've learned from past experiences, and to find a partner who is willing to meet these needs with you. There's no way to see whether someone can be there for you if you expect them to be a mind reader. And if they can't meet your basic needs, then you shouldn't be entering into a committed relationship with them. We need to stop being afraid of scaring away the wrong people.

So what are your needs in a relationship? What if we told you the biggest thing that irks you in modern dating translates to *exactly* what you need? This may sound counterintuitive, but think about your biggest disappointments while dating. This will help you turn what you *don't* want into what you *do* want. Maybe you hate the ambiguity of not knowing when you'll see the person or hear from them again. This could demonstrate a need for prioritization, contribution, and/or security (yes, it's okay to have many needs!). If ghosting really bothers you when dating, think about what that may mean: is it important that someone keep their word when they say they'll reach out or make plans? This translates to a need for trust or security. If it kills you when it feels like you're the only one carrying a conversation on a dating app, could this mean that you have a vital need for good communication or connection? Did it feel terrible when your last fling minimized your career or brushed off your hobby? This could indicate your need for acceptance or respect. If you felt lonely in your previous relationship, perhaps you need more intimacy or prioritization. As the relationship psychologist Dr. John Gottman has said: behind every complaint is a deep personal longing.

You can also dig into your past relationships. Maybe you had a partner who could never commit to you the way you wanted. Or your last relationship felt stagnant as it was missing that growth you needed from a partner. So, take note of your history; you may see recurring themes from many situations unfold. Think about how you can tell when things are going well and when they are not. If you haven't already, tie that experience to a specific need. Here's a list of some common needs in a relationship that, as humans, it's only natural for us to desire. These fifteen needs, in no particular order, can help get you started:

1. **Support:** Having a partner who listens to you, understands your feelings, and offers empathy and encouragement.
2. **Intimacy:** Physical touch, sexual intimacy, loving words, kind gestures, and other displays of affection.
3. **Connection:** A sense of closeness and emotional intimacy that you experience when you feel genuinely seen, heard, and appreciated by your partner.
4. **Acceptance:** A feeling that your partner accepts you as you and that they value your differences.
5. **Security:** Knowing you can count on your partner, and they are committed to your relationship.
6. **Consistency:** When a partner maintains a regular pattern of behavior, showing dependability and predictability.
7. **Contribution:** The act of providing for each other mentally, emotionally, physically, and/or financially so one person isn't carrying all the weight.
8. **Trust:** The ability to rely on another person and have confidence that they will do as they say.
9. **Prioritization:** Spending quality time together, feeling valued, and knowing that your partner factors you and your relationship into their decisions and actions.
10. **Communication:** Sharing your feelings, needs, and expectations; listening to your partner; and resolving conflict together.

11. **Independence:** Maintaining your sense of self, having the freedom to do your own thing, and embracing your alone time when needed.

12. **Honesty:** Telling your partner the truth and being open with them about how you think and feel.

13. **Respect:** Feeling that the other person values your opinion and admires you as a person outside of what they're getting from a relationship.

14. **Fun and humor:** The lighter side to your connection that helps you remember that through all of life's stress and mundanity, allowing you to enjoy yourselves in each other's presence.

15. **Growth:** A feeling like you're both developing, and helping each other become the best versions of yourselves.

The reality is that even all fifteen of these are not too much to ask for in the slightest. When dating, we're so afraid of being too needy so *we ask for far too little.*

Needs and boundaries are often seen as scary words, but they don't have to be. Instead of thinking of them as demands of the other person, consider them essential in bringing people closer. A relationship-partner would want to do whatever they could to meet these needs because they require the same in return! That being said, narrow your list down to your **top three core needs**: Did any stand out? Did any spark other ideas? Listen to that feeling in your gut as you read this list or meditate on this for a minute.

The right person will want to meet your needs. But you can't expect someone to meet your needs if you don't know them yourself. Now it's time to own them.

Julie's Corner

When I evaluated my core needs, I realized I needed a true partnership, not just another boyfriend. I had taken a solo trip to the Calistoga hot springs in Sonoma to reflect on my last relationship. As I floated in the water, I thought about how it felt like my ex and I were in the forever-dating stage instead of building a life together. I wanted a partner where it was a given that we were spending every weekend together. I envisioned coming home to them, sharing our days, and cooking dinner together. I imagined celebrating each other's birthdays, job promotions, or any other special occasion without a doubt that we were each other's go-to person. By gaining clarity on what I actually needed, I changed what I was looking for. And no longer was I attracted to people who couldn't give me that.

FINDING YOUR DATING NORTH STAR

Now that we've uncovered your Dating Why, aka the reason you're dating, and your core needs, let's combine them to form your Dating North Star:

I date because I want [Dating Why] and need [Three Core Needs].

It's as easy as taking your Dating Why and combining it with your top three core needs. For example, for Eli it was "I date because I want to be prioritized by someone who just gets me and need mutual respect, trust, and support." Your Dating North Star acts as your intention while dating. This is what's going to help you stay grounded through the hiccups and heartbreak along the way. This will also help you recognize a good partner when you see them—and cut loose the ones who aren't measuring up. Having a Dating North Star will enable you to enjoy dating—as the focus is on what *you* want as the main character in your love life. Remember, your North Star isn't some future goal but how you'll make informed decisions today. You can use it as a compass to check whether you're on the right path to where you want to go. And if not, it'll allow you to course correct accordingly.

Your Dating North Star may change over time as you get more and more dating and relationship experience. If you're still having trouble articulating your Dating Why and needs, that's okay, too! Continue reading the book, as it'll keep fueling ideas for you.

> **BDE (Big Dateable Energy):**
> To know where you want to go, you need to
> know why you're trying to get there.

USING YOUR DATING NORTH STAR
TO FIND YOUR PERSON

Now that you have a feel for your Dating North Star, let's figure out who you want to bring along for the ride. Many factors may come into play—for example, they need to be in the same life stage, want the same things out of a relationship, have financial literacy and life competency, and so on. They should also be your lover, roommate, and best friend. No wonder it feels like looking for a needle in a haystack! But have no fear, your Dating North Star is here to guide the way and make the search feel less daunting. Because after all, not much else matters if the person isn't aligned with your North Star.

Your Dating North Star gives you the baseline of what you need from a partner. And if someone cannot cross that barrier, then they aren't the partner for you, plain and simple. Back to Eli. Through his North Star exercise, he realized he wanted to be prioritized by someone who just got him—and he needed mutual respect, acceptance, and support. This was not something he had ever prioritized in the past. He was an influencer with close to a hundred thousand followers and was incredibly career-driven. Yet, he kept running into dates who undermined his career by not asking more questions or, worse, kept asking about his *real* job. The irony was that many of his dates didn't have their sh*t in order while he was building his own business! But he kept dating them anyway as he focused more on chemistry and attraction rather than honoring his core needs. After completing this exercise, he realized that if someone wasn't supportive of his ambitions, they were a no for him, no matter how hot or exciting they may be.

By using his Dating North Star, Eli was now taking an active role in his dating life instead of passively waiting for things to fall into place. He could make decisions—from the partners he chose to which behaviors he'd stand for—according to his definition of what was essential for him in a romantic relationship. He could hold people to standards of how he wanted to be treated instead of surface-level characteristics. This is exactly the shift that aligns you with the love life that would make you happiest.

You may be thinking, it's already hard to meet someone, you want me to eliminate *more* people? This isn't the case. You're simply changing how you evaluate potential partners, not adding another criterion to your list. Moving away from their potential (but they were sooo good on paper), you're now gauging their viability in the present moment. Let's say your North Star is building a life with someone who makes you feel supported, secure, and empowered. If you see from an early stage that they keep canceling dates at the last minute, how can you build a life with someone so unreliable? It's not that you have to write them off immediately; in fact, we encourage you to have a conversation with them and share that this is important to you. But if they show no interest in showing up differently (or are incapable of it), you know this person can't even meet the baseline requirement of being in a relationship with *you*.

Sure, you can't always avoid heartbreak. But when it's clear you and the person you're dating aren't remotely on the same page, it can save you unnecessary hardship and allow you to refocus on someone in line with your North Star. If you both have similar goals, values, and expectations, it increases the likelihood of a successful and ful-filling relationship. It's actually that simple. It's when we skip this step of gaining this clarity (or try to justify situations we know aren't in line with our needs!) that dating becomes difficult. By knowing your North Star before you meet that person, you can ensure they are living up to your standards instead of just getting swept up in the chemistry. This lets you approach relationships with a clear mindset, making the entire process more enjoyable and less anxiety-inducing. Because now you're just trying to find someone aligned with your North Star instead of trying to fit a square peg into a round hole.

Using your North Star to assess the relationship isn't limited to when you first meet someone. You may learn new things about them, or maybe your North Star will change. That's why it's essential to have a constant dialogue about what you want out of a partnership and check in with yourself and your partner. If the relationship feels out of alignment, that's a sign you're deviating from your North Star. Staying true to your North Star means staying true to yourself, which is all that matters in the end.

THE PERFECT PARTNER EQUATION (PPE)

While it makes sense to have a baseline from your Dating North Star, we need more information to conclude whether someone is the right type of partner for us. It's not enough to say: they want a long-term partnership like I do, therefore we should be together. We want you to have it all–the partner who is on the same page as you and also one who gets you excited!

As you've probably gathered, we're not referring to your standard list of traits. What if we were to give you a better way to focus in on qualities that align with your Dating North Star? We will use our Perfect Partner Equation framework to help identify your *actual* type–someone who is perfectly imperfect for you.

There's just so much more information you can glean from a person when using your PPE instead of a list. As we established from the Settling Paradox, having a laundry list of superficial qualities does not guarantee you the best partner. This PPE view allows you to gather information on who they are *relative to you*, which is ultimately what's most important in a relationship. Take Drea, our resident Dreamer, who was onto her next fling, declaring that she had *finally* met her person. Or at least she thought. At first, he was super attentive, texting Drea constantly throughout the day, and was always suggesting a new activity to take her on a date. They went to improv shows and wandered the Smithsonian for hours, hand in hand. But as the months progressed, she started to see the red flags, so much so that his outwardly good but sometimes shockingly evil nature earned him the nickname Mr. Hyde from Drea's friends.

He was a loving, caring Golden Retriever type (aka Dr. Jekyll), but when things didn't go his way, Mr. Hyde came out, revealing his short temper–often even breaking up with Drea in the heat of the moment. The following day, he would say he was drinking too much or in a bad mood and would revert to his sweet self. Sure enough, Mr. Hyde would return, starting a vicious cycle. Even though Mr. Hyde wanted to be exclusive with Drea, this was not the type of relationship she wanted. Drea had more drama than ever before in her life! She found herself playing into Mr. Hyde's antics, going on other dates to make him jealous, and saying hurtful things to him when he got angry or broke up with her. Drea hardly recognized this side of herself. Who was she becoming? One of Drea's good friends finally sat her down to address that she was not her best self with this person. She needed this wake-up call to end things for good with Mr. Hyde, like she should have done five months ago.

In Drea's case, this relationship didn't have the legs to last. Her needs weren't getting met, and she was losing herself. The problem with her list was that it was shortsighted and flawed. She was missing some key components that aligned with our Perfect Partner Equation:

Mr. Hyde had some features from her initial list that drew Drea to him, but did they align with her values and needs? Definitely not. And she sure as heck wasn't factoring in how she wanted to feel or how she wanted the relationship to operate. There's a reason for a trifecta of fundamentals, feelings, and future. Without all three in sync with your North Star, the equation won't work. So, what do each of these elements mean, and how can you use them to find that person who's perfectly imperfect for you?

Fundamentals

Fundamentals are typically two layers above our surface-level lists. They are the undeniable qualities that describe someone's character and values *in relation to you*. They are not someone's future potential, or tainted by their past, but rather how they're showing up *right now*. We currently get so focused on the facts about someone, we lose track of how these attributes relate back to us. Ultimately you don't need to date someone's résumé or social media feed. It's all about how the qualities they hold impact a relationship *with you*.

While we aren't fans of the list (if you haven't gathered by now!), understanding what's fundamental for you in a partner is pivotal. This will help you know what matters to you—and learn what's non-negotiable. The key here is seeing how you can align certain traits with your core needs and values. For instance, you may have on your list that you want someone who likes to travel. What is that actually saying about this person and what it means to be in a relationship with them? Is it that you want someone with an adventurous spirit who will open your worldview? Or someone who has work-life balance and will spend intentional time with you? Or someone who is self-sufficient with the means to go on trips with you? There's so much more you can unpack when you look at these features from this perspective!

So, let's take the time to refine your list accordingly. How can you take what you currently have on your list and bubble it up to one of your values? This can range from the incredibly superficial (no judgment!) to the latest buzzword (we get you want someone emotionally available, but what does that even mean to you?). For example, maybe you're stuck on someone's education level or occupation; perhaps you're looking for someone you respect and view as intelligent or ambitious. Does someone with a PhD and a high-paying job automatically possess all these qualities? Not necessarily. What's more important could be that you're with someone who values learning, or someone who is committed to their career. And what's even *more* important is how that translates to operating in a relationship. Does it mean they contribute financially to your relationship? Or are they someone you can rely on financially as you build a life together? So look for the deeper reason in everything from why you must have someone six feet tall to needing to be with a fellow snowboarder. While it may seem essential that your partner goes to music festivals with you now, you want to find a shared value that will stand the test of time. It's not that your desires aren't important, but by understanding the *why* you can open your parameters and focus on what you actually need.

Another way to understand your values is to reflect back on other relationships. Consider the best dates you've been on, past partners, or anybody you enjoy being around–what traits are most important to you in all your relationships, even platonic ones? Identifying the characteristics of these people will help you further understand the type of person you gel with and what's important when having a relationship with them.

Putting it into practice: Try to think of the core five to ten traits you need in a partner and turn them into fundamentals. Consider what this trait actually means *for* you when in a relationship. Here's an example of how you can view your typical traits as fundamentals:

Your Typical "List" Trait	The Fundamental You're Looking For
They're kind.	They treat me with humanity.
They have a growth mindset.	They're open to learning new things or new perspectives with/from me.
They get along with my friends and family.	They treat my friends and family with respect.
They go to therapy.	They're not afraid to have hard conversations.
They like the same music I do.	They're someone I can share experiences with.
They're a good communicator.	They stay in consistent communication with me.
They're hot.	They are someone I'm sexually attracted to.
They're empathetic.	They're constantly seeking to better understand me.
They're witty.	We have engaging conversations.
They're active.	They prioritize health for both of us.
They have a good career.	They contribute financially to our well-being.
They're stable.	They want to build a life together.
They're fun.	They're multifaceted and able to show various sides of who they are to me, including the sillier side.
They're emotionally available.	They are open to sharing their emotions and hold space for me to share mine.

From whatever list you created, circle the five that are most important to you. This will help you look for the fundamentals in a partner instead of looking for traits that may not even translate to what you need! To be clear, this is not the be-all and end-all of who you want your partner to be. The idea is to have a feel of what works/doesn't work for you while also being open to someone who may surprise you. After all, we also have two more parts of the equation to focus on!

Feelings

We're taught to think about what we want, but we tend to overlook how we want to feel in someone's presence. And we're not just talking about the rainbows and butterflies you feel from the chemistry, but the holistic feeling of being around this person. When anyone tells you to listen to your gut, they're telling you to listen to your body. And if you ignore what your body's telling you, you will inevitably end up in one of those "everything is perfect on paper, but something feels off" relationships. Or even worse—one that feels like you're on top of the world one moment, only to feel a giant pit in your stomach the next.

When we talked to the men's coach Connor Beaton on *Dateable* about the signs that someone is emotionally available, he encouraged people to be conscious of how they feel in their body around the person they're dating. When someone is unsure of what they want or not forthcoming about it, they'll seem more chaotic and you'll feel mistrust. If they're doing the work to be clear about what they want, then you'll feel more at ease, with a sense of safety and security. Your intuition is giving you a physical sensation that shouldn't be ignored.

By tuning in to your feelings, you can discern when someone isn't stepping up to meet your needs, saving you from hours of overthinking about the level of interest or emotional availability, or any other speculations circulating that group chat of yours. As discussed earlier, finding a partner who honors your emotional needs is imperative. Think back to that ideal relationship that inspired your Dating Why. *How do you want to feel in this person's presence?* And even more important, *How do you want to feel when you're apart from each other?* Especially for the Dreamers out there, it's easy to get wrapped up in the butterflies and chemistry when you're together. The actual test is when you're apart. Do you feel at ease and confident? Do you feel anxious or on edge? You may have found a keeper if you feel a sense of calm, security, and peace. And if you don't feel these things, press pause and really observe how you feel instead. It doesn't mean you need to end a relationship that is giving you some early anxiety, but how can you communicate your needs more to offer your partner the opportunity to understand and meet them?

Putting it into practice: Take your core needs and tie each of them to how you want to feel. Some examples could be:

- I need consistency and want someone reliable =
  I want to feel secure
- I need acceptance and want someone who is not judgmental =
  I want to feel respected
- I need quality time and want someone communicative =
  I want to feel prioritized
- I need intimacy and want someone attractive =
  I want to feel desired
- I need support and want someone with a growth mindset =
  I want to feel challenged (in a good way)
- I need connection and want someone who I can have good banter and conversations with =
  I want to feel alive
- I need security and want someone who is career-oriented =
  I want to feel safe

These are just a few examples. Now it's your turn! Choose the top three ways you want to feel around someone and use this as a "gut check" as you date. Having that first out-of-body experience of tuning in to your feelings during a date may seem challenging at first. However, with increased practice, it becomes progressively easier. Not only will this help you find the right partner; it'll also help you set boundaries, communicate accordingly (bye to that person who suddenly is "too busy"), and make choices that will help advance your relationships or . . . end them.

Future

And the last part of the equation is the future. This part of the PPE takes us beyond the dating phase and into "doing life" together. Sure, things can change and the future is unpredictable, but if your visions for the future are so wildly off, it's essential to know this information early on. For example, if you envision a monogamous relationship set in the suburbs with three kids and a goldendoodle, and they want to explore the world of nonmonogamy untethered, there will be a huge disconnect even if everything else lines up. Determine where there is flexibility for compromise and where there are hard lines of how you want the relationship to look. It's imperative to know that ahead of time. So think about what type of relationship you want and how it would operate.

DID YOU KNOW?

According to experts, there are now at least fifteen types of relationships, and we think that's just scratching the surface. Within monogamy alone, biologists have described three types:

- Social monogamy (i.e., the couple who live together, have sex only with each other, and share their basic needs such as food and shelter).
- Sexual monogamy (i.e., the couple who remain sexually exclusive with each other but keep their lives more separated).
- Genetic monogamy (i.e., two partners who have offspring only with each other).

You can live together in the same studio apartment, or you can have a long-distance relationship across the world. You can be co-dependent or independent based on how intertwined your lives are. Within polyamory (i.e., engaging in multiple romantic and typically sexual relationships), there are nine common configurations, including triads, quads, hierarchical poly, and anchor partners. Some ethically nonmonogamous (ENM) relationships involve having feelings and being in a full-blown relationship, whereas open relationships typically make sex more of the focus. Add sexuality to the mix—you could be asexual, demisexual, pansexual, bisexual, or trisexual (as Samantha Jones said in *Sex and the City*, "I'll try anything once"). So do some research! Keep asking yourself questions. Find areas where you're curious to learn more. Get excited to explore!

Just because monogamy works for some people doesn't mean it works for everyone. Just because some people build a family with kids doesn't mean a childless relationship is not a family. Just because your coworker, friend, or sibling found love one way doesn't mean their journey will suit you.

We can't emphasize enough how lucky and privileged we are to have the freedom to date the way we want. So honor that privilege and consider what's essential for you. Take a minute to visualize the future of your ideal relationship. What does life look like with that person? How do you wake up and spend an average day? What types of activities do you do together? How do you celebrate together? How do you two navigate conflict? When times are tough, how do you show up for each other? When your kids (if you want kids) are screaming their heads off in the middle of the night, how do you tag-team the situation? When something devastating happens, how will you be there for each other? Do you want to stay monogamous forever or be open to nontraditional relationship configurations? Do you prefer to live more independent or interconnected lives?

When selecting a life partner, we often overlook these crucial inflection points. It's natural to avoid contemplating moments such as when a loved one falls ill or when the demands of parenthood leave us sleep-deprived. Such considerations feel like a significant shift from the carefree conversations over cocktails about your shared passions for travel. But understanding the type of relationship you want to build will determine long-term compatibility. Achievers rejoice! This is a time your future thinking will help you while dating. Don't worry, though, if you don't have a full vision. Part of this will be answered once you're in a relationship, but much can be considered when you're single to strengthen your POV.

Putting it into practice: To complete the Perfect Partner Equation, reflect on three to five aspects you'd like integrated into whatever life you build with someone else. Thinking about how you want to navigate a relationship one year, five years, or ten years down the line is a worthwhile exercise. Life will throw you some curveballs, and you may change your mind as you grow or meet the person you will share your life with, so this future ideal doesn't have to be your final answer. However, crafting a vision for your future life and relationship that resonates with your needs serves as a compass, so you don't get sucked into someone else's life plan.

This PPE framework is designed to help you gain clarity on your dating journey. When the world is unpredictable and who you meet is out of your control, what you *can* control is having a solid sense of what and who you're looking for. With her PPE, Drea now had a well-rounded understanding of what she needed in a partner. She wanted someone who was as giving as she was, communicated openly, and was emotionally mature. Drea wanted to be with someone who made her feel safe and secure and prioritized her in their actions. Although she didn't know whether a second marriage was in the cards for her, she knew being in a loving, reciprocal partnership was more important. Look how much more clarity this gave Drea! While she couldn't have predicted Mr. Hyde's behavior 100 percent, she could have checked in with her PPE and realized the moment it started to feel misaligned.

Of course, this equation is theoretical for now; it's up to you to put it into practice. Remember, it takes time to unlearn all the bad dating habits we've acquired. So, if you find yourself falling back into old habits (looking for features on your list or going for people who aren't remotely close to your PPE), reflect on why you're still drawn to certain attributes and use this as an opportunity to reframe them again.

> **BDE (Big Dateable Energy):**
> You attract what you seek.

BECOME THE PERSON YOU'D WANT TO DATE

There's one last piece to all of this that will set you up for dating success. Now that you have a vision of what you want with the Perfect Partner Equation, you also need to *become* that person. Want someone who communicates well? Start welcoming conflict head-on. Want someone who makes you feel secure? Text them back as soon as you see their message. While it's essential to make sure we're *getting* what we want from a relationship, we also need to make sure we're *giving*. It's time to check yourself on your dating habits and behaviors to ensure they are aligned with your Dating North Star. For example, we hear of so many daters who never save their date's number into their phones because they assume most dates don't work out anyway. That's a terrible strategy if you're trying to form a connection! How can you ask for someone to respect and value their time with *you* if you don't do the same for them?

Your friends can also shed insight into whether you're being the person you are in other facets of life while dating. For months, Tori had been looking forward to a trip to Mexico with her best friend. It had been an insane quarter at work, and she couldn't wait to get to the beach with a margarita in hand. But instead of relaxing and bonding with her best friend, Tori agonized about hearing from Lynda, the woman she had gone on a couple of dates with recently. Being the Thinker she was, she feared being away would ruin the momentum of their budding relationship. Tori hadn't told Lynda she wanted to stay in touch during her vacation because she didn't want her to know she was thinking about her on the trip. But she *was* preoccupying her mind: Tori checked her phone repeatedly to see if Lynda had texted. Eventually, Tori's best friend called her on it: "You've been waiting months to go on this trip, and now you're not even enjoying your time here! You're such a go-getter in work and all other parts of life. Heck, you just asked for that killer promotion–and got it! Why are you being so passive in your dating life?" At this moment, Tori realized she took pride in being forthcoming and acting with conviction and she needed to do the same in her love life.

Let's also examine your lifestyle patterns: if you're always saying you want to be in a relationship yet you're always on the go, how can you expect to build a stable, consistent partnership? How can you be with someone if you're not available (physically or emotionally)? The same goes if you bury yourself in work or party all the time. If a relationship is what you desire, you need to be able to make room for it. We've noticed there's often a distinct period that we'll call the "relationship prep period," where you naturally find yourself drawn to a more domestic lifestyle–making room for a partner. It's like when parents start nesting during pregnancy; they are literally making way for their new family member. We've noticed it with our friends and even ourselves. It may feel unnatural when you start opting for quieter dinners out, going to the theater instead of the bar, or any other "couple" type activities. You may find yourself drawn to hanging with friends more one-on-one or even engaging in activities on your own. This shift to a quieter pace of life may signify that you're now more ready for something serious.

If there's one thing you can take away from this chapter, it's this: *Love is both about finding the right person and becoming the right person.* Before you pack your calendar with dates, get clear about what you truly want in a partner, and then go embody these characteristics and qualities within yourself.

Yue's Corner

In my twenties, while living it up in NYC, I was your typical "cool girl" playing Relationship Chicken, never wanting to show my cards or share my needs. While I professed I wanted a relationship, I had zero communication skills and bounced at any sign of conflict (in fact, I would often jump on a plane hoping for everything to be magically resolved upon my return!). Over the next decade, I realized in order to be in a healthy relationship, I had to become the person I would want to date. As a Maverick, I needed to learn to embrace conflict and truly let my partner in. I went from comparing myself to everyone around me to celebrating their choices. I went from trying to read minds to communicating my needs—especially with the help of therapy. But most importantly, I became the person I wanted to date.

LOOK UP AT THE STARS!

Now that you have a clear direction, you can decide and act based on what's important to you, based on your Dating North Star and Perfect Partner Equation. Don't be surprised if you go on fewer dates as you get more intentional about what you want, and to who you give your time. Gaining clarity helps you date with purpose. You can openly and honestly express your needs and desires and find more meaningful connections with compatible partners who share your same values. That person is (in fact, many persons are) out there— and now they can finally be visible to you.

We have this idea we call the Stargazing Theory. There are two components to finding your person. One is the search part: optimizing your dating apps, going to the right events, or expanding your social circle, as you never know who you will meet. The more often forgotten aspect is *seeing* this person as your person. When we go stargazing, we act like stars magically appear in the sky when they've been there all along. But it's just light pollution or environmental factors that prevent us from seeing the stars. The same could be true about finding your person. Even if your person appeared right before your eyes, it's irrelevant if you can't see them.

What prevents you from seeing this person as your person is all the mental pollution: societal constructs, pressures within yourself, limiting beliefs, insecurities, family pressures, what your friends say (it's a lot!). When you remove that mental smog blocking your view and gain that clarity within yourself (as we did with the Dating North Star), you now know what's polluting your mind versus serving it. You can stop focusing on the endless, mindless search and instead clean the clutter from within so the right people can simply appear. Now that you have this newfound clarity, you'll be able to recognize a good thing when you see it. And who knows, it may spotlight that someone who is already in your orbit.

We hope this chapter has given you some much-needed clarity about why you're dating, your needs, and who would make a great partner for you. While it's tempting to want it all, the Dating North Star framework helps you prioritize what's most important to you. Remember, the right relationship is *created*, not found. But to create it, you need the right foundation. The Dating North Star and Perfect Partner Equation are designed to provide exactly that, especially as we move through the rest of the book.

KEY TAKEAWAYS

1. Having a Dating North Star will direct your actions and behaviors. Get clear on why you date and your core needs, so you can start aligning your actions accordingly.

2. Say goodbye to your lists filled with hundreds of traits that don't matter! By focusing on your Perfect Partner Equation (fundamentals + feelings + future), you'll have a clear idea of who you are looking for while staying open to the package they may arrive in.

3. Pay attention to how you feel when evaluating partners. It's easy to focus on the chemistry and butterflies when you're together, but take notice of any unpleasant feelings as well, especially when you're *not* with the person.

4. Become the person you want to date. Before you expect certain qualities in others, you need to make sure you're showing up that way yourself.

5. Getting clear means you build the relationship of your dreams. No longer are you fitting into the mold of someone else's relationship; you're creating a vision to DIY the type of relationship that works for you. Eventually someone will be ecstatic to join you on this wild ride!

Chapter 7:

Showing Up

IT'S TIME TO DISCOVER:

1. **The Inner Roll Call:** Naming and understanding the aspects of your personality that can show up while on dates.
2. **Your V-Card:** Being vulnerable in a way that feels authentic to you and fosters connection with others.
3. **Meet and Greets:** A low-pressure way to think about first dates that will allow you to have fun.

Now that we've created our Dating North Star and learned we need to become the person we want to date, let's show up in that very way. When going on a date, we often think about where we're meeting up and what we're wearing, but very rarely are we mindful of the energy we're exuding. On a recent date, Maya was pleasantly surprised when an incredibly attractive man arrived at the coffee shop to meet her. He looked better than his profile photo, and she was excited by the prospect. After getting her usual oat milk latte, she asked the standard date questions to assess his relationship readiness. She also ran through her mental checklist of other deal-breakers and red flags: Financially stable? Check. Didn't do any hard drugs? Check. Worked out regularly? Check. She stayed for more than her typical five-minute date—in fact, she stayed a whole hour! After Maya left the date, she was ecstatic as he checked all the boxes. Except for the biggest one of all: he had no interest in seeing Maya again.

You see, it just so happens that we know Colby, Maya's date. It wasn't that he found Maya unattractive or not interesting, but that her vibe was off-putting. He felt like she came from a place of selection, not connection. It was as if he had to answer her questions a certain way—or else he'd fail the test. He didn't like the feeling of auditioning to be her boyfriend. So the next day, when she texted, he told her he didn't see a romantic connection.

Maya was confused—she thought the date went super well. She had dressed up, asked all the important questions, and gave him her full attention. But Maya wasn't aware of how she was showing up. When you keep track of your dates on an Excel spreadsheet and treat dating like a numbers game, people can feel it. If you go on a date thinking it will be another dud, guess what? It's probably going to be another dud. If you hide behind a date persona and play games, someone looking for a real relationship won't find you to be a viable match. So, how do you start to bring your best self to dating?

IS THIS YOUR REAL SELF OR YOUR DATE SELF?

For whatever reason, there's this unspoken etiquette to dating, from what topics we broach to what stays off-limits, and how we must present ourselves when we meet a new romantic prospect. We think we have to put on a persona when we go on dates, message on apps, or "flirt" at the bar. Have you ever observed a first date as an outsider before? It's painfully obvious as both people stiffly engage in small talk, eat politely, and laugh on cue. We say things we think the other person wants to hear to appear more attractive, intelligent, and interesting. We send messages full of emojis and try to be witty yet nonchalant. Or we answer with one-word responses to come off mysterious and busy. We would never text our friends and family this way! We don't analyze every sentence, editing out parts that don't paint us in the best light.

According to the Institute of Core Energetics, the founding organization that bridges body-oriented psychotherapy with spirituality, we have three layers to who we are: the mask self, the lower self, and the higher self. Our mask self is the default layer we choose to present in public, which is precisely that–the "presented" layer. It's the side of us we want others to see when we're putting our best foot forward (you know, at a job interview or a first date). As Chris Rock said, "When you meet somebody for the first time, you're not meeting them, you're meeting their representative."

The problem with the date persona is that we act the way we think other people want us to act. It's a projection of what we think people like without even knowing what they like. And that is why our date persona comes off performative and contrived, since it does not authentically represent who we are. As we discovered in discussing the Validation Trap, dating isn't a popularity contest. You don't need everyone to like you; you need one person to connect with the weird, nerdy, quirky, adventurous, extroverted, introverted . . . whatever type of person you are. In today's dating world, where we only get seven seconds to make a first impression and, most times, only one date, it's more important than ever to show our authentic selves in this small window. More often than not, our best selves are our actual selves, not the persona we bring to the date. Playing it safe by not being yourself isn't memorable, and people certainly don't feel connected to you when you're hiding behind a mask. When we fall into this date persona, that's when our dates feel generic and boring. You've been on dates where you feel like, *Here we go again, the same convo*. Well, your date probably feels the same way. How can our dates feel great when we have the same date talk repeatedly?

And this extends to all parts of the dating process. We've heard of people hiring dating coaches or ghostwriters, or even enlisting AI to write their messages on dating apps. Why would you want someone else to represent you when you're the one who will eventually show up IRL? Does that sound like a good foundation for love? We are so concerned with "hooking" the person that we forget about connecting with them instead. Why do we feel like we must be somebody else to attract someone, only to show our true selves once in a relationship? Seems a little contradictory, right? After all, it's going to be hard to hide your supposed hatred for reality TV when you're living with your partner of three years and *The Real Housewives* is on repeat.

Some of us may cling to how we *should* act while dating (there we go again with those damn shoulds!). If you find that you have no problem making friends and you're naturally a great conversationalist, yet none of your dates seem to be sticking, you may be bringing the date version of yourself. Maybe you've heard dating advice that you shouldn't talk too much about yourself or your career because especially for hetero women, we've been told to stay in our "feminine" and not intimidate our dates. Sure, you may not want to talk about the nitty-gritty of your job (because it's boring more than anything else), but holding back because you are told you *shouldn't* talk about something is anything but authentic. You only end up repressing parts of your personality. When you're trying too hard to be someone you aren't, that's when dating becomes challenging and exhausting.

How do you start to find your most authentic, best self? Here are two questions to ask yourself:

1. **Who are you when no one is around?** We all have unique and silly quirks about us that we sometimes hide. If you like to bust into random dance parties by yourself, do it! Don't wait until no one is watching, because one day you may be living with a partner who will hopefully find this as entertaining as you do.

2. **How would your closest friends and family describe you?** It's worth it to survey your closest circle. Ask them what value you bring to their lives and when they've seen you come most alive. Or you could be even more direct, asking questions like: How do you describe me to other people? What would you say about me to someone you're setting me up with? We may think we know what our friends would tell us, but it's much better to hear directly from them (plus they may surprise you!).

So show up as the wonderful version of you—the one your friends love and can't wait to hang out with. That's when you can stand out and allow the right person to see you for who you are instead of blending in with the sea of other daters.

> **BDE (Big Dateable Energy):**
> The unfiltered you will do the filtering for you.

WHAT PART OF YOU IS SHOWING UP?

Even when you show your authentic self, you have many facets of who you are. According to the licensed marriage and family therapist Lair Torrent, we all have many sides to our personalities, and they can get triggered in different situations. When we talked to him on *Dateable*, Lair suggested doing an "inner roll call." You may find that some sides of you show up more at work than with friends; it's human to have different parts to you (cue the lawyers, who probably don't want to be constantly battling it out with your partners). You have the power to decide which aspect of you meets the dating world.

It's no wonder that our inner critic will show up if we're skeptical of dating apps or the intentions of the people we're meeting. If we're coming straight from work, where we had a disagreement with our boss, our frustrated or frazzled self may arrive for dinner. Is there a part of you scared of putting your heart on the line or worried that you aren't worthy of love? Your wounded child, desperate for connection, has entered the chat. It's not always a reflection of who you are, but rather who you are in that instance.

To ensure you bring your best, most authentic self to dates, consider the following scenarios:

What type of people bring out the best in you?
Why do they make you feel your best? What qualities do they have that make you come alive? When you've identified who can bring out the best in you, look for these qualities in the people you date. Or call a friend who brings out your best side to get into a good headspace before a date.

What type of people bring out the worst in you?
Can you identify these qualities and know how to avoid them? If you find that avoidant people bring out your anxious side, you know to intentionally stay away from that type of behavior.

What type of environment brings out the best in you?
Some people thrive in loud bars, while others prefer to be in nature. If you know certain environments work in your favor, put yourself

in those places on dates. Let your environment work for you, not against you!

Monitor how you talk about dating with friends and the emotions you feel on dates. And if you find that while on a date, a side of you is coming out that's not what you want to bring, go to the restroom, regroup for a minute, and roll-call the part of you that's more conducive to enjoying the date. As Lair suggests, saying "Hello, inner critic, I see you. I hear you. But I don't want you to come out right now for this date" is an effective way to recognize the state you're in. If you know certain environments bring out the negative sides (like your job!), build in some buffer time between work and dates so you can get into the right headspace. Take a walk. Listen to music. Get yourself into the mindset you want to go into the date with.

We exert all this energy and time updating our profiles (where, let's be honest, there's a point of diminishing returns). But, and we mean this in the nicest way possible: it's not your profile, it's you. All you need to do is be mindful of how you show up and learn how to set yourself up for success. When we get so wrapped up in dating (especially when it's not working out), we fail to see all the parts of us that are amazing.

A WORD ABOUT ALCOHOL

Often what gets in the way of us showing up authentically is alcohol. While a drink or two can loosen you up, think about your relationship to alcohol and dating. Does it change how you show up for a date? Does it cloud your judgment? Does it make the connection seem deeper than it actually is? We believe the true test of chemistry is a #soberfirstkiss, a concept we've been proponents of since the early episodes of *Dateable*.

Coming from two people who once relied too much on alcohol while dating (listen back to our "Rock Bottom" episode if you want proof), we know it clouds your vision and doesn't enable you to show up as your most present, connected self. With the right person, you don't need alcohol to show them that you're a blast to be around. And by not drinking as much on dates, you can show your other sides that were once repressed by booze.

DATE THE WAY YOU WANT TO BE DATED

Just like how we can become the person we want to date, we can also date the way we want to be dated. It's easy to complain about dating, but it's also likely we're doing the exact same thing that bothers us the most, whether we realize it or not. How many times have you stopped messaging midconversation on a dating app? Or took a long time to get back to someone you weren't interested in? Have you ever ghosted someone despite complaining all the time about how terrible ghosting is? Whenever something irks you, pause and ask, *Am I also guilty of this behavior?* If yes, then you need to change yourself first.

It's easy to fall into the mindset of *Why should I make this effort if others don't do the same?* But as we established with Relationship Chicken and the lowest common denominator mindset, this approach will not get you the love life you want. Instead of playing at the same level as other bad daters, rise above and date the way *you* want to be dated! Show up the way you want others to show up for you. When you live in alignment with your Dating North Star, you'll see how you show up differently.

Our Energizer, Eli, remembers the time he was put in his place that forever changed how he dated. He had plans to meet up with a Tinder match but was running late (he was actually double-booked and coming from another date!). Eli decided to cancel because there was no way he could make it on time. Others did this to him all the time, so it was no big deal, right? Then his date wrote him a game-changing text: I understand that your day may have gotten away from you, but I was looking forward to meeting up, which I prioritized in my day. If this is your way of you saying you've changed your mind, I totally get it. But if you would still like to make this date happen, I will leave the ball in your court on setting it up and showing up.

Damn. Eli had never been called out like that. He had been so wrapped up in other people's bad dating behaviors that he failed to look at how he was behaving by overbooking dates. This was the shakeup he needed to do better. After all, Eli had realized from his Dating North Star that he needed mutual respect. How could he expect this from others if he wasn't showing up this way himself? After this experience, he became more intentional about setting up *fewer* dates to ensure he followed through and gave each date the proper attention and respect. In the past, Eli would jump to setting up a date as soon as he matched with someone. Now he would take a step back to determine whether this was a viable prospect before meeting up. He started implementing a pre-date call to gauge if there was a baseline connection and level of mutual respect. Eli could now go into the actual date excited, giving this person the full attention they deserved. And if the person did not meet his Dating North Star, he could set them free respectfully and funnel his attention to more deserving prospects.

The only thing you can actually control in dating is yourself. If you can uphold your actions to the highest standards, you will not settle for someone who doesn't match that. For your own actions, you will make sure that you give people the respect they deserve, follow through with plans, communicate regularly, let people know where you stand, and always close the loop. Even if it's not a romantic match, you can strive for connection. And you will make sure that you will not accept ghosting, flakiness, lack of accountability, or just plain rudeness. You're filtering out the people who aren't showing up for a healthy, sustainable relationship like you want. For every action you take, think, *Would I want someone to treat me this way?* When you raise your standards, you attract the people who are at that level. Energy attracts energy. Dating often can be a mirror of ourselves. You get back what you put in.

One simple way you can date the way you want to be dated is to focus on this motto: "I will leave each person I meet better than before they met me." If you felt a connection after a date, you could text something like: I had a really good time getting to know you, especially [insert something specific]. I would really like to continue getting to know you. Are you free next Wednesday night? And if you don't feel a connection, it goes a long way to say: Thanks for such a fun date. I really admire that you [insert something specific]. While I don't think a romantic connection is there, I am glad I met you! What a better way to show up, whether the date was good or not. When you employ energy of self-respect, confidence, and human decency, you'll know you're acting at your best. And that's how we raise the common denominator of what's acceptable dating behavior.

THE THREE WORST DATES

Now that we've established that how we show up for dates doesn't always reflect the connection we want, let's go through some of the most common disaster dates. Check yourself if you've been guilty of showing up this way:

1. **The Daterview:** We've talked about it before but it deserves repeating because this type of date is so painful. When we resort to the superficial "daterview," asking the basics such as where are you from, what do you do for work, where did you go to school,

it's not just that it's boring and repetitive (which it is); it's also dehumanizing. It feels like someone is interviewing you for the job of an ideal mate. Just like on a job interview, they have an idea of who they want to hire, and you feel nervous because you're not sure if you're giving the right answers to fit the role. Dates shouldn't feel like you need to prove yourself. You shouldn't ever wonder whether you're stacking up. Not only does it make the person on the receiving end feel like sh*t, but it also gives the impression that you have a very rigid way of dating. Just like Maya's date with Colby, even if the person checks all your boxes, this is no way to show up for someone looking for connection. No one wants to be asked on the first date where they want to be in five years or why their last relationship didn't work out.

Instead, think about ways of involving the other person in your date talk. For example, if you ask someone where they went to school, it's very much a Q&A at that point. Not fun. You can involve your date more if you say something like, "I've really enjoyed hiking ever since I went to college at [XYZ], where I was surrounded by nature. Do you remember hobbies you discovered at school?" This conversation then gives the opportunity for your date to tell you about their college experience without formally telling you where they went and what they majored in. Another hot topic is work, and daters love to directly ask where someone works and what they do for a living. Again, what if you could involve your date in the conversation? "I had a pretty rough day at work. It's tax season and being an accountant is like being Santa during Christmas. I've been looking for ways to decompress. Have you tried anything that works for you?" This is an effective way to divulge a little about you and set up your date to share as much as they'd like about their work environment. It's also nice to ask for some input or advice so they feel like they're already a part of your life in some way.

2. **The Solo Act:** We've all been on that date before, where it feels like a one-person Broadway show. Maybe you're trying to impress the other person by sharing your résumé and touting your accomplishments. Or you've come prepared with that winning story, and you can't wait to make them laugh. But it's not your job to entertain your dates, and the sentiment isn't typically appreciated. You've probably been on a date where you've barely gotten a word in; it doesn't feel great, right? People don't want to be steamrolled by you; they want to feel seen and heard. Dates should be a two-way street where we listen and share. If you're showing up trying to impress, you can leave your comedy routine at home. Your date doesn't need a two-drink minimum.

   Instead, prioritize strengthening your active listening skills. Hear. Every. Word. Sometimes when we're so focused on what to ask next or how to respond in an entertaining way, we don't actually listen to what the other person is saying. In fact, *most* of us have terrible listening skills on dates, where we only hear the last two to three words of a sentence. Don't believe us? Name three facts about the last person who you went on a date with that you learned while on the date. Not so easy, right? Make it a point to go into your next date to intentionally hear every word they're saying. And at the end of their sentence, where are you curious to learn more? Ask more questions in that direction. Or did you hear something that really stood out to you? Acknowledge and explore. We will dive deeper into active listening skills later in this chapter.

3. **The Therapy Session:** We're told to be vulnerable on dates, but there's a line between opening up to someone and then spilling all our deep, dark secrets. It's never good when someone prefaces what they're about to say with "I probably shouldn't talk about this, but . . ." The person you just met doesn't need to hear about your mediocre sex life with your ex, financial challenges, or the

big fight with your parents. And they certainly don't need to hear about how hard dating is (we've sadly heard this all too often come up on dates). We sometimes conflate this with vulnerability, but in reality, we're just not reading the room.

Instead, focus on how you've overcome challenges. Think about how you would want to talk about these issues if you're in a relationship together. Do you really want to keep revisiting the same problems over and over again with your partner? Or do you want to be solution-oriented and talk about a path forward? If you've had bad experiences with dating apps (c'mon, who hasn't), talk about what you've learned from these experiences. It's one thing to lament people disappearing from messaging on apps. But it's another to say, "I've had challenges with getting consistent communication from people so that's why you stood out, because you were consistent in messaging me and I appreciate you for it!"

You may be nodding, as you've been on all these dates before. But the real question is, have you ever been the one showing up this way? We often think we're above it, but it's not always true. It was a huge reality check for Maya when she heard Colby's feedback. She had no idea how she was coming off. As a Maverick, it was hard for her to let people in. But she realized that if she wanted a relationship with the legs to last (which she discovered from her Dating North Star that she did!), she needed to make some changes. Maya was hiding behind the daterview, peppering the other person with questions instead of letting that person get to know her, too. She challenged herself to approach dating the same way she interacts with her friends; she would show her dates the real Maya, and instead of judging, she'd let the conversation naturally unfold. Some of her strongest friendships came out of surprise connections, and she wanted to experience the same in dating.

Now take a minute to reflect on your last couple of dates. Were your actions the best representation of yourself? Genuine connections can only happen when you wholeheartedly embrace and express your true self.

Yue's Corner

For Dateable, *I went on a blind date with a guy named Andrew, who agreed to a post-date interview. I thought he was loving all my witty jokes and interesting stories, until . . . in the middle of the date, he called me out in a gentle, yet poignant way. "So when will you show me the real you, Yue?" I was shocked. As an avid poker player, Andrew saw through my act. I always thought I was good at dating, but I realized I was being performative and formulaic. He wasn't looking for someone to entertain him; he was looking for someone to connect with. I began to listen more and share parts of myself that were more vulnerable and, at times, less confident. But that's what Andrew connected with and by the end of the date, he wanted to go out again. If I hadn't heard this feedback, I'd continue this pattern as the "entertainer" and wonder why great guys like Andrew didn't want to go on a second date.*

SHOW US YOUR V-CARD

In addition to being your most authentic self, let's dive into what else it takes to show up in a way that fosters connection. You've probably heard the advice: be vulnerable. Vulnerability is such a buzzword, but what does it even really mean? According to Brené Brown (who made us all obsessed with the term): **vulnerability is the emotion that we experience during times of uncertainty, risk, and emotional**

exposure. The act of dating in itself is vulnerable. Putting your true self out there is most certainly vulnerable. Yet for whatever reason in dating culture, we've lost the actual definition. So before we go into what vulnerability looks like, let's talk about what it's not:

Vulnerability is not about exposing your weaknesses. We once had a dater tell us he had a great idea for his dating profile. He was going to list out all of his weaknesses: his general tardiness, lack of upper body strength, and subpar cooking abilities. While it would make his profile stand out, would it help him attract the right people? Vulnerability is supposed to feel organic and human. But this approach of publicly volunteering his weaknesses on a dating profile felt contrived and pessimistic.

Vulnerability is not trauma dumping. Another dater told us about her first date with a guy who felt so comfortable, he spilled everything about his last relationship, including asking his ex to get an abortion. It was a traumatizing experience that took a toll on their relationship and he regretted making her go through with it. All of this was shared before the first drink, mind you! He also asked nothing about his date and proceeded to tell her this was one of the best dates he'd ever been on. When you barely know someone's name, yet know extremely personal details about them, that's headed into trauma-dumping territory (i.e., the unsolicited act of expressing traumatic thoughts and stories to someone, leaving the receiver trapped without the option to exit). Discussing your previous traumas so early on will not facilitate a connection—it can actually create a divide.

Vulnerability is not about TMI. Once a dater shared that she was proud of her vulnerability since she shared on Instagram about her STI. She set up an entire Instagram Live to share her experience with her followers. She didn't understand why this level of vulnerability wasn't getting her a flood of DMs from potential suitors. Now, it's a different situation if you're talking one-on-one with a friend or partner about sexually transmitted infections. It's another to broadcast all your information to people you may not even know in real life, who didn't ask to hear about this personal issue.

Now that we got that out of the way, how can we be vulnerable on dates? *Vulnerability is about being true to yourself. It's consciously choosing not to hide your emotions or desires from others.* Telling someone you had a good time (when in fact you did) is vulnerable. Sharing that you're nervcited (you know, nervous and excited at the same time) about the date is vulnerable. Letting someone know you're upset is vulnerable. Dreamers, with all your emotions, this is your time to shine! Instead of covering up your feelings, share them in a way that allows for actual vulnerability!

Underneath the need to be vulnerable is showing your date that you are emotionally available, the number one thing people are looking for in a partner, according to our *Dateable* community. Here is what actual vulnerability looks like:

Make your inner dialogue your outer dialogue. Share that you've had a hard day at work, but you're excited to be here now on the date. You can express that first dates are inherently awkward, so let's be nervous together! And tell them that you're having a great time! Putting out your experiences without a need for reciprocity shows that you are simply expressing how you feel. When you share your genuine emotions—both positive and negative—that's putting yourself out there.

Share what you're going through. Open up about what you are currently working through or processing. For instance, what is it like to have aging parents or to be the lone person in your friend group who moved away from your hometown? Getting real about life (without trauma dumping!) makes someone feel closer to you. You can share any challenges you've faced, lessons you've learned, or moments of personal growth.

Ask for advice. Let people in by asking for advice. This shows that you have some humility that you don't know everything. It also tells someone that you value their opinions and are open to new ideas. Sharing anything you're unsure of, struggling with, or not confident about makes you vulnerable by default.

Show affection and your intentions. Make the move. Send the text. Do whatever to be crystal clear that you're into someone. Share your expectations for the relationship—whether short-term or long-term. You're inherently vulnerable when you put your heart on the line.

We often overthink what it means to be vulnerable. If you find yourself shying away from it (or partaking in faux vulnerability, as we showed with earlier examples), it's worth asking where this is coming from. Are you trying to cradle yourself from getting hurt? Being vulnerable means taking a risk and putting yourself out there to connect with another human being. When you open up, you can get hurt, but there is also a chance for connection and growth.

HACKING HUMAN CONNECTION

Now that we know what vulnerability is and what it isn't, how do we use it to connect with others? While one part is being vulnerable and sharing your feelings and desires, the other side of connection is being genuinely interested in what the other person has to say and letting them be seen and heard. A top reason for dates not progressing is "lack of emotional connection." It's frustrating getting a text like that but what does it actually mean?

The American journalist Celeste Headlee, renowned for her viral TED Talk on how to have better conversations, asserts that the ability to converse is not merely a soft skill but rather a fundamental human necessity, second only to food and water. We think that if we're good speakers, then we're good conversationalists—but this could not be further from the truth. Listening is the most challenging part of the interaction. As mentioned earlier, daters can be some of the worst listeners if they're too busy thinking about what they're going to say next or how they're being perceived. Connection is not built on what you're saying, but rather on how you're relating to the other person.

Here's a hack for you: **the most interesting person in the room is the most interested**. When you are listening to your dates, they feel seen and heard. It's tempting to want to come up with conversation starters in advance or overthink how the conversation should go (Thinkers, we're looking at you!), but this strategy often falls flat. We once talked to a dater who was so concerned about what he was going to say next that he missed one important detail about his date: her dog was just put down. Instead of replying with empathy and compassion, he nodded his head and asked about her dream vacation spot. Ummm . . . awkward. When you focus more on listening, you'll respond from a place of connection by default. Your dates will start to see you as a better conversationalist—despite talking less. If you can master the skill of active listening, you will not only walk away from dates feeling like you learned new things, but your date will also feel like they've connected with you. Here are a few tips on active listening:

- Shut down any thoughts about "what am I going to say next."
- Observe their body language and whether it seems consistent with the story.
- Pay attention to their change of tone and emotions.
- Think about why they are telling you this.
- Embrace the silence and pauses. You do not need to fill it with empty words.

When we spoke with communication expert Celeste Headlee on *Dateable*, she shared some sound advice: forget what you want to say and focus on what you want to know. This will allow you to craft a response based on what your date shared. Think about this as a collaborative process and a baton that's being passed back and forth. Questions are your allies as long as they are in response to the topic of conversation.

By now, you've learned to go beyond the date talk, show vulnerability, and be a good listener. Here are a few more tips for forming a deeper connection:

Don't underestimate small talk. Celeste pointed out that small talk is very different from the dreaded daterview, as it comes from a place of curiosity. It's not a checklist of questions; you're pointing out observations. If you look at the person in front of you, you can ask about things they've chosen for themselves, such as their tattoos, jewelry, or shoes. Small talk allows you to meet someone where they are and see how the conversation takes off from there. Additionally, when someone chooses to express themselves in an obvious way (statement jewelry, sports team jersey, or a tattoo sleeve), they also signal that they're open to conversation about these choices.

Share stories. People remember stories, not facts. Stories also allow us to convey the emotions we feel in the moment, instead of listing off our résumés or generic information easily found online. They are a great bonding technique and leave much more of an impression and room for follow-up. When practicing storytelling, try to expand on how you felt in those pivotal moments instead of just stating the facts.

Their presence is a present. Time is precious and if someone chooses to spend time with you, it is a gift they're offering you. Be there with them: in the moment. Refrain from checking your phone, glancing at bypassers, and other mindless distractions. How you interact directly with others affects the energy of the relationship. Staying present and giving someone your full attention will enhance your connection.

Have something just for you two. Is there an inside joke or a shared language you've created from this date? Maybe your date went to the wrong bar because there are two bars with similar names. Now you've got something you can share just the two of you, which becomes an inside joke. Did something funny happen during the date, like the waiter spilled your wine? Now you can always reference not wearing white. When you share some insider intel that's unique to you two, it strengthens the bond even more.

Be a team. Speaking of acting as a unit, think of other ways to accomplish that on your date. If you feel comfortable enough, you could meet up somewhere first (whether it's one of your places or another, more neutral location) and then go to the restaurant together, so it starts to feel like you're already showing up as a unit. Any chance to be a team together is a good moment for connection.

Ask for feedback. What strengthens human connection is when people feel understood and seen. Daters spend so much time trying to guess what the other person is thinking, which pushes people farther apart. During a conversation, try asking for feedback. If you were the one who planned the date, ask what they thought of the idea. If you're feeling a little nervous about the date, ask whether they're feeling the same. When you ask for feedback, it opens up the possibility for an open conversation.

Notice we didn't once tell you to change anything about who you are as a person (because, damn, you're fabulous the way you are). Nor did we instruct you about what conversations to have or give you any templates. There isn't a script you need to use: just be mindful of what it means to connect with another human. These techniques are entirely doable; you're probably implimenting some already subconsciously. Experiment with different ways of establishing connection and be mindful of how you're showing up.

MAKE DATING FUN AGAIN

We don't know about you, but we're sick of hearing about "fine" dates. Too many of you go on them—and it's disheartening for both parties if you leave the date apathetic. Our theory is that when we go on these dates that are just mediocre, it's because we're showing up as our mediocre selves. We want you to start having, as Mark Manson coined, f*ck yes or f*ck no experiences. It's time that we make dating fun again.

One of our favorite podcast guests on *Dateable* was Jeff Harry, a play expert who helps adults release their inner child. In conversation with him, we discussed ways to use the initial dates to connect with a new person rather than assess their potential as a life partner. Jeff defines play as a "joyful act where you're fully present in the moment, where there is no purpose, no result; you don't have anxiety about the future, you don't have regrets about the past, and you're fully in the zone." One of his favorite examples was going to the airport and handing out flowers to strangers with his date. Even if you're saying *I'd never do something like that*, the point is that fun dates create memories that bond people together. Even if you opt for a standard drink date, why not bring this playful energy to dating?

Part of the problem with dating is our expectations. You're trying to find someone you love spending time with; you need to get out of the mentality of seeing dating as a chore or assessment. It's hard to enjoy and have fun on dates if the goal is to decide whether this is your forever person. As you may recall, our resident Achiever, Andrew, was so focused on getting into a relationship that it destroyed the enjoyment of meeting and connecting with new people.

He recently met up with his friend Marc, who had been married for over a decade. Unfortunately, his wife was diagnosed with late-stage breast cancer, and although she was fighting it, Marc was distraught. He didn't know what the future held, but he knew that he needed to stay present and enjoy every single minute with his wife. He turned to Andrew and said, "If I have one piece of advice for you while dating, it's to enjoy every moment while you can. You never know when this will be the last time." This was a huge wake-up call for Andrew. Had he been so focused on the future that he forgot to live in the now?

In order to help him, we encouraged him to treat each date as a meet and greet, where he was simply meeting someone new, instead of putting pressure on the first date. We asked him to focus on how grateful he was to get this time with a new person, not worrying about the usual nerves and anxiety that go into a date. When you think about it, in what other environment would someone so eagerly meet up with you? Trust us, once you're out of the dating pool, you will miss the thrill of meeting new people! When Andrew started to show up with the mentality of asking, *Who do I have the privilege of getting to know?* it put him in such a better headspace for connection. It was no surprise to us when more of Andrew's first meets turned into second dates! This new energy of gratitude put him into a state of what he could *give* instead of focusing on what he could get. It's about seeing people as human beings, not as if they're auditioning for a role. Even if you never see this person again, you could have a conversation that changes your life or sparks a fresh perspective. You have the freedom to connect with anyone in the world. That's a luxury!

The best part about dating is that you get to cocreate your experience with the other person. As Jeff Harry mentioned, playfulness on a date for some people could mean going to a bookstore and reading together for hours, whereas others might participate in more introspective play, such as asking each other the thirty-six questions to fall in love. It's all about meshing your ideas together to form memories. It's a "yes and" conversation to see where the date takes you. Stay in the moment and get comfortable with uncertainty. Your bond begins to form when you start building these shared experiences.

Being open to what may happen puts you in a place of curiosity, which lets you show up in the best way possible. Think about when you travel. What do you do when you're a tourist in a foreign city? You let go of your checklists and to-do lists. You say yes to exotic food you've never heard of. You're open to new experiences and people. You wander down random streets and maybe you meet the love of your life! You can take this mindset into every date by taking a "dating vacation." How would you interact with people on the apps differently if you were in a foreign city? What other date activities would you be motivated to do? What new places or areas of town have you not yet explored? Can you limit swiping to only two days a week while you're out living your best life? You probably would start showing up a lot better for these dates because you'd appreciate them more. Even if you never leave your home city, try new ways to date and, most importantly, have fun.

Julie's Corner

For too long, I focused on trying to go deep and share everything about myself on the first date. I probably had a mix of the daterview, solo act, and therapy session all rolled into one! I thought this was the way to form a connection, but I realized that the best dates—the ones that turned into relationships—did not start that way. One of my most memorable dates with a past partner of mine began with talking about pranks we had both pulled on our friends. This created a comfortable baseline where we could naturally connect and eventually our conversations got deeper. With all the pressure around dating, we lose sight of the fact that dating is supposed to be fun, and we can reveal ourselves over time.

BRING THAT BIG DATEABLE ENERGY!

As you can see, mindset is everything when it comes to dating. When you show up as your best, most authentic self and have fun while dating, you'll naturally ooze that dateable energy. How you show up is so much more than what you're wearing or how you style your hair. Show your vibrant personality that your friends know and love! Say yes to new opportunities and bring your full self. Don't be surprised when you start to draw new people in left and right. That's the power of showing up in a way conducive to connection.

Before we close out this chapter, we'll leave you with a ritual. Before going on a new date, create a pre-date checklist to get into a good headspace and set three intentions for the date:

1. I am excited to meet someone new.
2. I will show up as my best self.
3. I will learn something new regardless of whether it's a romantic connection.

So light a candle and ritualize this pre-date setup! Then you'll be well on your way to showing up to dates in the best way possible!

KEY TAKEAWAYS

1. We focus so much on what we do on dates, but the most critical aspect is the energy and attitude you bring. Show up in a way that's conducive to connection.
2. Date the way you want to be dated. It's easy to fall victim to bad dating behavior, but the only way to find someone above it is to be above it yourself.
3. The root of vulnerability is emotional availability. Remember that vulnerability is a two-way street, and there's a difference between oversharing and building a deeper connection.
4. The most interesting person is the most interested. Make sure that your dates feel seen and heard and remember to ditch the daterviews, solo acts, and therapy sessions. Because after all, you're here to connect with another human being!
5. Let's make dating fun again! Think about the first date as a meet and greet to alleviate some of the pressure. Showing up with the mentality of *Who do I have the privilege of getting to know?* will always put you in a better headspace for connection.

Chapter 8:

Investing Appropriately

IT'S TIME TO DISCOVER:

1. **Fail-Fast Mentality:** When you can quickly identify a situation that will not work, so you can move on to something better suited for you.
2. **The Date Lens:** The difference between what makes someone a good date versus a great long-term partner.
3. **The Only Seven Things That Matter:** The ultimate gut check to determine whether someone is worth investing in further.

One of the biggest challenges with modern dating is figuring out how to invest your time and energy–and who you decide to give your heart to. These days, you could be filling your funnel with new prospects, talking to more people on the apps, or investing more into the person you had a great first date with the other week. You could spend hours building your dating profile or use that time to meet people IRL. You could go on a second date with the person you were lukewarm on, or you could call it and swipe for your next option. With so many crossroads when you date, how do you determine which direction to take?

You've probably heard the phrase "the paradox of choice" thrown around quite often. Numerous studies show that an abundance of options, instead of making you happier, causes you to become more stressed and confused. As your typical Thinker, Tori would spend hours contemplating, analyzing, and dissecting everything from someone's dating profile to the text they sent. Her head was filled with questions from *Am I on the right dating app?* to *Should I send another text when I haven't heard from her in three days?* to *Are they the right long-term match for me?* (mind you, they had only been out one time!). All these options put her into a state of analysis paralysis and resulted in more inaction than anything else.

The ironic part was that Tori was a go-getter in her career. As a female engineer who was always the only woman in the room, she learned how to find her voice, champion her needs, and ask for what she wanted (case in point: that big promotion she knew she'd earned!). Tori had a vision and wasn't afraid to ask questions, hold people accountable, and even fire underperforming employees. Yet in her love life, she struggled to make any decisions. She continued to dwell on people who didn't show signs of being good partners and let the "relationship" slip into situationship territory instead of pulling the cord. And she didn't double down and make her intentions clear with the people who could have been suitable long-term matches.

Tori was a Thinker by default (she was an engineer, after all!), but she found it easier to trust her instincts at work. We get it: it's hard to trust our decision-making while dating, especially when we haven't had the best track record in love. We want to give the person another chance (even when they haven't done anything to show they deserve one), or we sit passively waiting for the other person to decide if *they* like *us*. By the end of this chapter, we want you to be able to act with conviction and make decisions that benefit *you*. We'll help you learn to trust your instincts and feel more confident in your choices. This is a pivotal step in the process as it'll help you put situations into perspective, and you can use our decision-making frameworks when you're stuck. So, how do you start doing this?

YOU'RE THE CEO OF YOUR LOVE LIFE

Like Tori, you may already be a boss at your job (literally or figuratively), so how can you harness that energy in your love life? You make the call when a decision needs to be made. You control how your time is spent. And you fire that damn person who isn't showing up in the way you need. However, many of us do not adopt this mentality for our love lives. Instead of the CEO, we've become the assistant (waiting for assignments) or the PR rep (spinning the story in favor of that person). We see daters bending over backward for dates over the fear of missing out. They'll cancel plans with friends or skip an activity they love. It's easy to say *just this once*, or *I'm prioritizing dating*. They'll excuse bad behavior by creating a story in their defense: *they are just not ready for a relationship right now*. But you lose yourself in the process. As daters, we tend to put our emotions in the hands of mere strangers. Waiting for them to text. Wondering whether they like us back. Gutted when they didn't respond right away.

But when you're the CEO of your love life, *you're* in control—not the apps, your mother, or the person who may or may not be ghosting you as we speak. You're the decision-maker. At every decision point, you have the option to either be in the driver's seat or be a captive passenger. When you decide to be the CEO of your love life, a few things start to change:

- *Instead of wondering*, you ask.
- *Instead of waiting*, you initiate.
- *Instead of moping around*, you live your damn life.

You start to focus on the people who are showing up, and leave the ones who aren't. You start prioritizing your time—because this is your most valuable asset as a busy CEO. When you spend hours analyzing their last text, wondering if they will ask you out again, or questioning whether you'll scare them off with a DTR convo, you are occupying your thoughts with things that are out of your control. That *is* time wasted. By spending time in the unknown, we stay in limbo, not moving in either direction.

So instead of being mind readers, it's time to be info seekers! Go to the source, not your group text. Get curious and treat this as an opportunity to learn the other person's POV. Now let's take a look at a few situations and how the new you (aka the CEO of your love life) would act:

You had a nice date and are excited to see them again. They said they felt the same but four days have gone by, and still no text. What do you do?

New CEO You: Text or call them. That's the only way to get your answer. "Hey, I had a really nice time with you. Would you be down to go out again Saturday? Let me know tonight so I can book something for us." Ask with conviction and have a concrete intention. In this statement, there's no question that you're interested, want to hang out again on Saturday, and that you're planning the date. You've also given a deadline, so if they don't respond, you'll have your answer and then move on!

They planned a date for Thursday, and it's now Wednesday. Still no word of where you're going and what you're doing. What do you do?

New CEO You: Ask what the plan is. Stop thinking, *Oh, they'll let me know soon enough.* Instead of going by other people's timelines (whenever that is), you can request information based on *your* timeline. Say, "Looking forward to tomorrow! What's the plan? I want to plan my day accordingly." Boom. You're not only asking the question, you're creating boundaries for how you would like to organize your time.

The person you went on three dates with is now ghosting you. You can't figure out a reason why. You ask your mom, group chat, therapist, and best friend's cousin what this could mean. You spend hours debating whether you should text them again. What do you do?

New CEO You: When someone ghosts, there's one thing we all have to accept: you may not hear from them ever again. So what would make you feel better in this situation? If you want to let them know of your disappointment, do it! If you want to leave it alone and move on, do it! There's no need to marinate in sorrow. There's also no need to vent about it with your friends. That energy and precious time can be used on people who are additive to your life. Find out what would close the door for you and drive away. SCREEEEEEECH!

As we've observed from Relationship Chicken, it can be challenging for many of us to make moves, especially hetero women who've been told to "lean back" and let him lead. Taking action has been ingrained in us as bad: you're coming off too thirsty, aggressive, or whatever other BS you've been fed along the way. Trust us, sending the text will not make someone lose interest if they are indeed interested (in fact, they'll be thrilled you're interested in them, too!).

We want to make this loud and clear: taking action is the only way to live your life. All investments carry some risk, and it's imperative to put yourself out there and take a chance—even if it feels like you're being rejected. But as we discussed: rejection is just redirection. In Silicon Valley start-up culture, there's a "fail-fast" philosophy originated by Eric Ries, an entrepreneur and author of *The Lean*

Startup. The whole premise is that it's better to learn quickly and pivot if necessary instead of spending years developing a product that people may not even want. This was not a foreign concept to Tori, who had a decade's worth of start-up experience under her belt. So why couldn't she bring this same mentality to dating?

She would never passively wait for an answer in her professional life. She'd ask the right questions to get the necessary answers. Tori realized she owed it to herself to make educated decisions in her personal life, too. Even if she got an answer she didn't want, it was better than no answer at all. So when she fell back into old patterns of waiting for that text message from her recent date Susanne, she knew she had to put on that CEO hat. Tori and Susanne had one of those dates that shut the bar down. The conversation flowed effortlessly, and it felt like they had known each other for years. The date ended in an intense make-out sesh, and they talked about checking out a photography exhibit at the de Young Museum in Golden Gate Park. Susanne said she would reach out, but three days later, nothing. Tori felt the spiral starting but then she caught herself. She took out her phone and texted Susanne that she had a great time the other night and wanted to see if she was still interested in going to the museum. To her surprise, Susanne immediately replied, saying she was just about to reach out. They set up a date for that Saturday.

Lucky for Tori, she got the answer she wanted to hear. Even if you don't, having a fail-fast mentality allows you to learn and move on quicker to someone ready to invest in you. If you don't get the response you're hoping for (e.g., there's no chemistry or emotional connection), you can be grateful that they've cleared your path for someone more suitable. The key is to know when to hedge your bets, which means deciding when to take control and when to relinquish it. There's an important balance:

When to Take Control	When to Relinquish Control
Messaging first on a dating app.	Not checking in again if they don't answer.
Saying hello if you see someone interesting out and about.	Not hovering around if they aren't receptive.
Suggesting a video or phone call before you meet in person.	Exiting the conversation if it's clear they want a text-only buddy.
Asking the person on a date.	Letting them plan or bring up the next date if it feels like it's always you asking.
Saying you had a good time on the date and asking whether they'd want to do it again.	Not asking again if they brushed off your question.
Texting to see how they've been when you haven't heard from them in a bit.	Stopping if you're the only one ever reaching out.
Following up again to see if you have plans after they stopped responding to your texts.	Not sending more than one follow-up text.
Having the DTR convo(s).	Not staying in an undefined relationship if the person couldn't commit within a reasonable time frame and you want more.

This is the moment in your dating life to spend less time ruminating and more time taking calculated risks. Harnessing a CEO mindset for your love life (or life in general!) is extremely powerful. The next time you're at a crossroads, deciding whether you should go on that next date, pursue a relationship, or whatever you have going on, channel that inner CEO to determine who and what to invest in.

WHAT GIVES YOU THE BEST ROI?

Now that you are in the mindset of being in control, how do you allocate your time to optimize your dating experience? In today's dating world, there's always another option or way to meet new people. We often see daters dwelling on whether they should use dating apps or try to meet people in the wild. We strongly believe it doesn't need to be an either-or—especially if you're using your time effectively. Like it or not, technology is here to stay. And last time we checked, dating apps have an excellent track record of helping people find love (according to the Knot, one in four couples meet online!). Part of the frustrations with dating apps stems from feeling like it's a considerable time investment for a poor ROI. We hear daters constantly complain about how much time they spend swiping, resulting in so few dates (or dates they maybe wish they never went on in the first place). So, how do you invest your time more wisely?

We realize this is contrary to the advice given by many dating experts, but here's where we don't think you need to invest as much time as you think you do:

> **Your profile:** We hear people talk of spending hours creating the perfect dating profile, paying thousands of dollars to dating coaches and headshot photographers. We'll be blunt: spending all that time or money won't move the needle. Make sure you have a couple of solid photos and have a friend (preferably of the sex you're trying to attract) look them over to make sure you're accurately portraying yourself. Yes, a solid profile is important to a certain degree, but we see daters spend a disproportionate amount of time in this area

fine-tuning their profiles even when they have plenty of matches! Just get it to a place where you're getting enough traction; there's a point of diminishing returns.

Other people's profiles: Same goes for dissecting other people's profiles. We already established with the Settling Paradox that dating apps are inherently designed to focus on qualities that don't matter. You cannot tell whether someone will be your person just from their profile. And frankly, the last thing you need from a good partner is their ability to create a shiny dating profile (after looking at thousands of profiles, we can assure you that they have no correlation to someone's potential as a good partner!). We tend to make a lot of assumptions that people aren't serious if they don't have a compelling profile. But they could also be new to dating apps because they've been in serious relationships! Even if they don't have the most attractive photos, if you're *attracted enough*, it's worth talking to them further. Remember, your type isn't always your type, or they could be way more attractive IRL (yes, it does happen!).

Opening lines: Would you ever walk up to someone on the street and ask what superpower they'd have in an apocalypse? So why do we feel the need to develop these ultracreative opening lines that often fall flat? We get so stuck on the semantics—what to say, how to approach—that no action happens at all. So get rid of the pressure to say the wittiest opening line ever. We don't overanalyze every word someone says in the real world (and we're pretty sure you'd be psyched if someone attractive came up and said, "Hey!"). Remove the unrealistic expectations on dating apps and focus more on getting to know people.

The best way to efficiently use the apps is to *filter through the conversation*, not the profile. What if you looked at swiping like inviting someone to a house party? You don't need to decide immediately whether they have long-term potential; all you have to do is determine if they look interesting *enough* and if you're attracted *enough*. We promise you this isn't settling; it's simply accepting dating apps for what they are–a way to introduce you to new single people. We're not ones for rules, but we feel strongly about our thirty-second principle: spend no more than thirty seconds on each profile before deciding whether you want to match. This is how you can best work within the limitations of dating apps without wasting your time. In those thirty seconds, you'll get a gut feeling about how their profile speaks to you. You're not scrutinizing every line or every picture; you're looking at the profile vibe as a whole. This will help open up your options, and you can see who stands out through your conversations.

If you're enjoying your interactions with someone, then this is a green light to invest more time and energy. If they're barely responsive and giving you one-word answers, then it's time to cut it off (and aren't you glad you didn't spend an hour imagining a life with this person based on their profile alone?). See who meets your energy and who is willing to put in the effort–even being open to a phone call can weed out the people who want to be your forever pen pal! Get a Google Voice number if you're hesitant to give out your actual number. Nobody has time for a texting black hole–especially you as the CEO of your love life. This progression will help you see who is willing to eventually meet in the real world. Not to mention, it'll allow you to stand out from the other daters stuck at a standstill.

Initiating gives you a considerable advantage on apps. Even saying things such as "I find it a lot easier to chat via text instead of this app. Would you be down to do that?" or "I really want to finish the story, but it may be better for in person or a phone call. Which would you prefer?" helps turn matches into dates. A good rule of thumb is to exchange three to five tidbits you wouldn't have known from the profile (e.g., Why did you move to this city? What got you into this line of work?) and then move the convo off the app. This strikes the right balance: you will establish some sort of rapport, but not too much texting that you enter the stagnant zone. This doesn't mean you have to drive the whole interaction (in fact, that should be a sign to stop investing in this person), but learning to take the initiative in a world where everyone is afraid to make the first move will ultimately save you time, and allow you to invest in the best matches for you.

BDE (Big Dateable Energy):
You control the dating apps; they don't control you.

MAXIMIZING IRL INTERACTIONS

We always get asked: "Why can't I meet someone in real life?" While it seems like it should be so simple, we overcomplicate this one and that's why so few daters attempt IRL connections. There are two key ingredients to successfully meeting people in the wild: (1) an environment conducive to connection; and (2) you being approachable. Think about where it's easy to engage with new people. Where do you feel most in your element? Many daters only go out on the weekends, only to find crowded bars and hang out with the people they came with. Here's a hot take: go out on rainy nights or on a Tuesday. This may seem counterintuitive because fewer people will be out. But that makes it easier to chat with strangers (especially when you can make small talk about braving the torrential downpour).

Also take inventory of where you've *actually* talked to new people you've jived with. Anywhere with friends of friends (think: house parties, birthday parties, group picnics, dinner parties, and park days) tends to be a great bet as you're already connected to the group somehow, and making introductions will be less forced. Or think about places where you'd like to spend time with your future partner (e.g., museums, farmers markets, street fairs). Maybe there will be an instant connection, a reconnection, or simply an expansion of your network. We also like any activity where you consistently see the same people, as we know connection and attraction takes time to build. Maybe it's a weekly hiking group, pickleball, art organization, or a personal development group such as Toastmasters. Perhaps it's creating your own supper club (after all, there's something quite intimate about conversing with strangers over a meal, versus trying to mingle in a large crowd). Have a dinner party at your place and invite everyone bring a platonic plus-one. It's much easier to meet people when it's on your territory. Whatever it is, find something you love doing. Even if you don't find a love interest there, you never know who is in someone's network.

Once you have the environment nailed down, make sure you're approachable. Most of us walk around with "do not talk to me" energy. We're in our own worlds and aren't connecting with the environment around us. How you show up will directly affect your ROI. It doesn't do much to exert all your energy going out to meet new people if you don't look like you *want* to meet people. So be open and *approachable*. Put away your phone. Take out your earbuds. Wear something that can be an instant convo start (maybe that hat from your alma mater or your Coachella T-shirt will be handy after all!). Give off the vibe that you are open to conversation. Go to events alone. Make it a personal challenge to talk to at least one new person. At the minimum, you'll exercise those social muscles. Remember that others want to meet you, too—especially if they're also out in the wild. Recalling Rejection Therapy, harness that "nothing to lose" mindset and view everything as an opportunity for growth. Expanding your IRL strategy is a great way to invest time. Just make sure your meet-cute story doesn't overlook the signs of whether someone is worthy of your time and effort.

SHOULD YOU GO ON ANOTHER DATE?

So you've been on a date or two with someone new. Maybe they have many qualities you're looking for and are in line with your Perfect Partner Equation, but the "chemistry" isn't quite there yet. Perhaps it's unclear whether they have the same values as you, or you're unsure if they get your sense of humor. Remember, early dating is inherently awkward, and establishing a connection takes time. That doesn't mean you need to force a date that isn't clicking, but we like to use the motto "If it's a maybe, it's a yes."

When Maya was in her daterview mode, she went on a date with Tom. Like clockwork, she left after five minutes, citing Tom as "boring." Maya didn't give much thought to Tom until she saw him months later at her rock-climbing gym. She recognized him but couldn't quite place where she knew him from. Tom remembered Maya, though, and asked if she needed someone to spot her. As they were climbing, Maya noticed how helpful and supportive Tom was. She felt safe in his presence. When she finally realized they had gone on a date a few months back, she wondered why she had left so early. Tom was sweet, kind, and low-key funny! Not in the charismatic, boisterous way Maya was used to, but he'd crack a joke every now and then that made Maya chuckle. Of course at this point, Maya didn't know if Tom was her forever person, but she knew he was at least a strong maybe, so therefore, he was a yes.

They had so much fun that they went around the corner for coffee after they finished climbing. Maya learned from Tom that their initial date was his first online date—ever. He was new to dating after ending a five-year relationship with someone who didn't want to get married, but he was ready to take that next step. This time around, they closed down the coffee shop because they were so engrossed in conversation. Maya couldn't remember when she felt so in sync with another person. But most importantly, she felt he brought out the best sides of her, the calm and compassionate Maya. Before they parted ways, it was Maya who asked to see Tom again.

Luckily for Maya, she got a second shot with Tom. At the time of this publication, Maya and Tom are still rock-climbing partners— and so much more. If she was stuck in her Maverick ways, holding people to unattainable standards and not being vulnerable herself, she would have missed out on her best relationship yet. And that's because we're using a date lens when evaluating dates, not looking at the big picture of what makes them a wonderful partner. It's quite ironic that we judge someone's potential based on how much fun we had or whether we felt that elusive chemistry. When you think about it, early dates do not realistically reflect actual life with someone in the slightest. The only thing a date can accurately measure is if you enjoy spending time together. That's it.

So stop overthinking the first few dates! If you're having fun with them and there are no alarming red flags (e.g., signs of physical violence, bigotry, radical beliefs), go on that second date. The behavioral scientist turned dating coach Logan Ury strongly suggests the second-date default. As she shared on *Dateable*, many people are slow burns and don't give off that initial spark—in fact, these are often the type of people who may make great long-term partners. The only question you need to ask yourself on the first few dates is: *Would I enjoy spending more time with this person?* And if your answer is yes, then continue to go with it! If you're unsure, remember *a maybe is a yes* and see how they are in different environments. We suggest a mix of three types of dates: an activity date, an errand date, and a day-trip date. The activity date will assess how well you two experience new things together. Running errands will give you a glimpse of what it's like to do the day-to-day with this person. And planning a day trip will reveal both of your planning (and possibly conflict resolution) skills. By going on a variety of dates, you'll see more sides of the person than if you're going for dinner and drinks every time (or even worse, a movie, where you don't even utter a word to each other). If you're really brave, take a trip to IKEA. You'll see how your date navigates stress in no time! And who knows, that *maybe* may shortly turn into a *hell yes*!

TURN OFF YOUR INTERNAL TRANSLATOR

People tend to tell you the truth in early dating, although we often choose not to hear them. Have you ever had someone outright say they aren't ready for a relationship? We've both made the mistake of taking this on as a challenge to prove our own worthiness. Especially to the Achievers out there, it's a losing battle to try to change someone's mind, convince them to be with you, or not listen to what they're actually saying.

Sometimes people will be blunt about what they are or aren't looking for; other times, it does take you asking the right questions to understand your date better. We had a listener share that our podcast helped her find her person because she stopped asking questions such as "Do you like hiking?" and instead asked "What have you learned about yourself in the last ten years?" She said the variety of responses made it more than clear who was—or wasn't—worth investing in. Not to mention, it helped her stand out and form deeper connections! While we don't want you to go into daterview mode, asking a few more questions from a place of curiosity will help you better understand where they're coming from and what they may be looking for. Just be prepared to answer the same questions yourself!

Whatever they say, you must take it at face value before your "internal translator" steps in. Someone says one thing, and our handy translator tells us what we want to hear. But if we're aware, we can reverse the translator and truly hear people out. Let's try the reversal process:

WHAT THEY SAY: LET'S JUST TAKE THINGS SLOW AND NOT RUSH INTO ANYTHING RIGHT NOW.

WHAT WE HEAR: I'M IN THIS FOR THE LONG HAUL WITH YOU.

NO, REALLY HERE'S WHAT THEY SAID: I'M HAPPY TO STRING YOU ALONG IF YOU LET ME.

So invest in people for who they are today, not for the project you see them as. It's the same idea as the fundamentals in our Perfect Partner Equation: accept people for who they are and not the potential of who they could become. If someone tells you they haven't been emotionally available since their last bad breakup, this is not a sign for you to try to fix them! Also, pay attention to what questions they ask you. People who are relationship minded will show a genuine interest in getting to know you. They ask questions about you. They are responsive to your communications. They make an effort. People who are not interested will not do any of the above, and you can spend your time elsewhere. More later in this chapter.

Yue's Corner

Looking back, I realized my cheating ex had been honest from the start—I just chose not to listen. In our DTR convo three months into our relationship, he expressed commitment issues and didn't want to use labels. I took it as a challenge to prove my worth to him, but the relationship ultimately ended in him doing exactly what he said in the beginning: being unable to commit. Now fast-forward to my current relationship. Three months in, we did a "couples retreat" in Sedona. It was our chance to hash out uncomfortable topics as a newly formed partnership, from finances, to fears, to past relationships—fostering radical honesty. This set the tone for our relationship, allowing us to freely and openly address any issues, concerns, or nagging thoughts. It feels so phenomenally liberating to not have to guess how someone feels about me or try to read their mind.

DON'T BE AFRAID
TO SCARE AWAY THE WRONG PEOPLE

Dating is as much about attracting the right people as it is about filtering out the wrong ones. When you're the CEO of your love life and determining whether to invest in someone, initiating meaningful conversations and telling people what you want is a must. And if that scares someone away, you did your job of filtering out someone not right for you. If the person you've been seeing wants to be exclusive but they aren't quite ready to have the official label, it's still vital that you share what *you* want. We often see daters starting the dreaded DTR convo with "What are we?" or "Where do you see this relationship going?" But it's time to flip the script and put your needs at the forefront. Make sure your intentions are crystal clear, and if someone cannot meet you where you're at–then you'll know that it's okay to let them go. Only that way can you invest in someone else who is ready and capable.

We hear of daters afraid to share their needs because the last thing they want to do is scare away someone promising. But if something is bothering you, or you're experiencing anxiety (or even worse–putting your life on hold!), it's time to speak up. Share what's necessary for you in a relationship to see whether the person you're dating can show up that way. You don't need to say it in an aggressive or confrontational way. Let it be a conversation, and use this information to better understand if this is someone you want to invest your time and energy into. If they can't meet your needs, use this as a data point to gauge whether this relationship is right for you. Their reaction (and further actions) will tell you all. But remember, people aren't mind readers; you need to allow someone the opportunity to step up first! And if they can't? Then, don't hold on to people failing to meet you where you want.

So tell that person you're dating what qualities you look for in a partner and how you want to communicate. Do you like waking up to a good morning text? Share that. Hate getting bombarded by text messages? Suggest chatting over the phone or waiting to see each other in person for the big stuff. When you share what you need from a partner, it's like giving someone a map to your heart, and if they fall off the map, you know they weren't the right person for you. Investing is about attracting, not chasing. It's not about putting demands on people but rather setting them up for success.

Julie's Corner

Right before meeting my current partner, I experienced a whirlwind connection with someone from a dating app. We were both counting down the days until my return from the holidays, but as soon as I came back, he was suddenly too busy with work. I found myself initiating all the texts, waiting for him to be free. Then I caught myself: I wanted someone who prioritized spending time with me! If he couldn't find an hour to meet up, this was not the right person. So I sent him a message sharing that I was looking for someone who could prioritize a relationship and if that wasn't him right now that was okay. He could reach out when work calmed down, but I couldn't guarantee I'd be available then. He responded nicely and wished me the best. I was expecting this response, but it felt empowering to stand my ground. And soon after, I met my partner, who consistently treated me like a priority.

ARE THEY A GOOD PARTNER
OR LOVE BOMBING?

So where's the line between someone who shows interest and prioritizes you and someone who shows *too much* interest? We've all been warned about "love bombing," which, according to the Cleveland Clinic, is a form of psychological and emotional abuse that involves a person going above and beyond to manipulate you into a relationship with them. And once they've gained your trust, the switch can flip, and this person can suddenly belittle, control, or devalue you. Attention from the person you like is a good thing, but trust your gut when you feel like you're being showered with over-the-top behavior that feels overwhelming or insincere. Many dating-app scams often start this way (remember Tinder Swindler, how strong that guy came on before asking the women to wire him money?).

When we talked to Dr. Diane Strachowski on *Dateable* (better known as the Back to Love Doc), she shared that even she (as a therapist!) was susceptible to manipulation. Before her husband, she dated a man who sent her two dozen roses every day when they first met. But those roses had thorns. Often, excessive gifts or words of affirmation are a way for someone to gain leverage as they want something in return. In Dr. Diane's case, she found herself eventually watching this man's children as the makeshift second parent without ever agreeing to take on this responsibility. So are we supposed to question everyone who sends us flowers? Of course not. We're not saying this to be skeptical about everyone you meet, but pay attention if something doesn't feel right. Dr. Diane shared her DANGER signs to look out for:

- D: defensive
- A: attention seeking
- N: neglect
- G: gaslighting
- E: empathy failure
- R: rebound quickly

Sometimes, you can see the signs quickly; other times, it's not clear immediately. Drea was dating this new guy who seemed so great at the beginning. A mutual friend introduced them, but since she lived in DC and he was in San Francisco, their relationship started virtually. He took the initiative to schedule regular Zoom dates with thoughtful themes for discussion. He even ordered her DoorDash so they could have their first dinner date! By the end of their third virtual date, he confessed that he was already falling for her and had never met someone who made him feel this way. As the Dreamer she was, Drea was over the moon!

After about a month of doing video dates and daily phone calls, they decided to spend the weekend together in San Francisco, which happened to be the weekend before Drea's birthday. She was ecstatic and felt this was the start of her great love story. As she was getting on the plane, she got a text from him with a link to a spreadsheet. He had a robust plan of his favorite places, scheduled down to the minute. Drea was looking forward to this weekend but also wanted to carve out some time to see the friends she hadn't seen in years. She requested a few adjustments to the plan, and he seemed agreeable. She ended the text with a kissy-face emoji and thought about how lucky she was to be with someone so thoughtful.

Her first day in San Francisco was magical. She met his friends and coworkers for happy hour downtown, they shared a four-course Italian dinner in Nob Hill, and even took a trip to the top of Twin Peaks, where they had their first kiss. The next day, when Drea shared her plans to meet up with friends, his attitude completely flipped. He made her feel like she was deprioritizing him and that if her friends cared about her, they wouldn't steal her away. He was adamant about doing everything as planned, with total control over the situation. Drea chalked it up to his enthusiasm to be with her. She canceled plans with her friends, and they had a great rest of the weekend.

It wasn't until she was back in DC, on her birthday, that she noticed the real DANGER signs. This was the only day he didn't call or text her—despite knowing it was her birthday (Neglect). But when she asked him about it the next day, he responded with "Oh, I've been busy, and I already wished you a happy birthday last week" (Defensive + Empathy failure). He turned it around on her, saying that it wasn't necessary to wish someone a happy birthday on the actual day and that she was overreacting (Gaslighting). But to make her feel better, he was going to send her a present in the mail (Attention seeking). Two days later, a teakettle was delivered by Amazon, something she had never expressed a need or interest in. His gift message was, "Hope some tea will calm you. Happy Birthday!" It was clear from those events that he had no interest in Drea or creating a relationship with her; he just wanted to fill the role of "girlfriend" in a relationship that only suited himself. Less than a month later, he was already in a new relationship (Rebound quickly).

In the past, Drea may have not noticed the signs—or chosen not to see them. It was easier to stay in her fantasy world than to accept reality. But Drea now knew she wanted to feel valued in a relationship because she had her Perfect Partner Equation in mind. Fundamental: he was putting himself first and not focusing on any of Drea's needs. Feeling: she felt deprioritized and belittled by his behavior. Future: she could not picture a relationship with someone who would dismiss her needs so quickly. It was so clear he was not an ideal partner for her. In fact, this birthday experience gave her déjà vu: her ex-husband would take her out for her birthday to a restaurant *he* liked, or to go see a show *he* wanted, but never did anything to make her feel special—even on the day dedicated to her! For the first time in her life, she recognized that she didn't want to repeat that relationship and wanted to be with someone who put in as much effort as she did. Someone who cared for her in a way that showed they truly knew her. Someone who would give to her freely and do whatever they could to make *her* happy, not just go through the motions to fulfill their own needs.

So, how do you know whether someone is genuinely interested in you? They will prioritize you in their actions. People can talk a big game (plenty of future fakers out there), but if they can't deliver on their promises, they're not proving to be a good partner. Relationships take time, and people take time to reveal themselves. Some even say there's a "three-month-rule," which is about the point when a new partner can't keep hiding their potentially abusive, toxic, and manipulative behaviors. We're not saying this to scare you but to be realistic: people tend to be on their best behavior early on. Each new experience of getting to know someone is an opportunity to ensure this relationship serves *you*, especially in these early stages. And the minute it isn't, you can always change your investment strategy.

BDE (Big Dateable Energy):
Actions speak louder than words,
but patterns speak the loudest.

THE ONLY SEVEN THINGS THAT MATTER

With all that said, how can you determine if someone could be the real deal? Maybe you've been dating for a few months and wondering if you should DTR. In our ten years of talking to couples who made it through the dating BS and our own experiences of finding great loves, we've come to understand that there are only seven things that matter when evaluating if someone could be a great partner:

1. **They are consistent.** Do they text when they say they will? Do they follow through with plans? Is their temperament even-keeled, or do you never know what side of them you'll see tomorrow? Too often, we let this stuff slide early on or justify it throughout a relationship. Consistency is the baseline for any healthy partnership—and the foundation of feeling safe and secure. You're not waiting for their text because you already have

consistent communication. You're not worried they won't ask you out again, as they've made it clear they want to be with you. You're not concerned about them ghosting you or ending things out of the blue, as you know where you stand. There's nothing to dissect with your friends, because there's nothing to figure out. When consistency happens, you can focus on the fun parts of being with someone new: getting to know them and creating inside jokes and memories—the stuff that leads to falling in love. Consistency is so important because it builds momentum. If consistent behavior isn't happening (or there isn't a damn good explanation), nothing else on this list even matters.

2. **They bring out the best sides of you.** While we're all so multifaceted, with different parts of our personalities, a good partner will consistently bring out the best in us. Relationships are an additive to your life and should nurture your personal growth. This is often ignored in early dating because we think anxiety comes with the territory. However, it is concerning if you're constantly feeling insecure around someone and even worse when they're *not* around. While we can't blame the other person entirely (there's therapy to work on that!), we can see it as a sign that this isn't the right relationship for us. Some people trigger us in ways that aren't healthy or sustainable. Find the person that makes you feel like your best self.

3. **There's sexual chemistry.** Let's get real; for most of us, sex is the difference between a friend and a romantic partner. We discussed with the sex therapist and author of *She Comes First*, Dr. Ian Kerner, the importance of sex through the years of a long-term partnership. Yet he saw so many people deprioritize sex and attraction (mainly hetero men!), succumbing to the belief that you stop having sex after marriage. Dr. Kerner shared

that sex is the glue that holds relationships together; there shouldn't be shame in saying this is necessary for you. You do not need to have intense sexual chemistry right off the bat, but there needs to be a willingness to prioritize your special bond through intimacy. After all, being attracted to your partner is a must. Word of caution here: sex can't be the *only* thing you two have going on.

4. **They pass the Sunday test.** A lot of being in a long-term relationship is doing nothing together. Dates can be glamorous when you're out at a trendy bar or restaurant, but what happens when life settles in? The true test is when you're lying on the couch, running errands at Costco, or just having morning coffee on the balcony. Do you genuinely enjoy spending time with this person, or are you with them out of fear of being alone? With all the distractions and activities removed, does it bring peace to be around them? The baseline of a relationship is friendship—so can you picture building a friendship with this person while doing life together?

5. **They can navigate conflict with you.** When we chatted with the therapist Vienna Pharaon and her husband, the men's relationship coach Connor Beaton, about how to have a healthy relationship, our conversation went to a place we weren't expecting: navigating conflict. When there's friction (because there will be), you need someone who can be accountable instead of playing the blame game. Conflict is inevitable and will become a massive block if your partner doesn't take ownership and grow with you. Even in early dating, mini-conflicts are unavoidable. Share how you feel and see whether they welcome the conversation or run away. Do they genuinely want to seek understanding, or do they blow up when you broach the topic? Can you voice your needs calmly,

or are you walking on eggshells around them? These are all great data points for emotional maturity and availability. As Connor Beaton would say, "Find someone you can do conflict with." And even if someone (including yourself) hasn't found the best path to navigating conflict yet, what matters is that you both are committed to making it work. Instead of bailing when there's a fight or when times get tough, you push through together.

6. **They're aligned on what you're looking for.** You can't change someone. For a partnership to work, you must have similar expectations and goals for the relationship. This goes back to your Dating North Star. Even if you're not 100 percent sure about the semantics, what's more important is how you both see the relationship operating. What kind of culture do you both want to create? Are you aligned on the general vision of your relationship? For example, do you see building a family? Would you be open to moving elsewhere? What do you prioritize the most in the life you build together? And this is not a onetime assessment. You'll need to revisit these questions regularly to ensure you're heading down the same path. Overall, you want to feel on the same page as your partner so you can make decisions together.

7. **They want to be with you.** The right partner does not need to be convinced you're right for them. You can tell when you're a priority to someone—even in early dating when you're just getting to know each other. They're eager to make time for you. Reaching out to see how your day went. Showing you their favorite spots to invite you into their world. They're factoring you into their life by making space for you. The last thing you want to be doing is proving yourself to this person, competing for their attention. Recognize

when you're acting like their PR agent, overjustifying when you're not getting enough of their time or energy. At the end of the day, we all want to feel supported and valued. Especially by the person we're trying to build a life with!

By checking in on these seven things, it becomes increasingly clear who is worth investing more time and energy into. Energizers, this will help you take a beat and be more intentional about who you give your heart to. Even though the seven things serve as a baseline for investing in someone, understand you're still taking a gamble. All relationships are about taking a leap of faith. As relationships progress—whether for one week, one month, or one year—you'll continue to learn about the person you're with. We're all afraid to define the relationship out of making the wrong choice. If it's feeling good with someone—take the chance! True compatibility can only be determined when two individuals commit to nurturing the relationship.

> **BDE (Big Dateable Energy):**
> Find someone who treats you like a priority, not an option.

INVEST IN PEOPLE WHO INVEST IN YOU

If you can remember one thing from this chapter: focus your attention on those who match your energy. It's okay (in fact, good!) to be selective if you're selective on what matters. For example, saying you only want to invest in people who show up for you. So when they're down to text but never want to lock in a plan, you know that this person isn't in line with what you want. If you're looking through the lens of the seven things that matter, a potential partner who is lukewarm about hanging out isn't as much of a catch. If you have too many people messaging you on the apps (a good problem!), see who is consistent in their communication, who is taking the initiative, and who is receptive to your messages. It shows you have standards of how you want to be treated. Dating will be a lot more enjoyable if you aren't constantly spinning your wheels on the wrong people. You now have the confidence to determine whether someone is a fit for the right reasons! Understand that people don't fall into your life if you don't invite them in. You choose who you spend your time with, so choose wisely.

Once you find someone worth investing in, you may want to know whether this person is your forever person. The reality is that you may never know. Forever is daunting and unpredictable. Relationships reveal themselves in stages, so we encourage a more incremental approach. At the start of the relationship, the stakes are different than two years down the road, so once you get into a relationship, it's not set it and forget it. Every day, you both choose *how* to make this relationship work. Relationships can be right until they're not. Understand that investing is a continuous process where you can constantly evaluate if this person is right for you and whether you're meeting each other's needs.

If we know this, why does dating seem to take such an all-or-nothing approach? For instance, start-ups love working in sprints, which are short, time boxed periods (a strategy made popular by agile project management). Instead of trying to tackle a massive project at once, they break it down into dedicated sprints, with each time period incrementally taking the project closer to completion. Translating this idea into dating, we have a tactic we like to call the renewal period, where you and your partner can have conscious check-ins during whatever time period makes sense for your relationship (every three months, six months, etc.). Within that period, you set intentions and goals on how to deepen your relationship. When it's time to renew together, you can decide whether you want to continue this relationship for whatever further increment you've decided on—or recognize that while your time together was great, it wasn't intended to be forever. This should never be a surprise, though; this approach is grounded in open communication and being intentional with each other.

For Thinkers like Tori, breaking the relationship into these shorter sprints helps curb overthinking. It's been almost three months since Tori's museum date with Susanne, and they are hitting their first renewal period. In the past, Tori would have gotten in her head, wondering: *What if we fall out of love? What if we get married but then get divorced? What if something happens and Susanne changes?* Sure, all this *could* happen. But there is truly no way to know outside of evaluating as you go. Being in this sprint mentality keeps Tori in the confines of how she feels about the relationship *today*. She realized she didn't have to decide right now if Susanne was her forever person. She didn't have to stress about whether this relationship would last; she knew they'd have an open conversation to decide *together*. She may not fully know what the future holds, but she knows that Susanne makes her happy and is worth investing more in. Only with time will she know if their relationship is meant for a reason, a season, or a lifetime.

A healthy relationship requires both partners to invest time, energy, and resources. If you're dating someone mature and communicative—who wants to be with you as much as you want to be with them—even when the other shoe drops, you will have the tools to catch it! Dating and building a relationship with someone takes effort, but it becomes much easier when you have someone as invested as you in trying to make it work.

KEY TAKEAWAYS

1. You're the CEO of your love life. You can choose who, what, and where you invest your time and energy that's aligned with your Dating North Star.

2. It doesn't need to be either/or if you're using dating apps or meeting people IRL; optimizing each for the best ROI is more important.

3. First dates are inherently awkward. In those early days, base your decisions on *Do I enjoy spending time with this person?* That's it.

4. Don't be afraid to scare away the wrong people! State your needs. Say you want a committed relationship if you want one. This will only filter out the people who can't meet you where you're at.

5. The Only Seven Things That Matter is your ultimate gut check! Pair this with your Perfect Partner Equation to ground your decisions about someone and determining if they're worth investing in.

Chapter 9:

Persevering Through It All

IT'S TIME TO DISCOVER:

1. **The Inner Medium:** That voice telling you that what you're seeking is right around the corner.
2. **Your Love Army:** Your people who provide encouragement and support through your dating challenges.
3. **Masturdating:** The art of dating yourself, so you can fall in love with who you are and what you bring to a relationship.

So you've made it this far! You've let go of what's holding you back, gained clarity on what you need, assessed how you're showing up for dates, and learned tactics to invest in the right people. The last step is perseverance. As you probably know all too well, it's hard to meet the right person. While we wish they'd magically show up tomorrow, there's an element of dating that's purely out of our control: when and where you'll finally cross paths with that person who becomes *your* person.

As we established, challenges can be a good thing, but it's not to minimize how hard dating can be. We tend to get caught up in all the problematic aspects–the dates that don't go anywhere, the

promising prospect who suddenly vanishes, and even the relationship we thought was it but wasn't. These challenges can be extremely
demotivating, making it hard to keep dating.

So humor us for a minute as we try a different approach:

What if we told you that you'd meet your person within the next
year? What would you do differently? How would that change how
you showed up? You may be skeptical at first, but our guess is that
you'd feel this lightness that would allow you to approach dating in
a much more confident way. You'd be less attached to the outcome
of every situation because it was just a matter of when–not if–you
would meet your person.

When Julie finally ended her on-again, off-again relationship
with her ex (the one she believed for so many years was "the One"),
she was unclear about her romantic future. Lucky for her, we had a
medium and intuitive dating coach, Nikki Novo, as a guest on *Dateable* who gave us both readings before the interview. One of the first
things Nikki noted was that Julie was so close–her person was right
around the corner, and they would meet this coming year before her
next birthday. But! She would first go through a difficult period that
may feel turbulent, filled with the wrong people. She could risk getting jaded unless she accepted this was part of the process. To stay
on the path to finding her person, she needed to remain hopeful and
not let these experiences deter her. Then Nikki uttered three magical
words that stayed with Julie: "Just keep going." This gave her the
ammunition to move forward even when times were tough, and not
lose sight of what she really wanted.

You can believe in mediums or not, but approaching dating with
the "my person is right around the corner" mindset is game-changing.
It gives you the confidence to go into every date less attached to the
outcome, because you know your person is coming eventually. And
in the meantime, you're learning about yourself and trying different
experiences. This isn't about engaging in toxic positivity and sup-

pressing your emotions; it's more understanding that nothing in life is permanent. All you can do is believe that what's meant for you will come. Even if you have a more logical brain, the odds of eventually finding someone are highly in your favor if you're prioritizing dating (which we're pretty sure you're doing if you've made it this far!). Dating is a long game and your story is far from over. You get to see what each chapter unfolds; how much more exciting is that? While you can't control everything in dating (e.g., when you'll meet your person), you can control your mindset. And that's what separates the sea of daters: from the ones stuck in the same endless loop to the ones rising above.

So, as you embark on this journey, we want you to channel that inner medium, that voice telling you it will all be okay and you'll meet that person very soon. Because at the end of the day, we're optimistic about love and hope you are, too. We know you can have the love life you've always wanted, especially now that you're armed with everything from this book. We're not going to give you clichéd advice like "It'll happen when you least expect it" or "You'll find love when you stop searching for it," but we will leave you with some truths to remember as you keep going on your journey.

YOU'RE ON THE RIGHT PATH

When you've been on yet another date that doesn't pan out, or the relationship you thought was your forever person turns out not to be, your mind can question whether you're headed in the wrong direction. But the road to love is not linear, and setbacks are inevitable. As Nikki told Julie, it's pivotal to recognize and understand this is all par for the course. Now that you have your Dating North Star, you can feel confident that you're on the right path, even if there's a major setback or occasional bump in the road. You know where you're headed–even if the person you're seeing ends up not being along for the ride. And when you think about it: why give your power to someone who ghosted you or decided you weren't the right fit? Yes, rejection stings, but it's only temporary. When you can see past rejection as a reflection of who you are (goodbye, Validation Trap, we're not falling for that!), you'll start seeing it as a way to clear out the wrong people to make space for the right one.

But we get it: even if you intellectually understand this, it can be hard to stay positive while dating, especially when you've experienced the pain love can bring. When it comes to matters of the heart, we can't escape the occasional heartbreaks, setbacks, and disappointments. Instead of seeing that instance where you "wasted time" with the wrong person as taking you off path, how can you reframe each experience as leading you in the right direction? For instance, if you keep getting rejected, could it mean that you're taking more chances and putting yourself out there, which is actually getting you closer to the relationship you want? If your marriage or serious partnership didn't work out, could you see this as an opportunity for an even greater second shot at love? It's easy to throw in the towel when dating, relationships, and love feel painful, but this is when the true transformation happens. The more you recognize setbacks as a step in the *right* direction, the easier it'll be to keep going. And that's when the magic happens.

In the world of strength training, there's a fascinating concept known as hypertrophy. It involves the growth of muscle cells through intense workouts that push the muscles to their limits, causing damage to the muscle fibers. If you want to strengthen your muscles, you must first subject them to this kind of damage. It's an intriguing parallel to the realm of love. Just like how you need to push your muscles to their limits to make them stronger, you often have to push your love to its limits, even at the risk of experiencing some damage along the way. To truly embrace a profound and extraordinary love, you may find yourself facing heartbreak as a prerequisite. You might need to weather a few storms before you can have the love you've always wanted. Here's the remarkable part: you're not starting over; you're starting with invaluable experience. Because a broken heart builds a stronger heart.

We'd love to shield ourselves from these emotional damages, but let's face it: the most profound lessons we learn often come from those gut-wrenching breakups that no self-help article or assessment can prepare you for. Dating is all about those relational skills we develop through interactions with real, live humans. You can do all the self-improvement in the world on your own, but if you don't put it into practice, it's like being a med school grad who's never practiced on actual patients. It's scary to take a leap of faith, whether it's asking someone out, defining the relationship, or dropping those three powerful words, "I love you." Because, hey, there's always that chance of getting hurt. But you know what's even scarier? Not taking any of these risks at all. Sure, you won't face rejection if you never ask someone out, and you won't experience heartbreak if you avoid relationships altogether. But then you'll live a life paralyzed by fear, missing out on the greatness of human connection. So, how can you reframe these perceived setbacks to help you propel forward? How would your behavior change today if you actually welcomed heartbreak?

Know that you're on the right path, even if, at times, it feels like you're taking a detour. We wish we could tell you the secret to avoiding heartbreak, but there isn't one. Frameworks such as the Only Seven Things That Matter will lead you to the right person to be in a relationship with. But once you're in a relationship, it becomes a choice between two people to make it work. There's always a chance that you'll meet someone fantastic—only to discover over time that they're not the right person. The truth is that someone is right for you until they choose not to be. And the same applies to you! If someone hurts or betrays you, it doesn't always mean you picked wrong. It just means the relationship has run its course. You're still on the right path; you've just rerouted a bit.

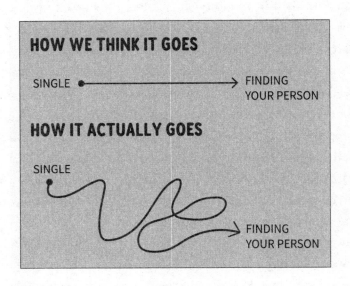

In the grand scheme of things, heartbreak serves a purpose: it puts us back on track. We may not always have control over what happens to us, but we do have control over how we respond and grow from those setbacks. It's all about cultivating resilience to bounce back and radiate even more brightly than before. If we can shift our perspective and view disappointments as opportunities to expand our hearts, we can move forward with newfound strength and wisdom. Remember, your life is unfolding exactly as it's meant to be. Embrace every experience in your love life–the ups and the downs–especially when you know you've shown up authentically and given your all. This approach is far more productive than succumbing to the inner critic that whispers "you're destined to be alone." The truth is, even the most prepared among us may face setbacks in our love lives. But what truly matters is how we overcome them. So practice self-compassion and remind yourself that whatever happens doesn't define your self-worth. Don't let the wrong partner discourage you from finding the right one. You're on the right path: it just may zigzag a bit more than you think it should.

> **BDE (Big Dateable Energy):**
> Expansion of the heart is always pushing you in the right direction.

YOU'RE NOT ALONE

One of the reasons dating can be such a challenging journey is that it can bring an overwhelming sense of loneliness. When times get tough, having a solid support system can make all the difference. We had one of our community members, Lakshmi, share about her own "Love Army," a hand-selected group of people who provide encouragement and support through her dating journey. You, too, can surround yourself with a group of people who will be there to guide, encourage, and uplift you throughout the challenges of dating. Your Love Army can be made up of your closest friends, family members, and trusted professionals such as doctors, therapists, or even your trainer, who can give you some tough love, but always with kindness. We absolutely adore this concept because let's face it, dating can feel incredibly isolating, especially when it seems like everyone else has it all figured out. But guess what? You're not alone! By building a supportive network of your own people, you gain valuable perspectives and fortify your resilience in the face of challenging times. Don't hesitate to gather your Love Army and let them lift you up when you need it most. Together, you can navigate the dating world with a whole lot more strength.

You get to decide who is the best to support you, but here are a few key members we'd recommend considering for your Love Army:

Couples as mentors: We could all use an excellent example of a healthy relationship; if you intentionally look for it, you will see examples around you. Seek out a couple you admire and spend more time with them. Learn how they've overcome difficult times while still strengthening their partnership.

Uplifting friends and family: As much as misery loves company, we cannot always surround ourselves with Negative Nancies. It'll just drag you down. Instead, identify the people in your life who energize you and offer a fresh perspective. That kind of uplifting and empowering energy is contagious. While venting is absolutely necessary sometimes it's important to get out of the endless negativity cycle.

Accountability partner(s): Find people who are in a similar phase of dating. This is why our online community Big Dateable Energy has been so instrumental for our listeners. The members offer positive support and act as sounding boards to help one another. You'll quickly see that you're never alone in your situation and learn from others who have overcome whatever you're going through. You can even share this book and discuss with your accountability partners!

Professional help: Whether it's a licensed therapist, counselor, dating coach, or other type of professional, investing in people whose job is to help and support you is imperative. Sometimes the only way out is through; you need to talk to someone with the proper training to effectively guide you. In addition, professionals can help you develop effective coping strategies to build resilience.

Your pets: Maybe they can't always talk, but pets show you a certain unconditional love. They can open your heart in ways you never imagined. There's a reason why pets are often emotional support animals!

Your support system is here to constantly remind you of your immeasurable worth, offer an empathetic ear, and, above all, ensure you never lose sight of what you truly desire. Because at the end of the day, someone is lucky to be with you. If you've made it this far in the book, we know you have a lot to give to a relationship. When you've been through the ringer with dating, it's easy to lose track of that. So lean on the people who know you best. They'll remind you of all you have to offer and assure you that if the person you're dating doesn't see that, then it's their loss, and something better for you is around the corner.

SELF-LOVE PRECEDES RELATIONAL LOVE

When we first started *Dateable*, our expectations were centered around stories of two individuals coming together, forging connections, and navigating the world of dating. We believed that by uncovering the secret dating tactics, tricks, and meet-cutes, we would find the ultimate answer. However, as the years went by, a major realization dawned upon us: the key to finding love lies in loving oneself first. Yes, we're aware it may sound like a cliché, but when we reflect on all the incredible daters we've had the privilege of talking to, we discovered a common thread. Each one of them had done the necessary work to cultivate their own happiness, regardless of whether they had a partner by their side.

While it's not necessarily true to say you're single because you don't love yourself enough, persevering through the ups and downs of dating will be that much easier if you're in a good place. When your cup is full, you're able to give that much more to someone else. Loving yourself is not as simple as reading an Instagram quote set over a video of the Maldives. It's an everyday practice. And it starts with some of the basics we tend to overlook, such as:

- Prioritizing yourself and what's important to you
- Being compassionate, kind, less judgmental, and more accepting toward yourself
- Giving yourself grace and forgiveness
- Talking about yourself in a loving way
- Setting healthy boundaries
- Practicing self-care and carving out time to recharge
- Being true to yourself
- Spending time with people who fill your cup

Self-love starts with self-compassion. If we can't treat ourselves well, how can we expect others to? We spoke with Ken Page, psychotherapist and author of *Deeper Dating*, on *Dateable* and he shared that the qualities we're often most ashamed of and try to hide are the key to finding real love. These are our core gifts that may arise when we feel we are too much or not enough. When we see these qualities as gifts, we can start to understand, honor, and treasure the many parts of ourselves. These gifts are the very essence of who we are—the places where we feel the deepest and yearn to express our most authentic selves. However, it's fascinating how we often run away from these gifts because they have been the source of our greatest wounds.

Think about it: have you ever been told by someone that you're "too much" of something or that you need to "tone it down" in certain areas? Well, friends, those are precious clues pointing right at your core gifts. Maybe you view your sensitivity and emotional nature as a hindrance to finding love. However, when you start recognizing these traits as core gifts—testaments to your ability to love deeply and genuinely—you can see what you bring to the table. Another example might be if you think you are too independent to be in a relationship (hey, Mavericks!). When you can start to see this fierce independence as your core gift—your love for life and personal growth–you can attract others who celebrate your gift. Embracing these core gifts allows us to attract individuals who appreciate and honor the essence of who we are. So, let us remember that our uniqueness, even in the face of societal expectations, can be our greatest asset in finding the love we deserve.

The more we embrace and love ourselves, the more we radiate that self-acceptance. And you know what happens then? We attract partners who do the same. Partners who appreciate and celebrate our core gifts. Partners who are truly good for us. And if they don't? It's as if those people unknowingly waved a flag saying, "I'm not the right fit for you!"

So take a moment to reflect on these two important questions:

> What is something about yourself
> that you genuinely love and admire?

> How can you show yourself that same
> love and appreciation today?

No matter what twists and turns unfold in your love life, there's one relationship that stands above all others–your relationship with yourself. You hold the power to control how you treat yourself and allow others to treat you. Advocating for yourself and speaking up become paramount because, let's face it, if you don't do it, who will? You are the one person you can count on for life, so it's essential to prioritize yourself. As we explored with the Validation Trap, seeking external love and acceptance becomes far less important when you've already cultivated it within. So, when that person you're into unexpectedly ghosts you, yes, it'll sting, but you'll rise above it. Your life will move forward because you recognize that your worth extends far beyond any one person's actions. Instead of feeling compelled to delete dating apps or give up on finding love, you'll remain resilient. You know that someday, you will find someone who loves you as deeply as you love yourself.

YOUR DREAM LIFE STARTS NOW

Many of us think that life begins only after we find that special someone. We believe that's when we can finally check off everything we've been dreaming of. Life is happening right *now*, whether you have a partner or not. Dating can feel so painful because we see it as a means to an end. But what if you can start living the life you want to live today? Right now?

Imagine the weight lifted off your shoulders if you could release the pressure of thinking that dating is the sole ticket to your happiness. When we remove that unnecessary burden, the whole process becomes more enjoyable and sustainable. One of the beloved pastimes within the *Dateable* community is what we affectionately call "masturdating." Now, get your mind out of the gutter (although, hey, self-love in all its forms is totally valid!). Masturdating is all about embracing your solo time and actively engaging with life, rather than sitting idly, waiting for sh*t to happen. It's a journey of self-discovery, where you take yourself out on dates and truly get to know and appreciate the wonderful person you are.

As you recall from Drea's recent love bombing situation where the guy she dated didn't take her into account in any of his planning, our resident Dreamer finally had the revelation that she was investing in people who weren't investing in her. She decided to take a much-needed break from dating and focus on the most important relationship of all: the one with herself. In the past, she had a habit of postponing her life while waiting for the perfect partner. But as she prioritized living life to the fullest, she finally began pursuing the interests she had long put on hold. Learning to surf was one of those dreams that Drea had always envisioned sharing with a future partner. She imagined the two of them laughing hysterically as they clumsily struggled to stay on the surfboard. It was during a solo surfing adventure to Costa Rica that she had an eye-opening realization.

During her very first surf lesson, something remarkable happened. Drea laughed so uncontrollably that she almost peed her pants. In that hilarious moment, she couldn't help but wonder, *Why on earth did I delay experiencing such pure joy while waiting for a romantic partner?* It was from this experience that Drea unlocked the door to her own happiness. For the first time, she didn't have a fear of ending up alone, because she was too busy falling in love with herself. At the time of writing this book, Drea is still on her dating sabbatical, but she's using the time intentionally to get clearer on her needs and desires, and who she is to the core. We're confident that when she returns to the dating scene, she'll be able to put her needs at the forefront and attract someone willing to give to the relationship as much as she is. Now that's the rom-com ending we've been waiting for!

What are some ways you can start masturdating? Here are some questions to help you get your list started:

What's one thing you truly love to do? Think about what brings you joy and how you can do that more—and in ways you haven't tried yet. For example, if you know you love to dance and already go to dance classes, have you considered joining a dance retreat? If you love vintage shopping, have you considered joining the local vintage community? If you know you're passionate about climate change, have you considered creating content with other activists?

What have you been wanting to do or try but thought you would save for a date? What have you been putting off for when you get into a relationship? Go do it now! If you've hesitated to travel solo, as it felt like a "coupley" thing to do, book that trip! You may discover a side of yourself that you really love—and realize you make a great travel buddy!

What's something you think you need the courage to do by yourself? Are you open to doing this soon? For instance, do you want to try that new sushi spot everyone's been raving about but you're afraid to go on your own? Find a spot at the bar and bring a book to read (may we suggest this one?). Don't forget to look up from time to time; you never know who else is there, too!

Yes we hear those of you asking: What if I get too good at being alone? What if I lose the desire to even be in a relationship? First of all, there's nothing wrong with choosing to stay single. But being happy on your own puts you in the best place possible for a relationship. You're now coming into dating without trying to fill a void. You'll be more discerning with who you let into your life because you know your time is valuable. If you know you'll have a bangin' Friday night even in your own company, you won't feel so desperate to reach out to the person who treats you like an option, not a priority.

It's natural to feel a sense of trepidation about being alone, as the fear of loneliness often looms over us. However, it's important to distinguish between loneliness and solitude. Loneliness stems from a place of lack, where joy is contingent upon the presence of someone else. Solitude, however, is a conscious choice to spend time in your own company—a period of well-spent moments. In a physical sense, both loneliness and solitude involve being by yourself. But the mental state associated with solitude is one of control and empowerment. You *choose* to schedule alone time so you can be with yourself. You *choose* to prioritize your own well-being by finding hobbies, activities, personal goals, or rituals that nurture you. Solitude is a beautiful act of self-prioritization, an opportunity to replenish your energy and find solace within yourself.

If you're looking for the secret to love, this is it: a full life will make you less dependent on dating for fulfillment and happiness, which puts you in the best position to attract a partner. When the time eventually comes for you to encounter that special someone, you'll have so many magnificent experiences to share. There's an irresistible allure to individuals who have crafted a fulfilling existence for themselves. Don't wait for a partner to unlock the doors to your dreams. Start living your life to the fullest right now, because you deserve it. Remember, dating is merely one chapter of your journey, not the entire story. When you make yourself happy, you no longer need a partner, you simply want one.

Julie's Corner

A significant turning point for me was when I was happy being single. Over the years, I got more and more comfortable being on my own, but it wasn't until the pandemic that I felt totally at ease. I had that initial freak-out of being isolated, but then I had an epiphany: If this is life on my own, then it isn't so freaking bad. In fact, it's great! I got the opportunity to slow down, do activities that nurtured my soul, and bring a bit more balance to my life. When it was time to date again, the whole experience felt more enjoyable. I built up so much confidence by knowing myself and building a life I loved that I knew a relationship would only be additive. Being happy on my own also allowed me to recognize situations that weren't serving me. Fear was no longer driving my decisions. And when I finally did meet my partner, I knew it was right because he made my already great life even better.

DATING IS JUST A SLICE OF YOUR LIFE

Have you ever gone out with a friend who was too busy checking out the scene to be present with you? It's the worst, right? And if you're that person, all it does is burn you out (especially if you don't find anyone you like!), and it certainly doesn't make you an enjoyable person to be around. When we talked to the author Amy Spencer on *Dateable* about meeting your *media naranja* (translation: your "half orange" or your sweetheart, the perfect other half), she gave very unconventional dating advice: stop trying so hard. If your goal is to be in a relationship to be happy, why not beeline for the happy now? As someone who would plan her life around singles events, Amy realized she was not nourishing herself with the people and activities she loved. She was losing herself in dating. As soon as she started focusing on what gave her joy, she began radiating the energy that eventually brought her now husband. She met him at a small film screening she attended with her mom—an event she would have deprioritized before when she was relentlessly searching for love.

We couldn't agree with Amy more: your life doesn't have to revolve around dating to find your person. For so long, our (former) serial dater Eli would jump at every opportunity that he could as an Energizer. But after getting clear on what he wanted (from a partner and life) and getting a reality check of how disconnected he was on dates, Eli had a major awakening to schedule dates around his life, not the other way around. So when his long-term crush Paul asked him out for *this* Thursday, he politely turned him down, as he already had plans with his siblings for their weekly dinner. The old Eli would have dropped everything to go on a date with Paul. But instead, he offered another time he would be free. Sure, he had the fleeting thoughts *What if he's not available by next week? What if someone snatches him up?* But the new Eli knew that his life came first, and he wanted to honor his prior commitments (plus he was looking forward to catching up with his siblings!). If a romantic prospect couldn't wait a week to see him, he knew it wasn't the right fit. To his surprise, Paul was happy to meet Eli the next week and found it attractive that he put his family first. As we're writing this, Eli and Paul had a great first date and continue to see each other, exclusively. While he really likes Paul, Eli continues to prioritize his life with Paul in it.

Eli realized he needed to balance dating with other parts of his life to have a sustainable dating strategy. Not only is dating time-consuming, but it can become emotionally draining–especially if you've had your share of rejections or disappointments. And when we get hyperfocused on finding a person, we often don't allocate our time in the healthiest way.

Think about your battery life like that of your cell phone. When you have too many apps open, are running location services, your screen is too bright, and you have endless notifications, your battery drains exponentially faster (and that's when we freak out that our phone is at 10 percent!). As you start to manage dating with the rest of your life, determine at what point it drains you. For example:

- Dating apps: start draining me after two hours per day
- Going out: starts draining me after two days per week
- Social gatherings: start draining me after two to three times per month
- Introductions through friends: start draining me after two introductions per quarter

Determining the point of diminishing returns will help you time-box each area. This makes dating less all-or-nothing. We hear of daters all the time taking dating sabbaticals or deleting the apps, but if your goal is to find a partner, why give up on the one activity that could get you there? Instead of outright deleting the apps, limit your time on them. For instance, you can try limiting your swiping to only Sunday nights (that's the most popular time anyway!) and setting up first dates for Wednesday evenings when you don't have any other commitments. This way you make sure to reserve your weekend nights for friends or whoever makes you feel great. You may end up talking or meeting with fewer people, yes, but you'll meet more quality people because you're more intentional about who you give your time to. This conscious change in routine can make all the difference in creating a sustainable dating strategy.

Take inventory of how you're spending your time. Your time allocation for dating should never supersede any other bucket. Life is about balance. It'll be hard to keep going if you don't find that. We suggest having a running list of nondating activities you'd like to do—either by yourself or with other loved ones. Whatever you choose, do what nourishes your soul, because preservation of your well-being is crucial to your perseverance.

> **BDE (Big Dateable Energy):**
> Plan dating around your life, not your life around dating.

EVERY EXPERIENCE IS A GROWTH OPPORTUNITY

Another way to make dating a more enjoyable experience is to view it as a journey of personal growth—a set of training wheels for the extraordinary relationship that awaits you. Each opportunity along the way serves as a valuable lesson, allowing you to better understand yourself and refine your needs, values, and boundaries. This mindset alone will keep you going as you take on the mentality of a lifelong learner, excited about what more you can discover about yourself and others. Approaching dating as a path of personal growth enables you to engage in relationships with a more positive outlook and will give you the skills necessary for the type of partnership you desire.

We've had countless guests on our podcast share how they wish they had developed these skills better before entering into a life commitment with someone. Many shared that they married before learning how to communicate and relate in ways that nurtured a long-term relationship, which led to divorce. They wished they'd had the opportunity to better build up their sense of self and learn the skills we talk about on *Dateable* and in this book! So while you may want your great relationship to begin *now*, think about the benefits that dating brings instead of seeing it as a hindrance. Whether you're with someone for two hours, two months, or two years, every experience helps you grow. Even expressing your feelings of hurt to someone who has ghosted you can serve as practice for engaging in similar conversations with long-term partners (because, let's face it, even the happiest and healthiest relationships can encounter moments of pain). Rather than viewing these experiences as time wasted, recognize the knowledge you are gaining. Navigating ambiguity, addressing conflicts, and asserting your own needs are the skills that serve us in relationships–and beyond. They are the building blocks of resilience and personal strength.

To start seeing every experience as growth, adapt a more curious mindset. Unless we consciously stop ourselves, it's all too easy to go into victim mode, perceiving that things are happening *to* us instead of *for* us. For instance, you can ask yourself, *How can this contribute to my personal development?* instead of dwelling on the question *Why is this happening to me?* Identifying patterns and learning the lessons you need to know is pivotal to adjusting your approach to dating. Especially for the Thinkers, it's essential to consciously break free from your habitual thought patterns, self-doubt, and rumination cycles and approach dating with this newfound openness. None of this is wasted time; you can reframe "failures" as valuable experiences to help you find a better match. You'll then be able to put your thinking to good use: asking all the important questions and exploring yourself and others on a more profound level.

So when you're feeling down about dating, flip the questions around in a more empowering way. For instance, as you reflect on your dating experiences, how can you contemplate: *What if I . . . ? Could I . . . ? What would it feel like to . . . ? Would I genuinely enjoy it if . . . ?* By looking at dating this way, you can shift your mindset from a mind reader to an info seeker and learn more about yourself in the process. Think of it like a scavenger hunt for your dating life. How much more fun is staying flexible and open to the different possibilities? How much more enjoyable is seeing every aspect of dating as a learning experience or teachable moment that prepares you for the real deal? Now, that's motivation to keep going!

Yue's Corner

I was forty-two when my almost five-year relationship ended due to a cheating boyfriend. Even though I initially thought Did I just waste five years of my life? *and* How do I start over at 42? *I was quickly reminded of the fact that I had grown so much through this relationship. Not only did I shed some of my Maverick tendencies; I also learned to maintain my individuality in a partnership. Yes, it was brutal how it ended, but it was the ultimate test of my resilience and sense of self. Even in the midst of heartbreak, I discovered more about myself and what I truly wanted from a partner, making me even more optimistic about finding love, which I did find very shortly after.*

IT'S ABOUT PROGRESS, NOT PERFECTION

Feeling stuck is a common hurdle that can lead people to consider giving up on dating altogether. It's important to have positive reinforcement, because without it, it's tough to keep going! This is especially true when it comes to dating apps, where the lack of matches, meaningful conversations, or successful dates can be disheartening. While we shouldn't solely focus on outcomes, it's natural for us as humans to have some level of expectation. However, constantly dwelling on past disappointments and frustrations will only drain our energy. So, how can we shift our focus to celebrate the wins, no matter how small they may be?

Drew Davis, one of our community members, shared his story and tactics as a guest on *Dateable*. As a heterosexual man in his late twenties, he longed to find a partner and start a family. Being surrounded by coupled-up friends, it was hard for him not to compare his own situation and believe that the grass was greener on the other side. But Drew had a valuable insight to share: the best way to make your own grass greener is to nurture and care for it. He created a "wins" folder, a collection of reminders highlighting his accomplishments in dating and life. While his friends were celebrating significant milestones such as meeting a partner or getting engaged, he could genuinely celebrate their successes while also recognizing his own.

Inspired by this perspective, we initiated a weekly tradition with our *Dateable* community Big Dateable Energy to reflect on dating wins, regardless of their magnitude. Here's a glimpse into the types of wins that people shared each week:

- "I have my first date in five months set for Saturday! I'm trying to enjoy what it is instead of worrying about where it'll go."

- "Not feeling as anxious about dating!"
- "Was honest in my profile that I'm more of a homebody than a hiker."
- "Trusting my gut when the person I was seeing started to exhibit worrisome behaviors."
- "Listening to someone's actions about what they want."
- "Taking my time with the person I'm dating. Usually, I rush into relationships, but it feels different here as we're building a solid foundation and relationship."
- "Still unlearning 'the rules' and just texted to tell a guy to say I had a good time and would like to go out again. That's new for me!"
- "Learning more about what I like and desire in a new partner with each new person I meet."
- "Letting a ghost go without the need to send a closure text."
- "Ended a situationship when the guy wouldn't commit. Struggling but know it was right for my mental health."

By focusing on these wins, both big and small, it reminds us that progress is happening, even if it's not always obvious. When you feel like there's a slew of people ghosting you, start celebrating those who didn't. You'll begin to recognize that you have encountered some great people, regardless of whether they were a romantic match or not. You can also celebrate the fact that you've promised to *not* ghost. That is definitely worth popping a bottle of champagne for! The more we can find these small victories along the way, the easier it'll be to have the momentum to keep going. Also, make sure to celebrate your friends' "wins," too. Remember that love is not a zero-sum game. You can give and receive as much love as you want without taking away from other people's wins.

BELIEVE IN MAGIC

By remembering the wins, you can see the larger greatness that comes from dating. It's easy to get caught up in what *isn't* going well, instead of relishing in the magical moments. By thinking back to those memories–from that date where you couldn't stop talking to that one that ends with the steamy kiss–you'll immediately be reminded of why you're dating in the first place. Even if these magical moments don't last forever or lead you to your life partner, they remind you that love and connection are out there. The best part of dating is that you never know what's around the corner. You never know when you'll have that great first date or meet someone who will change your life forever.

As you may recall, our Achiever, Andrew, was trying to be more present on his dates and relinquish the need for them to progress a certain way. He was already trying to get out of the first-date mentality with his new "meet and greet approach," and was also open to more organic opportunities. One night, Andrew's best friend, Marc, invited him to a dinner party. At first, Andrew was reluctant to go, as the guest list was shaping up to be mostly couples. But he figured, why not? He could at least spend some quality time with Marc and his wife, Jessica, who was finally in remission from breast cancer. So Andrew grabbed a bottle of wine and headed to the party. He didn't think much about what he was wearing or the fact that he hadn't gotten a haircut in months, because heck, he wasn't expecting to meet anyone there anyway.

But as soon as Andrew showed up, Jessica introduced him to her friend Sophie, who had recently moved from Boston with her dog, Rupert. From the moment Andrew shook hands with Sophie, he felt a pull to her that he had never experienced before. He felt completely at ease (Sophie being warm and friendly also helped!). They somehow got into a conversation about their obsession with plants. He loved how animated she was when mentioning philodendrons, and her smile was infectious. For the rest of the night, they got lost in conversation with each other. It was one of those dating moments that just felt captivating beyond explanation. Andrew wasn't in his head thinking about what would come next; he was enjoying the present moment getting to know Sophie.

It may have taken over a hundred first dates for Andrew to find Sophie, but he did. And he isn't concerned in the slightest about a third-date curse, as he finally met someone he jives with in the most authentic way possible. Making space for magic is crucial. You don't need to abandon your entire dating strategy, but also invite in the unexpected moments of connection. We owe it to ourselves to be open to the unknown, welcoming the extraordinary into our lives. Believing in love and all the special moments along the way will make your dating journey so worth it.

> **BDE (Big Dateable Energy):**
> What's meant for you will come.

TRUST THE PROCESS

Persevering through it all is the crucial last step because love doesn't always operate on our timetable. Just like the Expectation of Love on Demand: you can't just order it up like a pizza (although wouldn't that be delightful!). You have to go through the highs and lows to truly appreciate what's waiting for you on the other side. There are no hacks or shortcuts, but everything along the way is an experience meant for you. Not every date is going to be a fairy-tale ending, and that's to be expected. Dating is an amazing opportunity for self-discovery. It's a chance to explore who you are, what you need, and what truly matters in a relationship. How can you grow if you never take risks or venture into the unknown?

This journey you're on is about staying true to yourself, taking chances, and embracing the courage to love wholeheartedly. These experiences shape you into a stronger and more resilient person, leading to a fulfilling life, with or without a romantic partner. When you view it from this perspective, you realize that the process itself is just as important as the outcome. Think of your dating life as the epic movie of your own existence. It's your personal love story unfolding before your eyes. And while it may have its fair share of challenges, setbacks, and heartaches, deep down, you know that one day, you will find the relationship that's meant for you.

We know it can be brutal out there, but we hope that with this book, you now possess a newfound perspective that empowers you to take control of your love life. As we bid farewell, we want to leave you with a parting gift—mantras to carry with you as you continue your dating journey. Consider it your mental checklist before every date, a reminder of what you deserve. If you can't give each of these items a resounding "hell yeah!" it might be worth rescheduling that date. Because as you remember, how you show up matters immensely.

- I feel energized.
- I'm open to meeting someone new.
- I'm ready to learn something new.
- I feel confident and self-assured, not defensive.
- I've released the stress from today and am fully present.
- I understand that not everyone is a match, but this is my path to finding my person.

Feel free to add to the list or modify it to align with your own values and aspirations. The goal is to create rituals that put you in a positive headspace so you're setting yourself up for success and

using your time in the most productive way possible. We're genuinely excited to witness how your unique love story unfolds. So, as
your inner medium would say: *Just keep going. Your person is just
around the corner, waiting to join you on this beautiful adventure
called life.*

KEY TAKEAWAYS

1. Have faith in the process of finding love. Your perseverance is
   dependent on your belief that love is right around the corner.
2. Heartbreak and setbacks are inevitable. They may leave you
   feeling shattered and vulnerable, but they also present a
   remarkable opportunity for growth. Cultivating resilience
   becomes paramount as it allows your heart to expand and evolve,
   even in the face of the most trying circumstances.
3. Having support is critical! Deploy your Love Army and get
   any professional help you need so you don't have to feel alone
   through your dating journey.
4. Your life already has so much love—including your love for
   yourself. So masturdate often, celebrate your wins, and
   appreciate the people in your life.
5. Date with curiosity. Treat every date as a learning opportunity.
   When you reflect on your journey, you'll realize the immense
   personal growth you've experienced and how it has paved the
   way for love. And remember to embrace the magic!

Conclusion:

You Design Your Love Life

While we may be at the end of the book, we know it's just the start of your great love story. If there's one thing you can be sure of, you're already dateable. If you've made it this far, you are the type of person who is introspective, vulnerable, and open to all that your love life has in store for you. Someone will only be so lucky to have you as their partner! Now it's up to you to get out of your own way.

By understanding your prevalent dating archetypes, you hold the power to say goodbye to those dating habits that no longer serve you. Whether it's the milestone-driven Achiever, the fairy tale-chasing Dreamer, the date-stacking Energizer, the hyperindependent Maverick, or the analysis-paralysis Thinker, you know *exactly* what traps you're falling for. You now understand that love doesn't happen on demand. There are no tricks, hacks, or shortcuts, but with the tools we've given you, you can cut through the noise and find the people worth investing in. It's time to stop settling for situationships—or any relationship that isn't additive to your life. Anchor yourself around your Dating North Star and use your Perfect Partner Equation to focus on the qualities that actually matter. Remember, your worthiness of love is not contingent upon having a partner—it comes from embracing your authentic self, free of the arbitrary rules, timelines, and societal expectations. You don't need to appeal to the masses, just who matters. When you invest your time and energy in cultivating a healthy connection, only those who truly desire the same will remain by your side. Then you can take that leap and stop playing Relationship Chicken. Let go of any preconceived notions and show up in a way conducive for connection. Trust in the process and trust in yourself, and you'll undoubtedly persevere through anything that is thrown at you.

We started off saying that our society is in a love crisis. We felt so compelled to write this book because we believe that we have the power to change modern dating for the better. While everyone else is frantically trying to survive, you can thrive. If you have a momentary freak-out that you're going to die alone: just remember you have a plan now. As you embark on your dating journey, we want to leave you with these three parting thoughts:

1. **You can be intentional yet not attached:** While we can't magically remove all the ghosters, breadcrumbers, and love bombers from the world (we wish we could!), you are still the one in control of your love life. You're the CEO—you invest as you see fit and fire anyone who isn't measuring up. You know where you're going, and you can take intentional actions to lead you down that path. You have your Dating North Star to guide you, after all! But if one date doesn't go as planned or someone doesn't return the sentiment, you are no longer attached to the outcome. You know they are a small fraction of your overall journey, and they're clearing themselves out of your path to love. In fact, you know there's a better fit just around the corner!

2. **You DIY your love life:** Let's place less emphasis on the DTR and put more energy into DIY'ing a relationship that works for you.

As you've seen in this book, there is no one right way to date, yet we're still following a script of how dating *should* work. With so many unspoken rules and timelines, it's no wonder dating is frustrating! With the DIY approach, you no longer have to follow dating logic that hinders human connection. No other relationship in life requires us to be this formulaic (ummm, have you ever gone on a fifth hang with a friend and expected to take your friendship to the next level?). If you met a new friend, you wouldn't debate whether you should follow up a day or two later—you'd just do it. And you certainly wouldn't overanalyze whether reaching out makes you look needy or desperate. So when in doubt, take control of the steering wheel and drive toward the direction you want. After all, you decide how dating works—not some TikTok influencer asserting outdated rules.

What if, with the next person you meet, you focus on finding creative solutions that work for both of you instead of playing the typical dating game? All your actions are anchored in connection and building something incredible together. You decide how fast (or slow) you want your relationship to go—together. You decide whether to be monogamous or monogam*ish*. That's the beauty of designing your love life: you build a relationship together that's unlike any other out there.

3. **You choose to believe in love:** Even through all the bad dates and the heartbreak, we're romantics at heart. And we bet you are, too. There's no better feeling than knowing you have someone on your team who loves you for all of you. We've poured our heart and soul into writing this book because we want you to experience the type of love you've always desired. We've both come out on the other side—not only experiencing great loves but, more importantly, knowing how to love harder despite setbacks.

Ultimately, we're both optimists when it comes to dating, because why would you choose the alternative? Whenever we tell anyone about our podcast, they immediately dive into how terrible it is "out there," expecting us to be in full consolation. But from hosting our podcast and having our share of experiences over the last decade, we've been able to see how much growth and personal development can come from dating. The healthy partnerships that prevail have such a strong foundation built on open communication, vulnerability, and equality; it's actually quite incredible. And by doing the type of work in this book, you've taken the time to know and fall in love with yourself first. Having that solid foundation of self-worth and self-work is building a strong base that supports the growth and strength of your relationship.

The two of us have become completely different daters than we were when we first started *Dateable*, and we're glad we've been given an opportunity to share all our learnings and aha moments with you. As a way to close out this book, here's a letter from your future self. Your person is coming–it's just a matter of time. Trust the process and know that everything you're learning along the way is setting you up for the type of partnership you've always wanted. If you're ever in need of a reminder, refer to this letter at any time. Or go to our website (www.howtobedateable.com) and print the damn thing out! That will be our parting words to you.

Dear [Your Name],

Hellooooo from your future self. Guess what? I'm here to tell you that you met someone incredible. It's by far the healthiest relationship you've ever had–one that you created and designed together–and now you can see clearly why all the others never worked out. Every day you feel lucky to have a true teammate and partner in life—someone who loves you for *you*.

Even though it wasn't easy, it was worth it. I know you're feeling frustrated by dating right now, but this is not time lost. I trust that you're dating with intentionality, and when setbacks happen (they're inevitable), you know that they're just making way for the right person. You're learning and growing; everything you're experiencing now will benefit your incredible future relationship. So keep this in mind on your quest for love:

You will find love.

You're deserving of love.

You're on your way to love.

Everything you're doing is putting you on the right path. You're about to experience so much, but I don't want to give too many details away. I'm only here to assure you that everything will work out the way it's supposed to. There are no shortcuts or secret doorways. Your journey is exactly what is needed to set you up for your person. So cherish it. Learn from it. And enjoy every moment because one day, you will look back and miss certain aspects of your single life. For now, do everything you *get to do* because you are single. When you do find love, the journey doesn't end. As your future self, even I am still learning, evolving, growing, and iterating. It's not easy, but it's worth it.

Sincerely,

Your Future Self

It has been our pleasure writing this book for you. The process is not meant to be easy; otherwise, love wouldn't be so coveted. Share this book with a friend who could benefit from the newfound approach you'll now be adopting. We hope that when you put that BDE (Big Dateable Energy) into the dating universe, it'll have that ripple effect to transform modern dating culture for the better. Let's all pledge to date better, love fearlessly, and make waves together. And most importantly: stay dateable.

The next step of your journey . . .

Congrats on finishing the book!
We hope you enjoyed it as much as we loved writing it.
As a thank you, we want to share a free gift to help you
with the next stage of your journey to finding love.
www.gift.dateablepodcast.com

Glossary

Anchor Partner: A person's primary or central romantic partner, around who other relationships may revolve within polyamorous configurations.

Anxious Attachment: One of the four primary attachment styles identified in attachment theory, where individuals have heightened fears of rejection, abandonment, or loss in relationships.

Asexual: A sexual orientation characterized by a lack of sexual attraction or desire toward others.

Attachment Theory: A psychological framework that aims to explain how humans form emotional bonds and relationships, particularly in early childhood and throughout the lifespan.

Avoidant Attachment: One of the four primary attachment styles identified in attachment theory, where individuals tend to avoid intimacy, emotional closeness, and dependence on others in relationships.

Bachelor Vortex: The need to progress to the next round of dating, whether you like the person or not.

Bisexual: A sexual orientation characterized by attraction to people of both the same and different genders or sexes.

Booty Call: A late-night request, typically by text message, for a casual hookup.

Boundaries: The personal limits and guidelines that you establish to maintain your emotional, physical, and psychological well-being.

Breadcrumbing: When you give someone just enough attention or communication to keep them interested or engaged, while simultaneously withholding a commitment or deeper level of engagement.

CEO of Your Love Life: When you're the one in control–calling the shots, making decisions, taking action–like you would be if you were the chief executive officer of a company.

Cool Girl/Nice Guy Syndrome: The act of playing it cool or being overly accommodating in an effort to not rock the boat, meaning you never state your needs.

Core Needs: The fundamental requirements that must be fulfilled in order for you to experience a sense of well-being, fulfillment, and happiness in your relationship.

Date Lens: The difference between what makes someone a good date versus a great long-term partner.

Daterview: A date that feels more like a job interview, where you're peppered with questions instead of letting the connection naturally unfold.

Dating ATM: Treating dating transactionally, tallying up every interaction and exchange.

Dating Chameleon: The date version of yourself, the one that tries to appeal to the masses, instead of showing who you really are.

Dating Fatigue: The feeling of exhaustion, frustration, or disillusionment that you may experience after prolonged or repeated attempts at dating without achieving the desired outcomes or finding a fulfilling connection.

Dating North Star: Your guiding principles for how you want to date and whom you choose to date.

Dating Profile: An online representation created on a dating platform or app with the purpose of attracting potential romantic partners.

Dating Sabbatical: A deliberate and conscious decision to take a break from dating, often by uninstalling dating apps or refraining from romantic relationships.

Dating Trauma: A series of micro-interactions and slights experienced while dating that, when compounded over time, eat at your self-confidence and self-worth.

Dating Why: What's really driving you to date in the first place.

Deal-Breaker: A characteristic, behavior, or circumstance that is considered unacceptable or intolerable in a potential romantic partner.

Demisexual: A term used to describe someone who experiences sexual attraction only after forming a strong emotional connection with a person.

DTR: An acronym for defining the relationship that refers to a conversation or series of conversations between two people romantically involved that establish the parameters, expectations, and commitments within the relationship.

Ethical Nonmonogamy (ENM): A relationship model where you have the consent and agreement of all parties involved to engage in romantic or sexual relationships with multiple people simultaneously.

Exclusivity: When two people have agreed to only date each other and are not seeing or romantically involved with anyone else.

Expectation of Love on Demand: The instantaneous and effortless connection that we believe we can have whenever we want.

Fail-Fast Mentality: When you can quickly identify a situation that will not work, so you can move on to something better suited for you.

Fearful-Avoidant Attachment: One of the four primary attachment styles identified in attachment theory, where individuals exhibit a combination of anxious and avoidant attachment behaviors, often experiencing conflicting emotions and behaviors in relationships.

Friends with Benefits (FWB): A type of relationship where two people engage in a friendship with occasional sexual activity or physical intimacy, without the expectation of a committed romantic relationship or emotional attachment.

F*ckboy (or -Girl): A person who f*cks around and gives mixed signals, who will do or say anything to have sex or get what they want.

Future Faker: Someone who makes promises or plans for the future within a relationship, but ultimately has no intention of following through on them.

Gaslighting: A form of psychological manipulation by another person that causes you to doubt your own perceptions, memories, or sanity.

Ghosting: When someone you've been on a few dates with disappears abruptly without any warning or explanation, ceasing all communication and contact.

Hookup: A casual sexual encounter or activity, often without any expectation of a romantic relationship or emotional attachment.

Imaginationship: When you fall for the fantasy of the person, creating a love story that's not grounded in reality.

Inner Medium: That voice telling you that what you're seeking is right around the corner.

Inner Roll Call: Naming and understanding the aspects of your personality that can show up while on dates.

Internal Translator: When someone says one thing, but you listen to what you want to hear instead.

IRL: An acronym for "in real life," referring to interactions that happen in the physical world. Also referred to as "in the wild."

Limiting Belief: A belief or conviction that someone has about themselves, others, or the world around them that holds them back or constrains them in some way.

Limitless Belief: The idea that anything is possible, and that you aren't confined to your past opinions and experiences.

Love Army: Your people who provide encouragement and support through your dating challenges.

Love Bombing: A manipulation tactic that involves overwhelming someone with signs of affection, attention, and praise in order to gain control or influence over them.

Love Crisis: A societal phenomenon where people looking for love are increasingly disillusioned with modern dating, leading to a significant decline in their desire or willingness to engage in romantic pursuits.

Love Language: The different ways in which people express and interpret love.

Lowest Common Denominator (LCD): Accepting bad dating behavior as the norm—and exhibiting the same behaviors you despise—to play at the same level as everyone else.

Masturdating: The art of dating yourself, so you can fall in love with who you are and what you bring to a relationship.

Meet and Greet: a low-pressure way to think about first dates that will allow you to have fun.

Meet-Cute: The expectation you'll meet like in a romantic comedy, with a charming or quirky encounter that leads to the beginning of your romantic relationship.

Microwave Relationship: A relationship that heats up so fast only to evaporate just as quickly.

Monogamish: A relationship style that falls somewhere between strict monogamy and an open relationship.

Monogamous: When you're in a committed relationship with only one partner at a time.

Numbers Game: The concept of increasing your chances of finding a compatible partner by increasing the volume of interactions and connections with potential dates.

OG: Acronym for "original Gangster," but over time it's come to refer more broadly to something or someone who was an originator in their field.

On-Again, Off-Again Relationship: A romantic partnership characterized by a pattern of breaking up and getting back together multiple times over a period of time.

One Percent Rule: Taking a small step every day to look for new opportunities to heal and grow.

Opening Line: The first message or conversation starter that someone uses to initiate communication with a potential romantic interest on a dating app or platform.

Pansexual: A sexual orientation characterized by the potential for attraction to individuals of all genders or regardless of gender.

Primary Partner: A person's central romantic partner that other relationships revolve around within polyamorous configurations.

Perfect Partner Equation (PPE): The factors that help determine who would make an ideal partner for you.

Pick-Me Behavior: When someone seeks validation, attention, or approval from others they are trying to attract or date.

Polyamory: When you engage in multiple romantic and typically sexual relationships.

Red Flag: Warning sign or indicator that the person probably can't have a healthy relationship, and that proceeding down the road together would be emotionally dangerous.

Red-Flag Hunt: Finding anything and everything that could be a red flag—and often ignoring actual relationship deal-breakers.

Rejection Therapy: Actively seeking out and putting yourself through a series of rejections, in an effort to desensitize yourself to the feeling of devastation each time.

Relationship Chicken: When you don't want to be the one to show your cards first, acting in the exact opposite way you would in a relationship in order to protect your heart.

Relationship Prep Period: When you naturally find yourself drawn to a more domestic lifestyle that ultimately makes room for a partner.

Relationship Scars: The emotional issues, negative experiences, and unresolved conflicts from your past relationships, which can manifest as distrust, jealousy, fear of commitment, or poor communication skills.

Relationshopping: The act of looking for your romantic partners the way you would shop for items online.

Roaching: A deceptive behavior where one person hides from their main partner the fact that they're dating or seeing multiple people simultaneously.

ROI: An acronym for return on investment.

Secure Attachment: One of the four primary attachment styles identified in attachment theory, where individuals tend to have a positive view of themselves and others, feel comfortable with intimacy and autonomy in relationships, and are able to communicate their needs effectively.

Settling: The act of entering into a relationship with someone despite feeling that they may not be the ideal match or partner.

Settling Paradox: A phase where you hyperfocus on surface-level qualities, often overlooking the qualities necessary for a healthy, long-term, emotionally fulfilling partnership.

Situationship: A romantic relationship that lacks clear labels and commitment, and is undefined, ambiguous, and uncertain by nature.

Slow Fade: When you gradually slow down communication with someone you've been seeing, eventually ending in not talking to them again.

Sober First Kiss: The coveted first kiss, where both people are completely sober.

Stargazing Theory: Removing the mental pollution of societal constructs, pressures within yourself, limiting beliefs, insecurities, and family pressures to actually see the person as your person.

Sunday Test: Determining someone's compatibility based on whether you would enjoy spending a Sunday with them doing absolutely nothing.

Swipe: The act of moving your finger across the touch screen of your device to indicate interest or disinterest in another user's profile while on dating apps.

Texting Black Hole: When you message endlessly or engage in a never-ending text conversation with someone you meet online, never to actually meet in person.

Textlationship: When you're dating someone but seem to text them more often than actually see them in person.

The One: The concept that there's one perfect person out there with all the qualities you are looking for.

The Only Seven Things That Matter: The ultimate gut check to determine whether someone is worth investing in further.

The Rules: A specific set of guidelines or principles to follow when dating.

The Solo Act: A date that feels more like a performance, where one person is driving the date, feeling the need to entertain or impress instead of connect.

The Spark: That elusive chemistry we're all chasing that ends up not being the best predictor of a good partner.

The Therapy Session: A date that gets too personal too quickly, divulging information that is better left for an actual session with your therapist.

Thirsty: When you appear overly eager or desperate for attention or affection from potential romantic partners.

Thirty-Second Principle: When you spend no more than thirty seconds on each profile before deciding whether you want to match.

Trauma Bond: The emotional bond with an individual that arises from a recurring, cyclical pattern of abuse perpetrated by intermittent reinforcement through rewards and punishments.

Trauma Dumping: The unsolicited act of expressing traumatic thoughts and stories to someone, leaving the receiver trapped without the option to exit.

Triad: A form of romantic or intimate partnership involving three individuals who are all mutually involved with one another.

Turbo Relationship: A relationship where you reach relationship milestones at an accelerated pace.

Uber Radius: Determining someone's desirability based on the distance between where each of you live.

Validation Trap: When you let dating define your worth instead of using it to find a good match.

Vanity Swipes: Racking up matches and likes to feel better about oneself, oftentimes never moving to an actual date.

Vulnerability: The emotion that we experience during times of uncertainty, risk, and emotional exposure.

Your V-Card: Being vulnerable in a way that feels authentic to you and fosters connection with others.

Zombieing: A situation where someone who previously ghosted or disappeared suddenly reappears without any explanation or apology for their previous disappearance.

References

Introduction

XIV   Brown, Anna, "Nearly Half of U.S. Adults Say Dating Has Gotten Harder for Most People in the Last 10 Years," *Pew Research Center*, August 20, 2020, https://www.pewresearch.org/social-trends/2020/08/20/nearly-half-of-u-s-adults-say-dating-has-gotten-harder-for-most-people-in-the-last-10-years/.

XIV   Fry, Richard, and Kim Parker, "The Rising Share of U.S. Adults Are Living without a Spouse or Partner," *Pew Research Center*, 2021, https://www.pewresearch.org/social-trends/2021/10/05/rising-share-of-u-s-adults-are-living-without-a-spouse-or-partner/.

XIV   Twenge, J. M., R. A. Sherman, and B. E. Wells, "Sexual Inactivity during Young Adulthood Is More Common among U.S. Millennials and iGen: Age, Period, and Cohort Effects on Having No Sexual Partners after Age 18," *Archives of Sexual Behavior* 46 (2017): 433-40, https://doi.org/10.1007/s10508-016-0798-z.

XIV   Julian, Kate, "Why Are Young People Having So Little Sex?" *The Atlantic*, December 2018, https://www.theatlantic.com/magazine/archive/2018/12/the-sex-recession/573949/.

XV   Centers for Disease Control and Prevention, "How Does Social Connectedness Affect Health," https://www.cdc.gov/emotional-wellbeing/social-connectedness/affect-health.htm.

XV   Harvard Study of Adult Development (1938).

XV   Robert Waldinger and Marc Schutlz, "What the Longest Study on Human Happiness Found Is the Key to a Good Life," *The Atlantic*, January 2023, https://www.theatlantic .com/ideas/archive/2023/01/harvard-happiness-study -relationships/672753/.

XV   "WHO Commission on Social Connection," World Health Organization, https://www.who.int/groups/commission-on -social-connection.

XV   Johnson, Sarah, "WHO declares loneliness a 'global public health concern,'" The Guardian, November 16, 2023, https:// www.theguardian.com/global-development/2023/nov/16 /who-declares-loneliness-a-global-public-health-concern #:~:text=The%20World%20Health%20Organization%20 (WHO,smoking%2015%20cigarettes%20a%20day.

XXVI Fileva, Iskra Ph.D., "Is Marriage a Bad Deal for Women?" *Psychology Today* May 2021, https://www.psychologytoday .com/us/blog/the-philosophers-diaries/202105/is-getting -married-bad-deal-women.

Chapter 1: The Expectation of Love on Demand

6   Eyal, Nir, *Hooked: How to Build Habit-Forming Products* (New York: Portfolio, 2014).

12   Ellen Fein and Sherri Schneider. *The Rules: Time-tested Secrets for Capturing the Heart of Mr. Right* (New York: Grand Central Publishing, 1995).

12   Argov, Sherry, *Why Men Love Bitches: From Doormat to Dreamgirl–A Woman's Guide to Holding Her Own in a Relationship* (New York: Adams Media, 2002).

12   Strauss, Neil, *The Game: Penetrating the Secret Society of Pickup Artists* (New York: Harper Collins, 2005).

14   Solomon, Alexandra Ph.D., "Marriage 101," December 11, 2018, in *Dateable*, podcast, https://www.dateablepodcast.com /episode/s7e22-marriage-101.

14   Solomon, Alexandra Ph.D., *Loving Bravely* (Oakland, CA: New Harbinger Publications, 2017).

19   Novo, Nikki, "Following Your Intuition (in Dating)," September 19, 2023, in *Dateable*, podcast, https://www .dateablepodcast.com/episode/following-your-intuition-in -dating-w-nikki-novo.

27   Lee, May, "Finding Love at Any Age," June 27, 2018, in *Dateable*, podcast, https://www.dateablepodcast.com /episode/s16e20-finding-love-at-any-age-w-may-lee.

Chapter 2: The Settling Paradox

31   Fechner, Gustav, *Vorschule der aesthetik* (Wiesbaden: Breitkoff & Härtel, 1876), https://www.wiwi.europa-uni.de /de/lehrstuhl/fine/mikro/bilder_und_pdf-dateien/WS0910 /VLBehEconomics/Ausarbeitungen/MereExposure.pdf.

31   Titchener, Edward B., *A Text-book of Psychology* (Macmillan, 1910).

31   Zajonc, Robert B., "Attitudinal Effects of Mere Exposure," *Journal of Personality and Social Psychology* 9 (1968): 1-27, https://doi.org/10.1037/h0025848.

34   New York University, "Scientists Identify the Neural Circuitry of First Impressions," March 2009, https://www.nyu.edu /about/news-publications/news/2009/march/scientists _identify_the_neural.html.

38   Gould, Wendy Rose, "13 Red Flags in Relationships," *Very Well Mind*, June 2023, https://www.verywellmind.com/10-red -flags-in-relationships-5194592.

42   O'Donoghue, Ted, and Matthew Rabin, "Doing It Now or
      Later," *American Economic Review* 89, no. 1 (March 1999):
      103-24, https://www.jstor.org/stable/116981.

43   Rego, Sara, Joana Arantes, and Paula Magalhães, "Is There
      a Sunk Cost Effect in Committed Relationships?" *Current
      Psychology* 37 (November 2016): 508-19, https://doi.org
      /10.1007/s12144-016-9529-9.

45   Nicholson, Jeremy, MSW PhD, "When Being Friends with
      Benefits Leads to Love, and When It Doesn't," *Psychology
      Today*, March 24, 2022, https://www.psychologytoday.com
      /us/blog/the-attraction-doctor/202203/when-being
      -friends-benefits-leads-love-and-when-it-doesnt.

47   Eastwick, Paul Dr., "The Science of Attraction," September 21,
      2021, in *Dateable*, podcast, https://www.dateablepodcast
      .com/episode/s13e6-the-science-of-attraction-w-paul
      -eastwick.

51   Sholes, Marc, "Why You're Choosing the Wrong Partners,"
      March 22, 2023, in *Dateable*, podcast, https://www
      .dateablepodcast.com/episode/s16e6-why-youre
      -choosing-the-wrong-partners-w-marc-sholes.

51   Sholes, Marc, *Reset Your Romantic GPS: Why You Steer
      towards the Wrong Partners, and How to Change Direction
      for the Better*, 2021.

52   Katz, Evan Marc, "Where Are All the Dateable People?"
      September 12, 2023, in *Dateable*, podcast, https://www
      .dateablepodcast.com/episode/where-are-all-the-dateable
      -people-w-evan-marc-katz.

54   Eastwick, Paul Dr., "Ideal Partner Preferences," http://
      pauleastwick.com/ideals.

54   Eastwick, P. W., E. J. Finkel, and A. H. Eagly, "When and
      Why Do Ideal Partner Preferences Affect the Process of
      Initiating and Maintaining Romantic Relationships?" *Journal*

of Personality and Social Psychology 101, no. 5 (June 2011): https://doi.org/10.1037/a0024062.

54   Isern, Heidi, "Why You Cannot Find 'The One,'" May 29, 2017, in *Dateable*, podcast, https://www.dateablepodcast.com /episode/s4e16-why-you-cannot-find-the-one.

54   Isern, Heidi, "Why You Cannot Find 'The One,'" *Heidi Isern* (blog), March 12, 2016, https://heidiisern.com/why-you -cannot-find-the-one/.

Chapter 3: The Validation Trap

58   Taitz, Jennifer PsyD, "How to Be Single & Happy," February 14, 2023, in *Dateable*, podcast https://www.dateablepodcast .com/episode/s16e1-how-to-be-single-happy-w-dr-jenny -taitz.

58   Taitz, Jennifer PsyD, *How to Be Single and Happy: Science-Based Strategies for Keeping Your Sanity While Looking for a Soul Mate* (New York: TarcherPerigee of Penguin Random House, 2018).

59   Lucas, Richard E., Andrew E. Clark, Yannis Georgellis, and Ed Diener, "Reexamining Adaptation and the Set Point Model of Happiness: Reactions to Changes in Marital Status," *Journal of Personality and Social Psychology* 84, no. 3 (March 2003): 527-39, https://doi.org/10.1037/0022-3514.84.3.527.

59   Lickerman, Alex M.D., "How to Reset Your Happiness Set Point," *Psychology Today*, April 21, 2013, https://www .psychologytoday.com/us/blog/happiness-in-world/201304 /how-reset-your-happiness-set-point.

59   Brickman, P., and D. T. Campbell, "Hedonic Relativism and Planning the Good Society," in *Adaptation-Level Theory*, edited by M. H. Appley, 287-305 (New York: Academic Press, 1971).

60   New York University, "Scientists Identify the Neural Circuitry of First Impressions," March 8, 2009, https://www.nyu.edu /about/news-publications/news/2009/march/scientists _identify_the_neural.html.

61   Pharaon, Vienna LMFT, "How Your Childhood Wounds Affect Your Love Life," May 9, 2023, in *Dateable*, podcast https:// www.dateablepodcast.com/episode/s16e13-how-your -childhood-wounds-impact-your-love-life-w-vienna -pharaon.

61   Pharaon, Vienna LMFT, *The Origins of You: How Breaking Family Patterns Can Liberate the Way We Live and Love* (New York: G.P. Putnam's Sons, 2023).

69   Carnes, Patrick Ph.D., *Trauma Bonds: Why People Bond to Those Who Hurt Them* (2016).

70   Manson, Mark, "Love Is Not Enough," April 28, 2020, in *Dateable*, podcast, https://www.dateablepodcast.com /episode/s10e12-love-is-not-enough-w-mark-manson.

70   Manson, Mark, *Love Is not Enough* (New York: Audible Original, 2020).

74   Mack, Robert, "Love from the Inside Out," August 16, 2022, in *Dateable*, podcast, https://www.dateablepodcast.com /episode/s15e1-love-from-the-inside-out-w-rob-mack.

74   Mack, Robert, *Love from the Inside Out* (Coral Gables, FL: Mango Publishing, 2022).

75   Chapman, Gary D., *The Five Love Languages* (Woodmere, NY: Northfield Publishing, 2010).

Chapter 4: Relationship Chicken

84   Strauss, Neil, *The Game: Penetrating the Secret Society of Pickup Artists* (New York: Harper Collins, 2005).

84 Ellen Fein and Sherri Schneider, *The Rules: Time-tested Secrets for Capturing the Heart of Mr. Right* (New York: Grand Central Publishing, 1995).

89 Singh, Sonica, "The Lowest Common Denominator (in Dating)," in *Dateable*, podcast, https://www.dateablepodcast.com/episode/s15e4-the-lowest-common-denominator-in-dating.

94 Emba, Christine, "Rethinking Sex," September 20, 2022, in *Dateable*, podcast, https://www.dateablepodcast.com/episode/s15e6-rethinking-sex-w-christine-emba.

94 Emba, Christine, *Rethinking Sex: A Provocation* (New York: Sentinel, 2022).

97 Nate Klemp and Kaley Klemp, "The 80/80 Marriage," October 19, 2021, in *Dateable*, podcast, https://www.dateablepodcast.com/episode/s13e10-the-80-80-marriage-w-nate-kaley-klemp.

97 Nate Klemp and Kaley Klemp, *The 80/80 Marriage: A New Model for a Happier, Stronger Relationship* (New York: Penguin Life, 2021).

98 Matos, Greg PsyD., "The Rise of Lonely, Single Men," December 6, 2022, in *Dateable*, podcast, https://www.dateablepodcast.com/episode/s15e17-the-rise-of-lonely-single-men-w-dr-greg-matos.

98 Matos, Greg PsyD., "What's Behind the Rise of Lonely, Single Men," *Psychology Today*, August 9, 2022, https://www.psychologytoday.com/us/blog/the-state-our-unions/202208/whats-behind-the-rise-lonely-single-men.

98 Brown, Anna, "Nearly Half of U.S. Adults Say Dating Has Gotten Harder for Most People in the Last 10 Years," *Pew Research Center*, August 20, 2020, https://www.pewresearch.org/social-trends/2020/08/20/nearly-half-of

-u-s-adults-say-dating-has-gotten-harder-for-most-people
-in-the-last-10-years/.

98   Murakami, Sukura, "It's 'Now or Never' to Stop Japan's
Shrinking Population," *Reuters*, January 23, 2023, https://
www.reuters.com/world/asia-pacific/its-now-or-never-stop
-japans-shrinking-population-pm-says-2023-01-23/.

98   Burton, Bonnie, "To Boost Birth Rate, Japan's Government
Considers AI to Match Spouses," *CNET*, December 11, 2020,
https://www.cnet.com/science/to-boost-birth-rate
-japans-government-looks-to-ai-to-match-spouses/.

99   Levy, Luke, "For Valentine's Day, I Went on a Government-
Organised Date. It Got Weird," *Kopi*, 2020, https://www
.google.com/url?q=https://thekopi.co/2020/02/20
/sdu-date-firstperson/&sa=D&source=docs&ust=1706811
6817128378&usg=AOvVaw2IJtBk_orlobfjN5jGp-47.

99   "Chinese Government Organises 'Blind Date' to Help Youth
Get Married," *The Hindui*, September 23, 2017, https://www
.thehindu.com/news/international/chinese-government
-organises-blind-date-to-help-youth-get-married
/article19741187.ece.

105   Peel, Raquel, "Are You Sabotaging Your Love Life?"
November 1, 2022, in *Dateable*, podcast https://www
.dateablepodcast.com/episode/s15e12-are-you-sabotaging
-your-love-life-w-dr-raquel-peel.

Chapter 5: Letting Go

125   Rosen, Corey, "Your Story, Well Told," May 11, 2021, in
Dateable, podcast, https://www.dateablepodcast.com
/episode/s12e14-whats-your-story-w-corey-rosen.

128   Bowlby, John, *Maternal Care and Mental Health*, Geneva:

World Health Organization, 1951, https://lccn.loc.gov /a52007766.

128   Ainsworth, Mary, "Infant-Mother Attachment," *American Psychologist* 34, no. 10 (1979): 932-37, https://psycnet.apa .org/doi/10.1037/3-066X.34.10.932.

128   Levine, Amir, M.D., and Rachel Heller, M.A., *Attached: The New Science of Adult Attachment and How It Can Help You Find–and Keep–Love* (New York: TarcherPerigee of Penguin Random House, 2012).

129   Pharaon, Vienna LMFT, "How Your Childhood Wounds Affect Your Love Life," May 9, 2023, in *Dateable*, podcast, https:// www.dateablepodcast.com/episode/s16e13-how-your -childhood-wounds-impact-your-love-life-w-vienna-pharaon.

129   Pharaon, Vienna LMFT, *The Origins of You: How Breaking Family Patterns Can Liberate the Way We Live and Love* (New York: G.P. Putnam's Sons, 2023).

137   Jiang, Jia, *Rejection Proof: How I Beat Fear and Became Invincible through 100 Days of Rejection* (New York: Harmony, 2015).

138   Schultz, Makena, "Reflection or Rumination?" *Michigan State University*, February 17, 2017, https://www.canr.msu.edu /news/reflection_or_rumination.

139   Taitz, Jennifer PsyD., "How to Be Single & Happy," February 14, 2023, in *Dateable*, podcast, https://www .dateablepodcast.com/episode/s16e1-how-to-be-single -happy-w-dr-jenny-taitz.

139   Taitz, Jennifer PsyD., *How to Be Single and Happy: Science-Based Strategies for Keeping Your Sanity While Looking for a Soul Mate* (New York: TarcherPerigee of Penguin Random House, 2018).

144   Stone, Gabrielle, "Coming Back Stronger after Heartbreak," April 25, 2023, in *Dateable*, podcast, https://www

.dateablepodcast.com/episode/s16e11-coming-back
-stronger-after-heartbreak-w-gabrielle-stone.

144   Stone, Gabrielle, *Eat, Pray, #FML* (2019).

Chapter 6: Gaining Clarity

151   Simone Milasis and Brandon Watt, "Relationship. Are you
sure you want one?" May 26, 2020, in *Dateable*, podcast,
https://www.dateablepodcast.com/episode/s10e16
-relationship-are-you-sure-you-want-one.

151   Milasis, Simone, and Brandon Watt, *Relationship. Are you
sure you want one?* (Access Consciousness Publishing, 2018).

153   Ohno, Taiichi, *Toyota Production System: Beyond Large-Scale
Production* (New York: Productivity Press, 1988).

154   The Gottman Institute, Online Abstracts of Published
Research Articles (2008).

166   Beaton, Connor, "Socially Distant Yet Emotionally Available,"
February 9, 2021, in *Dateable*, podcast, https://www
.dateablepodcast.com/episode/s12e1-socially-distant-yet
-emotionally-available-w-connor-beaton.

169   Davenport, Barrie, "15 Different Types of Romantic
Relationships You Should Know About," *Live Bold and
Bloom*, October 1, 2023, https://liveboldandbloom.com/10
/relationships/different-types-romantic-relationships.

Chapter 7: Showing Up

179   Loustaunau, Lisa, "The Four Phases of the Core Energetics
Approach: An Evolutionary Therapy," *USABP (United States
Association of Body Psychotherapy) Newsletter* (2014, revised

in 2019), www.coreenergetics.org/wp-content
/uploads/2019/06/Four-Stages-of-Core-Energetics
-Final-6_25_19.pdf.

181   Torrent, Lair, "Who's Showing Up for Your Date?"
February 22, 2022, in *Dateable*, podcast, https://www
.dateablepodcast.com/episode/s14e1-whos-showing-up
-for-your-date-w-lair-torrent.

181   Torrent, Lair, *The Practice of Love: Break Old Patterns,
Rebuild Trust, and Create a Connection That Lasts* (Lanham,
MD: Rowman & Littlefield Publishers, 2022).

191   Brown, Brené, *Atlas of the Heart: Mapping Meaningful
Connection and the Language of Human Experience* (New
York: Random House, 2021).

194   Headlee, Celeste, *We Need to Talk: How to Have
Conversations That Matter* (New York: Harper Wave, 2017).

194   Headlee, Celeste, "10 Ways to Have a Better Conversation,"
May 2015, TEDxCreativeCoast, https://www.ted.com/talks
/celeste_headlee_10_ways_to_have_a_better_conversation
?language=en.

196   Headlee, Celeste, "Death to the Daterview," March 1, 2022,
in *Dateable*, podcast, https://www.dateablepodcast.com
/episode/s14e2-death-to-the-daterview-w-celeste-headlee.

198   Harry, Jeff, "Make Dating Fun Again," April 6, 2021, in
Dateable, podcast, https://www.dateablepodcast.com
/episode/s12e9-make-dating-fun-again-w-jeff-harry.

Chapter 8: Investing Appropriately

204   Schwartz, Barry, *The Paradox of Choice* (New York: Harper
Perennial, 2004).

207   Ries, Eric, *The Lean Startup: How Today's Entrepreneurs*

Use Continuous Innovation to Create Radically Successful Businesses (New York: Crown Business, 2011).

210   Lee, Esther, "Dating Apps Are Officially the Most Popular Way to Meet a Spouse," *The Knot*, 2019.

216   Ury, Logan, "How to Not Die Alone," February 16, 2021, in *Dateable*, podcast, https://www.dateablepodcast.com /episode/s12e2-how-to-not-die-alone-w-logan-ury.

216   Ury, Logan, *How to Not Die Alone: The Surprising Science That Will Help You Find Love* (New York: Simon & Schuster, 2021).

221   "What Is Love Bombing?" *Cleveland Clinic*, January 31, 2023, https://health.clevelandclinic.org/love-bombing/.

222   Strachowski, Diane, "Is It Love or Love Bombing?" May 4, 2021, in *Dateable*, podcast, https://www.dateablepodcast .com/episode/s12e13-is-it-love-or-love-bombing-w-dr -diane.

226   Kerner, Ian, PhD, LMFT, "So Tell Me About the Last Time You Had Sex," July 5, 2022, in *Dateable*, podcast, https://www .dateablepodcast.com/episode/s14e20-so-tell-me-about-the -last-time-you-had-sex-w-ian-kerner.

226   Kerner, Ian, PhD, LMFT, *So Tell Me About the Last Time You Had Sex: Laying Bare and Learning to Repair Our Love Lives* (New York: Grand Central Publishing, 2021).

227   Connor Beaton and Vienna Pharaon, "How to Have a Healthy Relationship," November 30, 2021, https://www .dateablepodcast.com/episode/s13e16-how-to-have-a -healthy-relationship-w-connor-beaton-vienna-pharaon.

230   Beck, Kent, et al., *Manifesto for Agile Software Development* (2001), https://agilemanifesto.org/.

Chapter 9: Persevering through It All

234 Novo, Nikki, "What's Holding You Back?" November 17, 2020, in *Dateable*, podcast, https://www.dateablepodcast.com /episode/s11e14-whats-holding-you-back-w-nikki-novo.

234 Novo, Nikki, *The Final Swipe: Heal Your Heart, Find Your Person, and End the Dating Search for Good* (Nikki Novo Writes LLC, 2018).

242 Page, Ken, "Discovering Your Core Gifts," June 20, 2023, in *Dateable*, podcast, https://www.dateablepodcast.com /episode/s16e19-discovering-your-core-gifts-in-dating-w -ken-page.

242 Page, Ken, *Deeper Dating: How to Drop the Games of Seduction and Discover the Power of Intimacy* (Boulder, CO: Shambhala, 2014).

248 Spencer, Amy, "Meeting Your Half Orange," May 29, 2018, in *Dateable*, podcast, https://www.dateablepodcast.com /episode/s6e15-meeting-your-half-orange.

248 Spencer, Amy, *Meeting Your Half-Orange: An Utterly Upbeat Guide to Using Dating Optimism to Find Your Perfect Match* (Philadelphia: Running Press, 2011).

253 Davis, Drew, "Stopping the Comparison Game," November 22, 2022, in *Dateable*, podcast, https://www.dateablepodcast .com/episode/s15e15-stopping-the-comparison-game.

Acknowledgments

We could never have written this book without the help of so many people. First of all, to our editor extraordinaire Veronica (Ronnie) Alvarado. You believed in us from day one. Getting that email from you back in 2021, saying that you were an avid listener who knew our voices needed to be translated into a book, was still one of the greatest moments we can recall. We knew from the start that you were the right editor and Simon Element was the perfect publisher for us because of the passion, excitement, and genuine desire you held to help others create positive change in their love lives, too. We could never have done this without you, Maria, Nan, Alyssa, and the rest of the Simon Element Team. So thank you a million times over.

To the Park & Fine team (Mia Vitale and Sarah Passick), thank you for championing us and this book. A huge thank-you to Anna Petkovich who really helped incubate this book from the beginning. You all have played such an instrumental role in bringing this book to fruition.

A special thank-you to our *Dateable* friends + listeners Emily, Evan, Greg, Janis, Jason L., Jason S., Louise, Maria, Melissa, and Sonica for testing out a few iterations of the Dating Archetypes quiz. Your feedback was instrumental in creating a quiz that will help so many daters.

And before we get into our individual acknowledgments, it's the *Dateable* community who really gave us the ammunition to write this book. Your encouragement and success stories are what keep us going. Every time you share how much our podcast or work has helped you, it means more than you'd ever know. Witnessing first-hand the growth you've made in your personal lives is what gives us purpose. So thank you again for supporting *Dateable* over the years, in turn, enabling us to support the countless other daters out there who need it more than ever. Without you, we wouldn't be where we are today. #staydateable

JULIE'S ACKNOWLEDGMENT:

First and foremost, to my partner, John: You've been there through it all—to celebrate the news of getting this book deal to all the ups and downs along the way. You are my rock and support system; I could not have done this without you. Your words of encouragement and belief in me mean more than you even know. You've shown me what's truly possible in a relationship—and have served as such a catalyst for this book.

To Mom and Dad: I attribute so much of my work ethic and creative drive to you both. You both instilled these values in me from an early age, and I have carried them with me throughout the years. Without this, I would never have been able to write a book in the first place or have the confidence to know it's possible. So thank you for all your encouragement.

To Jeff and Hannah: Your excitement about this book and belief in me doesn't go unnoticed. From making a point to celebrate this accomplishment to your genuine enthusiasm every time we talk, you make me feel so supported. I feel so lucky to have siblings that feel more like best friends. And I absolutely love your dedication to *Dateable*. Hannah, you truly are one of our #1 listeners.

To Olivia: You've shown me a love different from anything I've ever known before. And who knows, with your wit and sense of humor (already!), you may take over as a *Dateable* host someday (wouldn't that make your parents proud?).

To my friends (you know who you are!) and extended family members: Thank you for all your encouragement, support, and belief in me and what we're doing with *Dateable*. It means so much to know I have you in my corner.

Last but certainly not least, to Yue: I honestly don't even know where to start. When we met, I knew our friendship would be special, but I certainly did not know all that would be in store for us! Thank you for everything you've taught me—from the skills you bring to our venture to you being a supportive best friend. There's no one else I'd rather be doing all this with!

YUE'S ACKNOWLEDGMENT:

To my incredible parents, who have both written books, I never imagined I'd share the title of published author with you. Thank you for paving the way *and* for showing me what unconditional love looks like.

To Louise and Emily, who dropped everything to drive me to/pick me up from the airport that fateful day, you were instrumental in my healing. I am so lucky to have you both in my life.

To my Mojo bear, you deserve credit for reopening my heart to love. Through thick and thin, you've had mommy's back.

To G, my epic plot twist, thank you for showing me a love I never knew existed. Your humility, honesty, and commitment restored my faith in relationships. I'm grateful our paths crossed again when they did.

And finally, to Julie, you are still my longest relationship to date (haha!). Who knew when we met a decade ago that we would publish a book together! Thank you for keeping me honest and for your commitment to us. Let's keep dreaming big together!

About the Authors

Julie Krafchick & Yue Xu are active daters turned dating insiders and top influential voices on dating, relationships, and connection in the digital world. They're the co-hosts and creators of *Dateable*, which has been named one of the best podcasts about modern dating and relationships by the *New York Times*, the *Huffington Post*, *Oprah Daily*, and more. They're also the hosts and executive producers of the dating experiment show *Exit Interview*.

Prior to *Dateable*, Julie Krafchick worked in the Silicon Valley tech scene for nearly two decades, understanding the ins and outs of how technology impacts human relationships. She's a trained qualitative researcher and app designer with an emphasis on human-centered design. Frustrated by dating herself at the time, she created the app 500 Brunches to facilitate more organic, in-person meetings for friends and dates, which grew into a thriving community (and was also how Julie and Yue met and developed *Dateable*).

Yue Xu was a dating coach and vlogger in New York City, working with clients all over the world. Her vlog, *Singlefied*, was featured on AskMen.com, Match.com, *New York Post*, Coffee Meets Bagel, the *Times* (London), BBC, and more. She is a TV host and producer and has worked on the shows *TechtheLead*, *The Gadget Show UK*, and *The Gadget Show China*.

Together you can find them at dateablepodcast.com and @dateablepodcast.